enVisionmath 2.0

SCOTT FORESMAN · ADDISON WESLEY

Volume 1 Topics 1-8

Authors

Randall I. Charles
Professor Emeritus
Department of Mathematics
San Jose State University
San Jose, California

Jennifer Bay-Williams
Professor of Mathematics Education
College of Education and Human
Development
University of Louisville
Louisville, Kentucky

Robert Q. Berry, III
Associate Professor of
Mathematics Education
Department of Curriculum,
Instruction and Special Education
University of Virginia
Charlottesville, Virginia

Janet H. Caldwell
Professor of Mathematics
Rowan University
Glassboro, New Jersey

Zachary Champagne
Assistant in Research
Florida Center for Research in Science,
Technology, Engineering, and
Mathematics (FCR-STEM)
Jacksonville, Florida

Juanita Copley
Professor Emerita, College of Education
University of Houston
Houston, Texas

Warren Crown
Professor Emeritus of Mathematics
Education
Graduate School of Education
Rutgers University
New Brunswick, New Jersey

Francis (Skip) Fennell
L. Stanley Bowlsbey Professor
of Education and Graduate and
Professional Studies
McDaniel College
Westminster, Maryland

Karen Karp
Professor of Mathematics Education
Department of Early Childhood and
Elementary Education
University of Louisville
Louisville, Kentucky

Stuart J. Murphy
Visual Learning Specialist
Boston, Massachusetts

Jane F. Schielack
Professor of Mathematics
Associate Dean for Assessment and
Pre K-12 Education, College of Science
Texas A&M University
College Station, Texas

Jennifer M. Suh
Associate Professor for
Mathematics Education
George Mason University
Fairfax, Virginia

Jonathan A. Wray
Mathematics Instructional Facilitator
Howard County Public Schools
Ellicott City, Maryland

PEARSON

Glenview, Illinois   Boston, Massachusetts   Chandler, Arizona   Hoboken, New Jersey

Mathematicians

Roger Howe
Professor of Mathematics
Yale University
New Haven, Connecticut

Gary Lippman
Professor of Mathematics and
Computer Science
California State University, East Bay
Hayward, California

ELL Consultants

Janice R. Corona
Independent Education Consultant
Dallas, Texas

Jim Cummins
Professor
The University of Toronto
Toronto, Canada

Common Core State Standards Reviewers

Debbie Crisco
Math Coach
Beebe Public Schools
Beebe, Arkansas

Kathleen A. Cuff
Teacher
Kings Park Central School District
Kings Park, New York

Erika Doyle
Math and Science Coordinator
Richland School District
Richland, Washington

Susan Jarvis
Math and Science Curriculum Coordinator
Ocean Springs Schools
Ocean Springs, Mississippi

Velvet M. Simington
K–12 Mathematics Director
Winston-Salem/Forsyth County Schools
Winston-Salem, North Carolina

ISBN-13: 978-0-328-82737-4
ISBN-10:   0-328-82737-1

18 19

Digital Resources

You'll be using these digital resources throughout the year!

Go to PearsonRealize.com

 MP
Math Practices Animations to play anytime

 Solve
Solve & Share problems plus math tools

 Learn
Visual Learning Animation Plus with animation, interaction, and math tools

 Glossary
Animated Glossary in English and Spanish

 Tools
Math Tools to help you understand

 Assessment
Quick Check for each lesson

 Help
Another Look Homework Video for extra help

 Games
Math Games to help you learn

 eText
Student Edition online

 ACTIVe-book
Student Edition online for showing your work

PEARSON realize. Everything you need for math anytime, anywhere

Contents

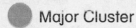
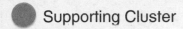
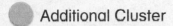

This shows how you can use ten-frames to make a 10.

TOPIC 1
Fluently Add and Subtract Within 20

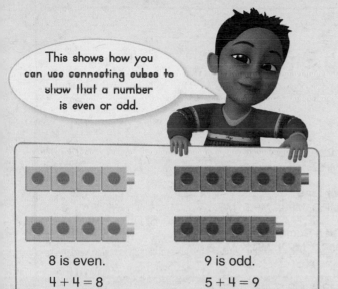

This shows how you can use connecting cubes to show that a number is even or odd.

8 is even.

$4 + 4 = 8$

9 is odd.

$5 + 4 = 9$

TOPIC 2
Work with Equal Groups

PearsonRealize.com

This shows how you can add two-digit numbers using a hundred chart.

$$54 + 18 = 72$$

51	52	53	54	55	56	57	58	59	60
61	62	63	64	65	66	67	68	69	70
71	72	73	74	75	76	77	78	79	80

TOPIC 3
Add Within 100 Using Strategies

© Pearson Education, Inc. 2

This shows one way to model a 2-digit addition problem.

TOPIC 4
Fluently Add Within 100

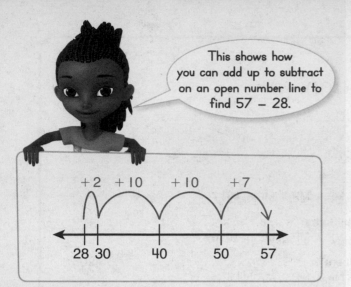

This shows how you can add up to subtract on an open number line to find 57 − 28.

TOPIC 5
Subtract Within 100 Using Strategies

© Pearson Education, Inc. 2

This shows how addition and subtraction are related. You can use addition to check subtraction.

TOPIC 6
Fluently Subtract Within 100

PearsonRealize.com

This shows how bar diagrams can be used to model and solve a two-step problem.

Mia sees 15 yellow birds and 16 red birds. Some birds fly away and now Mia sees 14 birds. How many birds flew away?

TOPIC 7
More Solving Problems Involving Addition and Subtraction

© Pearson Education, Inc. 2

This shows how to count on to find the total value.

Micah has the coins shown below. How many cents does Micah have?

50¢   75¢   85¢   90¢   91¢

TOPIC 8
Work with Time and Money

KEY

- ● Major Cluster
- ● Supporting Cluster
- ● Additional Cluster

The content is organized to focus on Common Core clusters.

Dear Families,

The standards on the following pages describe the math that students will learn this year. The greatest amount of time will be spent on standards in the major clusters.

Common Core Standards for Mathematical Content

DOMAIN 2.OA
OPERATIONS AND ALGEBRAIC THINKING

MAJOR CLUSTER 2.OA.A
Represent and solve problems involving addition and subtraction.

2.OA.A.1 Use addition and subtraction within 100 to solve one- and two-step word problems involving situations of adding to, taking from, putting together, taking apart, and comparing, with unknowns in all positions, e.g., by using drawings and equations with a symbol for the unknown number to represent the problem.

MAJOR CLUSTER 2.OA.B
Add and subtract within 20.

2.OA.B.2 Fluently add and subtract within 20 using mental strategies. By end of Grade 2, know from memory all sums of two one-digit numbers.

SUPPORTING CLUSTER 2.OA.C
Work with equal groups of objects to gain foundations for multiplication.

2.OA.C.3 Determine whether a group of objects (up to 20) has an odd or even number of members, e.g., by pairing objects or counting them by 2s; write an equation to express an even number as a sum of two equal addends.

2.OA.C.4 Use addition to find the total number of objects arranged in rectangular arrays with up to 5 rows and up to 5 columns; write an equation to express the total as a sum of equal addends.

Common Core Standards for Mathematical Content

DOMAIN 2.NBT
NUMBER AND OPERATIONS IN BASE TEN

MAJOR CLUSTER 2.NBT.A
Understand place value.

2.NBT.A.1 Understand that the three digits of a three-digit number represent amounts of hundreds, tens, and ones; e.g., 706 equals 7 hundreds, 0 tens, and 6 ones. Understand the following as special cases:

2.NBT.A.1a 100 can be thought of as a bundle of ten tens—called a "hundred."

2.NBT.A.1b The numbers 100, 200, 300, 400, 500, 600, 700, 800, 900 refer to one, two, three, four, five, six, seven, eight, or nine hundreds (and 0 tens and 0 ones).

2.NBT.A.2 Count within 1000; skip-count by 5s, 10s, and 100s.

2.NBT.A.3 Read and write numbers to 1000 using base-ten numerals, number names, and expanded form.

2.NBT.A.4 Compare two three-digit numbers based on meanings of the hundreds, tens, and ones digits, using >, =, and < symbols to record the results of comparisons.

MAJOR CLUSTER 2.NBT.B
Use place value understanding and properties of operations to add and subtract.

2.NBT.B.5 Fluently add and subtract within 100 using strategies based on place value, properties of operations, and/or the relationship between addition and subtraction.

2.NBT.B.6 Add up to four two-digit numbers using strategies based on place value and properties of operations.

2.NBT.B.7 Add and subtract within 1000, using concrete models or drawings and strategies based on place value, properties of operations, and/or the relationship between addition and subtraction; relate the strategy to a written method. Understand that in adding or subtracting three-digit numbers, one adds or subtracts hundreds and hundreds, tens and tens, ones and ones; and sometimes it is necessary to compose or decompose tens or hundreds.

2.NBT.B.8 Mentally add 10 or 100 to a given number 100–900, and mentally subtract 10 or 100 from a given number 100–900.

2.NBT.B.9 Explain why addition and subtraction strategies work, using place value and the properties of operations.[1]

Common Core Standards for Mathematical Content

DOMAIN 2.MD
MEASUREMENT AND DATA

MAJOR CLUSTER 2.MD.A
Measure and estimate lengths in standard units.

2.MD.A.1 Measure the length of an object by selecting and using appropriate tools such as rulers, yardsticks, meter sticks, and measuring tapes.

2.MD.A.2 Measure the length of an object twice, using length units of different lengths for the two measurements; describe how the two measurements relate to the size of the unit chosen.

2.MD.A.3 Estimate lengths using units of inches, feet, centimeters, and meters.

2.MD.A.4 Measure to determine how much longer one object is than another, expressing the length difference in terms of a standard length unit.

MAJOR CLUSTER 2.MD.B
Relate addition and subtraction to length.

2.MD.B.5 Use addition and subtraction within 100 to solve word problems involving lengths that are given in the same units, e.g., by using drawings (such as drawings of rulers) and equations with a symbol for the unknown number to represent the problem.

2.MD.B.6 Represent whole numbers as lengths from 0 on a number line diagram with equally spaced points corresponding to the numbers 0, 1, 2, …, and represent whole-number sums and differences within 100 on a number line diagram.

SUPPORTING CLUSTER 2.MD.C
Work with time and money.

2.MD.C.7 Tell and write time from analog and digital clocks to the nearest five minutes, using a.m. and p.m.

2.MD.C.8 Solve word problems involving dollar bills, quarters, dimes, nickels, and pennies, using $ and ¢ symbols appropriately. *Example: If you have 2 dimes and 3 pennies, how many cents do you have?*

SUPPORTING CLUSTER 2.MD.D
Represent and interpret data.

2.MD.D.9 Generate measurement data by measuring lengths of several objects to the nearest whole unit, or by making repeated measurements of the same object. Show the measurements by making a line plot, where the horizontal scale is marked off in whole-number units.

2.MD.D.10 Draw a picture graph and a bar graph (with single-unit scale) to represent a data set with up to four categories. Solve simple put-together, take-apart, and compare problems using information presented in a bar graph.

Common Core Standards for Mathematical Content

DOMAIN 2.G
GEOMETRY

ADDITIONAL CLUSTER 2.G.A
Reason with shapes and their attributes.

2.G.A.1 Recognize and draw shapes having specified attributes, such as a given number of angles or a given number of equal faces.[2] Identify triangles, quadrilaterals, pentagons, hexagons, and cubes.

2.G.A.2 Partition a rectangle into rows and columns of same-size squares and count to find the total number of them.

2.G.A.3 Partition circles and rectangles into two, three, or four equal shares, describe the shares using the words *halves, thirds, half of, a third of,* etc., and describe the whole as two halves, three thirds, four fourths. Recognize that equal shares of identical wholes need not have the same shape.

---

[1]Explanations may be supported by drawings or objects.

[2]Sizes are compared directly or visually, not compared by measuring.

Common Core Standards for Mathematical Practice

MP.1 MAKE SENSE OF PROBLEMS AND PERSEVERE IN SOLVING THEM.

Mathematically proficient students start by explaining to themselves the meaning of a problem and looking for entry points to its solution. They analyze givens, constraints, relationships, and goals. They make conjectures about the form and meaning of the solution and plan a solution pathway rather than simply jumping into a solution attempt. They consider analogous problems, and try special cases and simpler forms of the original problem in order to gain insight into its solution. They monitor and evaluate their progress and change course if necessary. Older students might, depending on the context of the problem, transform algebraic expressions or change the viewing window on their graphing calculator to get the information they need. Mathematically proficient students can explain correspondences between equations, verbal descriptions, tables, and graphs or draw diagrams of important features and relationships, graph data, and search for regularity or trends. Younger students might rely on using concrete objects or pictures to help conceptualize and solve a problem. Mathematically proficient students check their answers to problems using a different method, and they continually ask themselves, "Does this make sense?" They can understand the approaches of others to solving complex problems and identify correspondences between different approaches.

MP.2 REASON ABSTRACTLY AND QUANTITATIVELY.

Mathematically proficient students make sense of quantities and their relationships in problem situations. They bring two complementary abilities to bear on problems involving quantitative relationships: the ability to *decontextualize*—to abstract a given situation and represent it symbolically and manipulate the representing symbols as if they have a life of their own, without necessarily attending to their referents—and the ability to *contextualize*, to pause as needed during the manipulation process in order to probe into the referents for the symbols involved. Quantitative reasoning entails habits of creating a coherent representation of the problem at hand; considering the units involved; attending to the meaning of quantities, not just how to compute them; and knowing and flexibly using different properties of operations and objects.

MP.3 CONSTRUCT VIABLE ARGUMENTS AND CRITIQUE THE REASONING OF OTHERS.

Mathematically proficient students understand and use stated assumptions, definitions, and previously established results in constructing arguments. They make conjectures and build a logical progression of statements to explore the truth of their conjectures. They are able to analyze situations by breaking them into cases, and can recognize and use counterexamples. They justify their conclusions, communicate them to others, and respond to the arguments of others. They reason inductively about data, making plausible arguments that take into account the context from which the data arose. Mathematically proficient students are also able to compare the effectiveness of two plausible arguments, distinguish correct logic or reasoning from that which is flawed, and—if there is a flaw in an argument—explain what it is. Elementary students can construct arguments using concrete referents such as objects, drawings, diagrams, and actions. Such arguments can make sense and be correct, even though they are not generalized or made formal until later grades. Later, students learn to determine domains to which an argument applies. Students at all grades can listen or read the arguments of others, decide whether they make sense, and ask useful questions to clarify or improve the arguments.

MP.4 MODEL WITH MATHEMATICS.

Mathematically proficient students can apply the mathematics they know to solve problems arising in everyday life, society, and the workplace. In early grades, this might be as simple as writing an addition equation to describe a situation. In middle grades, a student might apply proportional reasoning to plan a school event or analyze a problem in the community. By high school, a student might use geometry to solve a design problem or use a function to describe how one quantity of interest depends on another. Mathematically proficient students who can apply what they know are comfortable making assumptions and approximations to simplify a complicated situation, realizing that these may need revision later. They are able to identify important quantities in a practical situation and map their relationships using such tools as diagrams, two-way tables, graphs, flowcharts, and formulas. They can analyze those relationships mathematically to draw conclusions. They routinely interpret their mathematical results in the context of the situation and reflect on whether the results make sense, possibly improving the model if it has not served its purpose.

Common Core Standards for Mathematical Practice

MP.5 USE APPROPRIATE TOOLS STRATEGICALLY.

Mathematically proficient students consider the available tools when solving a mathematical problem. These tools might include pencil and paper, concrete models, a ruler, a protractor, a calculator, a spreadsheet, a computer algebra system, a statistical package, or dynamic geometry software. Proficient students are sufficiently familiar with tools appropriate for their grade or course to make sound decisions about when each of these tools might be helpful, recognizing both the insight to be gained and their limitations. For example, mathematically proficient high school students analyze graphs of functions and solutions generated using a graphing calculator. They detect possible errors by strategically using estimation and other mathematical knowledge. When making mathematical models, they know that technology can enable them to visualize the results of varying assumptions, explore consequences, and compare predictions with data. Mathematically proficient students at various grade levels are able to identify relevant external mathematical resources, such as digital content located on a website, and use them to pose or solve problems. They are able to use technological tools to explore and deepen their understanding of concepts.

MP.6 ATTEND TO PRECISION.

Mathematically proficient students try to communicate precisely to others. They try to use clear definitions in discussion with others and in their own reasoning. They state the meaning of the symbols they choose, including using the equal sign consistently and appropriately. They are careful about specifying units of measure, and labeling axes to clarify the correspondence with quantities in a problem. They calculate accurately and efficiently, express numerical answers with a degree of precision appropriate for the problem context. In the elementary grades, students give carefully formulated explanations to each other. By the time they reach high school they have learned to examine claims and make explicit use of definitions.

MP.7 LOOK FOR AND MAKE USE OF STRUCTURE.

Mathematically proficient students look closely to discern a pattern or structure. Young students, for example, might notice that three and seven more is the same amount as seven and three more, or they may sort a collection of shapes according to how many sides the shapes have. Later, students will see 7×8 equals the well remembered $7 \times 5 + 7 \times 3$, in preparation for learning about the distributive property. In the expression $x^2 + 9x + 14$, older students can see the 14 as 2×7 and the 9 as $2 + 7$. They recognize the significance of an existing line in a geometric figure and can use the strategy of drawing an auxiliary line for solving problems. They also can step back for an overview and shift perspective. They can see complicated things, such as some algebraic expressions, as single objects or as being composed of several objects. For example, they can see $5 - 3(x - y)^2$ as 5 minus a positive number times a square and use that to realize that its value cannot be more than 5 for any real numbers x and y.

MP.8 LOOK FOR AND EXPRESS REGULARITY IN REPEATED REASONING.

Mathematically proficient students notice if calculations are repeated, and look both for general methods and for shortcuts. Upper elementary students might notice when dividing 25 by 11 that they are repeating the same calculations over and over again, and conclude they have a repeating decimal. By paying attention to the calculation of slope as they repeatedly check whether points are on the line through $(1, 2)$ with slope 3, middle school students might abstract the equation $(y - 2)/(x - 1) = 3$. Noticing the regularity in the way terms cancel when expanding $(x - 1)(x + 1)$, $(x - 1)(x^2 + x + 1)$, and $(x - 1)(x^3 + x^2 + x + 1)$ might lead them to the general formula for the sum of a geometric series. As they work to solve a problem, mathematically proficient students maintain oversight of the process, while attending to the details. They continually evaluate the reasonableness of their intermediate results.

Math Practices and Problem Solving Handbook

Math practices are ways we think about and do math.

Math practices will help you solve problems.

Math Practices

| MP.1 | Make sense of problems and persevere in solving them. |

| MP.2 | Reason abstractly and quantitatively. |

| MP.3 | Construct viable arguments and critique the reasoning of others. |

| MP.4 | Model with mathematics. |

| MP.5 | Use appropriate tools strategically. |

| MP.6 | Attend to precision. |

| MP.7 | Look for and make use of structure. |

| MP.8 | Look for and express regularity in repeated reasoning. |

There are good Thinking Habits for each of these math practices.

MP.1 Make sense of problems and persevere in solving them.

Good math thinkers know what the problem is about. They have a plan to solve it. They keep trying if they get stuck.

My plan is to use counters as trucks. I can act out the problem.

A store has some toy trucks.
Mike buys 2 of the trucks.
Now the store has 3 trucks.
How many trucks did the store have at the start?

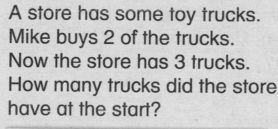

5 − 2 = 3
5 trucks

Thinking Habits

What do I need to find?

What do I know?

What's my plan for solving the problem?

What else can I try if I get stuck?

How can I check that my solution makes sense?

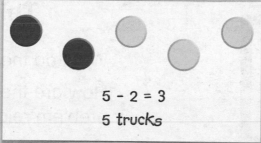

MP.2 # Reason abstractly and quantitatively.

I completed a part-part-whole model. It shows how things in the problem are related.

Good math thinkers know how to think about words and numbers to solve problems.

Tony has 10 apples. 6 are red. The rest are green. How many apples are green?

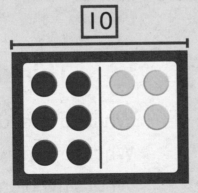

10 − 6 = 4

4 apples are green.

Thinking Habits

What do the numbers stand for?

How are the numbers in the problem related?

How can I show a word problem using pictures or numbers?

How can I use a word problem to show what an equation means?

Math Practices and Problem Solving Handbook

MP.3 Construct viable arguments and critique the reasoning of others.

I can use place-value blocks to check Paula's thinking. My explanation is clear and complete.

Good math thinkers use math to explain why they are right. They talk about math that others do, too.

Paula added 34 + 5.
She says she had to regroup the ones.
Is she correct? Show how you know.

34 has 4 ones.

4 ones and 5 ones are 9 ones.

Paula is incorrect.

You do not need to regroup ones.

Tens	Ones

34 + 5 = 39

Thinking Habits

How can I use math to explain my work?

Am I using numbers and symbols correctly?

Is my explanation clear?

What questions can I ask to understand other people's thinking?

Are there mistakes in other people's thinking?

Can I improve other people's thinking?

MP.4 Model with mathematics.

I can use ten-frames and counters to show the problem.

Good math thinkers use math they know to show and solve problems.

14 dogs are playing at a park.
9 dogs go home.
How many dogs are still at the park?

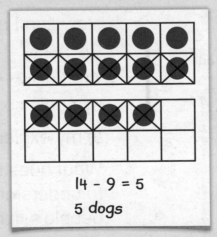

14 − 9 = 5
5 dogs

Thinking Habits

How can I use the math I know to help solve this problem?

Can I use a drawing, diagram, table, graph, or objects to show the problem?

Can I write an equation to show the problem?

Math Practices and Problem Solving Handbook

MP.5 Use appropriate tools strategically.

Good math thinkers know how to pick the right tools to solve math problems.

I chose connecting cubes to solve the problem.

Kai and Maddie each pick 6 apples.
Then Maddie picks 1 more apple.
How many apples do they pick in all?

6 + 7 = 13

13 apples

Thinking Habits

Which tools can I use?

Is there a different tool I could use?

Am I using the tool correctly?

MP.6 Attend to precision.

Good math thinkers are careful about what they write and say, so their ideas about math are clear.

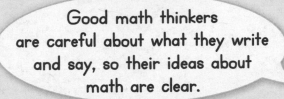

I can use the definition of a cube to help me describe what it looks like.

Circle each cube below.

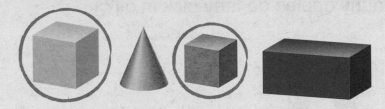

Describe what a cube looks like.

A cube has 6 flat surfaces.

Each flat surface is the same size.

A cube has 12 edges.

Thinking Habits

Am I using numbers, units, and symbols correctly?

Am I using the correct definitions?

Is my answer clear?

Math Practices and Problem Solving Handbook

MP.7 Look for and make use of structure.

It is hard to add three numbers at once. I can add any two numbers first. I added 6 + 4 first to make the problem easier.

Good math thinkers look for patterns in math to help solve problems.

Jeff saw 6 brown frogs, 3 green frogs, and 4 spotted frogs.
How many frogs did Jeff see in all?

Show your work and explain your answer.

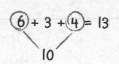

I made 10 then added 3 to make the problem easier.

Thinking Habits

Is there a pattern?

How can I describe the pattern?

Can I break the problem into simpler parts?

MP.8 Look for and express regularity in repeated reasoning.

I can compare the tens first. If the tens are the same, I can compare the ones.

Good math thinkers look for things that repeat in a problem. They use what they learn from one problem to help them solve other problems.

Compare each pair of numbers.
Write <, >, or =. Tell how you will compare each pair of numbers.

57 ⊙< 75   49 ⊙< 52

36 ⊙> 34   61 ⊙= 61

Thinking Habits

Does something repeat in the problem?

How can the solution help me solve another problem?

Math Practices and Problem Solving Handbook

Problem Solving Guide

Math practices can help you solve problems.

Make Sense of the Problem

Reason
- What do I need to find?
- What given information can I use?
- How are the quantities related?

Think About Similar Problems
- Have I solved problems like this before?

Persevere in Solving the Problem

Model with Math
- How can I use the math I know?
- How can I show the problem?
- Is there a pattern I can use?

Use Appropriate Tools
- What math tools could I use?
- How can I use those tools?

Check the Answer

Make Sense of the Answer
- Is my answer reasonable?

Check for Precision
- Did I check my work?
- Is my answer clear?
- Is my explanation clear?

Some Ways to Show Problems

- Draw a Picture
- Draw a Number Line
- Write an Equation

Some Math Tools

- Objects
- Rulers
- Technology
- Paper and Pencil

Math Practices and Problem Solving Handbook

Problem Solving Recording Sheet

This sheet helps you organize your work.

Name **Mary**

Teaching Tool
1

Problem Solving Recording Sheet

Problem:
John bikes for 17 miles on Monday.
He bikes for 15 miles on Tuesday.
How many miles does John bike in all?

MAKE SENSE OF THE PROBLEM

Need to Find

I need to find how many miles John bikes in all.

Given

John bikes 17 miles on Monday and 15 miles on Tuesday.

PERSEVERE IN SOLVING THE PROBLEM

Some Ways to Represent Problems
☑ Draw a Picture
☐ Draw a Number Line
☑ Write an Equation

Some Math Tools
☐ Objects
☐ Rulers
☐ Technology
☑ Paper and Pencil

Solution and Answer

$17 + 15 = 32$

I made a 10.
John bikes 32 miles in all.

CHECK THE ANSWER

I checked my drawing of blocks.
They matched the problem and show 32 in all.

 TT1

Fluently Add and Subtract Within 20

Essential Question: What are strategies for finding addition and subtraction facts?

Digital Resources

Solve Learn Glossary

Tools Assessment Help Games

Look at the different types of paper!

Different papers have different properties.

Wow! Let's do this project and learn more.

Math and Science Project: Material Math

Find Out Collect different types of paper. Talk about the uses of paper. Tell how strong each type of paper is. Tell how the paper feels. Tell if the paper can soak up water.

Journal: Make a Book Show what you find out in a book. In your book, also:

• Glue samples of paper and tell what you found.

• Choose a type of paper to make flash cards of addition and subtraction facts.

Name _____

Review What You Know

1. Circle the symbol for **equals**.

$$-$$
$$+$$
$$=$$

2. Circle the symbol for **minus**.

3. Circle the number that is the **whole**.

$$4 + 2 = 6$$

Subtraction Stories

4. There are 7 birds on a fence. 2 fly away. How many birds are left?

_____ birds

Addition Stories

5. Write an equation to solve the problem.

Kate draws 4 big stars. Then she draws 2 small stars. How many stars does Kate draw in all?

_____ + _____ = _____

Making 10

6. Write the numbers that show a way to make 10.

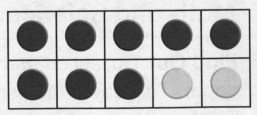

_____ + _____ = _____

My Word Cards

Study the words on the front of the card.
Complete the activity on the back.

A-Z Glossary

addend

$2 + 5 = 7$

addends

sum

$3 + 4 - 7$

$$\begin{array}{r} 4 \\ + 3 \\ \hline 7 \end{array}$$

sum ⟶ 7

equation

$3 + 4 = 7$

$14 - 6 = 8$

doubles

$4 + 4 = 8$

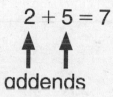

near doubles

$4 + 5 = 9$

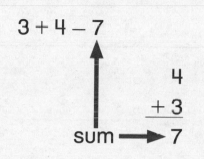

difference

$14 - 6 = 8$

$$\begin{array}{r} 14 \\ - 6 \\ \hline 8 \end{array}$$

difference ⟶ 8

Use what you know to complete the sentences.
Extend learning by writing your own sentence using each word.

An _____

uses an equal sign (=) to show that the value on the left is the same as the value on the right.

The answer in an addition equation is called the

_____.

Numbers that are added are called

_____.

The answer in a subtraction equation is called the

_____.

Addition facts that have two addends that are close are called

_____.

Addition facts that have two addends that are the same are called

_____.

Name _____

Solve & Share

Use cubes to show $4 + 5$.

What will happen to the total number of cubes if you change the order of the numbers being added? Explain.

I can ...
count on to add and add in any order.

Content Standard 2.OA.B.2
Mathematical Practices MP.2, MP.4, MP.7, MP.8

$4 + 5 =$ _____   _____ $+$ _____ $=$ _____

You can count on to find $6 + 3$.

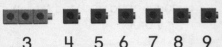

6   7   8   9

Or count on to find $3 + 6$.

3   4   5   6   7   8   9

Counting on from the greater number is easier!

An **equation** uses an equal sign (=) to show that the value on the left is the same as the value on the right.

$$6 + 3 = 9$$

$$3 + 6 = 9$$

You can change the order of the **addends**.

$$6 + 3 = 9$$

$$3 + 6 = 9$$

The sum is the same.

addend addend **sum**

You can add numbers in any order, and the sum is the same.

So, $6 + 3 = 3 + 6$.

You can write the facts this way, too.

$$\begin{array}{r} 6 \\ +3 \\ \hline 9 \end{array} \qquad \begin{array}{r} 3 \\ +6 \\ \hline 9 \end{array}$$

Do You Understand?

Show Me! Does $5 + 2 = 2 + 5$? How do you know?

☆ Guided Practice ☆

Count on to find the sum. Then change the order of the addends.

1.

$$3 + 1 = \underline{4}$$

$$\underline{1} + \underline{3} = \underline{4}$$

2.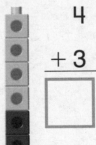

$$\begin{array}{r} 4 \\ +3 \\ \hline \square \end{array}$$

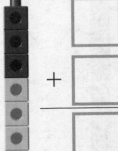

$$\begin{array}{r} \square \\ +\ \square \\ \hline \square \end{array}$$

© Pearson Education, Inc. 2

Name _____

Tools Assessment

Independent Practice

Count on to find the sum. Then change the order of the addends. Use cubes if needed.

3. 8 + 2 = ____

____ + ____ = ____

4. 8 + 5 = ____

____ + ____ = ____

5. 9 + 3 = ____

____ + ____ = ____

6. 8 + 4 = ____

____ + ____ = ____

7. 7 + 4 = ____

____ + ____ = ____

8. 7 + 3 = ____

____ + ____ = ____

9.
```
    7         □
  + 2    +  □
  ____    ____
   □       □
```

10.
```
    6         □
  + 2    +  □
  ____    ____
   □       □
```

11.
```
    5         □
  + 6    +  □
  ____    ____
   □       □
```

12. **Algebra** Write the missing numbers.

6 + ____ = 4 + 6

8 + 2 = ____ + 8

6 + ____ = 5 + 6

____ + 7 = 7 + 4

9 + 3 = 3 + ____

____ + 8 = 8 + 4

13. © **MP.4 Model** Joy has 8 bean plants and 6 corn plants in her garden. How many plants does she have in all? Draw a picture. Then write facts for this story with the addends in a different order.

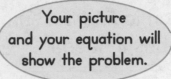

Your picture and your equation will show the problem.

____ + ____ = ____

____ + ____ = ____

---

14. **Higher Order Thinking** Find the objects in Box 1 and Box 2 that are the same. Write an equation to show how many of each object there are. Then change the order of the addends.

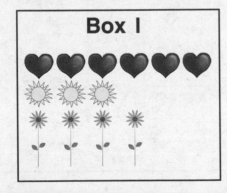

Box 1

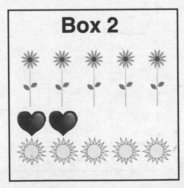

Box 2

♥ ____ + ____ = ____ = ____ + ____

✿ ____ + ____ = ____ = ____ + ____

✾ ____ + ____ = ____ = ____ + ____

15. © **Assessment** Kate has 7 fish. Nick has 5 fish. How many fish do Kate and Nick have in all?

Which shows how to count on to solve the problem?

Ⓐ 7, 8, 9, 10, 11, 12

Ⓑ 1, 2, 3, 4, 5

Ⓒ 7 − 5

Ⓓ 7, 8, 9, 10, 11

© Pearson Education, Inc. 2

Topic 1 | Lesson 1

Name _____

Another Look! You can count on to find a sum. Counting on from a greater number is easier.

I can add numbers in any order and get the same sum.

5   6   7

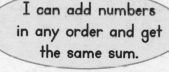

2   3 4 5 6 7

$5 + 2 = \underline{7}$

$\underline{2} + \underline{5} = \underline{7}$

HOME ACTIVITY Have your child use small clothing items, such as socks or mittens, to model counting on to find $5 + 4$. Then ask your child to explain why $5 + 4$ and $4 + 5$ have the same sum.

Count on to find the sum. Then change the order of the addends.

1.

$3 + 4 = \underline{}$

$\underline{} + \underline{} = \underline{}$

2.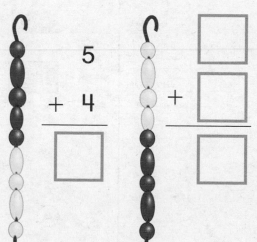

$\begin{array}{r} 5 \\ + \ 4 \\ \hline \end{array}$

$\begin{array}{r} \square \\ + \ \square \\ \hline \square \end{array}$

3.

$7 + 6 = \underline{}$

$\underline{} + \underline{} = \underline{}$

Write two addition facts for each story. Then solve.

4. © **MP.2 Reasoning** Danny collects toy train cars. He has 9 red train cars and 5 black train cars. How many train cars does he have in all?

_____ + _____ = _____

_____ + _____ = _____

_____ train cars

5. © **MP.2 Reasoning** Ana draws 3 red circles and 8 blue circles. How many circles does Ana draw?

_____ + _____ = _____

_____ + _____ = _____

_____ circles

6. **Higher Order Thinking** Draw a picture to solve. Then write two addition facts for the story.

15 cows live at a farm. Some of the cows are brown and some are white. How many of each color could be at the farm?

_____ + _____ = 15

_____ + _____ = 15

_____ brown cows

_____ white cows

7. © **Assessment** Which shape belongs in the second equation?

 +  = ○

 + ? = ○

              ▭   ⬡

Ⓐ   Ⓑ   Ⓒ   Ⓓ

© Pearson Education, Inc. 2

Name _____

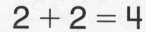
Solve & Share

You know that $2 + 2 = 4$.
Tell how knowing that fact can help you find $2 + 3$.

I can ...
use doubles and near doubles to add quickly and accurately.

Content Standard 2.OA.B.2
Mathematical Practices MP.4, MP.6, MP.7, MP.8

$2 + 2 = 4$ $2 + 3 = $ _____

Find 7 + 8 and find 7 + 9.

You can use a doubles fact to help you add.

Doubles

3 + 3   5 + 5

4 + 4

You can use the doubles fact to help find a **near doubles** fact.

Doubles Fact: 7 + 7 = 14

7 + 8 is 1 more than 7 + 7.

7 + 9 is 2 more than 7 + 7.

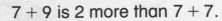

7 + 8 = 15 and 7 + 9 = 16 These are near doubles facts.

Do You Understand?

Show Me! How could you use the doubles fact 7 + 7 to find 7 + 9?

Guided Practice   Complete the doubles facts.
Use the doubles facts to solve the near doubles.

1. $2 + 2 = \underline{4}$ $2 + 3 = \underline{}$

2. $\underline{} = 4 + 4$ $\underline{} = 4 + 5$

3.
$$\begin{array}{r} 3 \\ + 3 \\ \hline \square \end{array}$$

$$\begin{array}{r} 3 \\ + 4 \\ \hline \square \end{array}$$

4.
$$\begin{array}{r} 5 \\ + 5 \\ \hline \square \end{array}$$

$$\begin{array}{r} 5 \\ + 7 \\ \hline \square \end{array}$$

Tools Assessment

Independent Practice

Complete the doubles facts. Use the doubles facts to solve the near doubles.

5. $6 + 6 =$ _____ $6 + 7 =$ _____

6. $5 + 5 =$ _____ $5 + 6 =$ _____

7. $8 + 8 =$ _____ $8 + 10 =$ _____

8. _____ $= 1 + 1$ _____ $= 1 + 3$

9.
$$\begin{array}{r} 2 \\ +2 \\ \hline \square \end{array}$$
$$\begin{array}{r} 2 \\ +3 \\ \hline \square \end{array}$$

10.
$$\begin{array}{r} 4 \\ +4 \\ \hline \square \end{array}$$
$$\begin{array}{r} 4 \\ +5 \\ \hline \square \end{array}$$

11.
$$\begin{array}{r} 8 \\ +8 \\ \hline \square \end{array}$$
$$\begin{array}{r} 8 \\ +9 \\ \hline \square \end{array}$$

12.
$$\begin{array}{r} 3 \\ +3 \\ \hline \square \end{array}$$
$$\begin{array}{r} 3 \\ +5 \\ \hline \square \end{array}$$

13.
$$\begin{array}{r} 5 \\ +5 \\ \hline \square \end{array}$$
$$\begin{array}{r} 5 \\ +7 \\ \hline \square \end{array}$$

14.
$$\begin{array}{r} 7 \\ +7 \\ \hline \square \end{array}$$
$$\begin{array}{r} 7 \\ +9 \\ \hline \square \end{array}$$

15. **Algebra** Complete the doubles and near doubles facts.

$9 + \boxed{} = 18$ $\boxed{} + \boxed{} = 19$

16. © **MP.4 Model** John drew 4 houses.
Then he drew 5 more houses.
How many houses did John draw in all?

Draw a picture and write an equation.

_____ + _____ = _____ houses

17. **Higher Order Thinking** Choose a doubles fact. Use that doubles fact to draw a picture that shows a near doubles story.

18. © **Assessment** Kate's dog had 6 puppies. Jim's dog had 1 more puppy than Kate's dog.

Which equation shows how many puppies in all?

Ⓐ $6 + 1 = 7$

Ⓑ $6 + 6 = 12$

Ⓒ $6 + 7 = 13$

Ⓓ $7 + 7 = 14$

Name _____

Another Look! You can use a doubles fact to solve a near doubles fact.

To solve a near doubles fact, you can add 1 or 2 more to the doubles fact.

HOME ACTIVITY Have your child use common objects, such as pennies or buttons, to show doubles and near doubles. Then ask your child to write equations to show the facts.

$6 + 6 = \underline{12}$

Doubles Fact

$6 + 7 = \underline{13}$

Near Doubles Fact

Write and solve the doubles facts and the near doubles facts.

1.

_____ + _____ = _____   _____ + _____ = _____

2.

_____ + _____ = _____   _____ + _____ = _____

3. $7 + 7 = $ _____

$7 + 9 = $ _____

4. $8 + 8 = $ _____

$8 + 10 = $ _____

In 5 and 6, write an equation to solve the problem. Use doubles facts to help you.

5. **Algebra** A number plus 6 equals 12.
What is the number?

_____ + _____ = _____

The number is _____.

6. **Algebra** 6 plus a number equals 13.
What is the number?

_____ + _____ = _____

The number is _____.

7. **A-Z Vocabulary** Which is a **near doubles** fact?
Circle the fact.

$4 + 4 = 8$ $4 + 5 = 9$

$2 + 7 = 9$ $0 + 5 = 5$

8. **Higher Order Thinking** Draw a picture to show the story.

Then write an equation for the story.

Jane has 5 books.
Fred has 2 more books than Jane.
How many books do Fred and
Jane have in all?

_____ + _____ = _____

_____ books

9. **© Assessment** Terry's dollhouse has 7 windows on the first floor and 8 windows on the second floor.

Which shows how Terry found the number of windows in all?

Ⓐ $6 + 6$ and I more is 13.

Ⓑ $7 + 7$ and I more is 15.

Ⓒ $8 + 8$ and I more is 17.

Ⓓ $9 + 9$ and I more is 19.

Name _____

Solve & Share

How can thinking about 10 help you find 9 + 3?
Use the ten-frames and counters to show how.

I can ...
make a 10 to help me add
quickly and accurately.

© **Content Standard** 2.OA.B.2
Mathematical Practices MP.1,
MP.2, MP.3, MP.5, MP.7

$$\begin{array}{r} 9 \\ + 3 \\ \hline \end{array}$$

You can make a 10 to help you add.

8
+ 5
─────
[?]

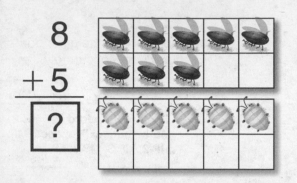

Move 2 counters to make a 10.

Add with 10.

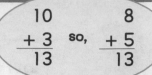

$$\begin{array}{cc} 10 & 8 \\ +3 & +5 \\ \hline 13 & 13 \end{array}$$ so,

Do You Understand?

Show Me! Why do you move 2 counters to add 8 + 5?

★ **Guided Practice** ★ Make a 10 to add.
Use counters and ten-frames.

1.   7
    + 4
    ─────
    [?]

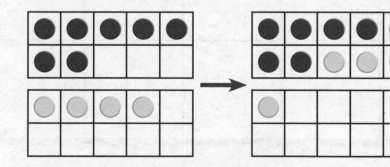

$$\begin{array}{ccc} 10 & & 7 \\ + \boxed{\text{I}} & \text{so,} & + \boxed{} \\ \hline \boxed{\text{II}} & & \boxed{} \end{array}$$

Topic 1 | Lesson 3

Tools Assessment

Independent Practice ☆ Make a 10 to add. Use counters and ten-frames.

2. 8
     + 4
     ☐

3. 3
     + 9
     ☐

4. 6
     + 7
     ☐

5. 5
     + 8
     ☐

6. 7
     + 5
     ☐

7. 5 + 9 = _____

8. 3 + 8 = _____

9. 4 + 9 = _____

10. 7 + 9 = _____

Algebra Which number is missing?

11. 8 + 5 = ☐ + 3

12. 6 + 9 = 10 + ☐

13. 8 + 9 = 10 + ☐

14. Higher Order Thinking Can you make a 10 to help you add 7 + 4 + 5? Explain.

_____

_____

15. Tan's team scored 16 points in a game. During the first half, they scored 9 points. How many points did the team score in the second half of the game?

_____ points

16. ⓒ **MP.1 Make Sense** The school has a clothing drive for charity. Ana's class donates 8 coats. Nico's class donates 5 hats. Adam's class donates 8 coats. How many coats were donated in all?

_____ coats

17. Higher Order Thinking Draw a picture to show how you can make a 10 to help you add 3 + 5 + 9.

18. ⓒ **Assessment** Mary wrote an equation. Which number makes her equation true?

$8 + 9 = 10 +$ _____

Ⓐ   5

Ⓑ   6

Ⓒ   7

Ⓓ   8

Think about making a 10. Find the missing addend!

© Pearson Education, Inc. 2

Name _____

Another Look! You can make a 10 to help you add.

This shows 8 + 4.

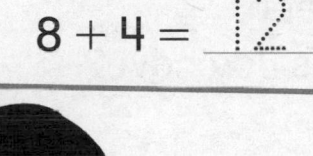

Show 10 + 2.
Move 2 counters to make a 10.

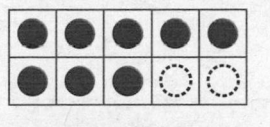

The sums are the same!

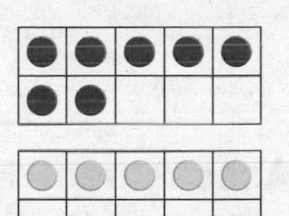

8 + 4 is the same as 10 + 2.

8 + 4 = <u>12</u>   10 + 2 = <u>12</u>

HOME ACTIVITY Have your child use buttons to make a group of 9 and a group of 5. Ask your child to show you how to make a group of 10 buttons to help find the sum.

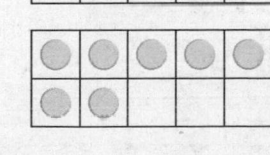

Make a 10 to help you add.

1. Find 9 + 7.   Move 1 counter to make a 10.

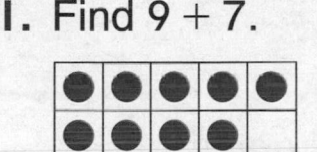   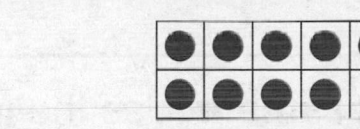

9 + 7 is the same as 10 + ___.

9 + 7 = ___   ___ + ___ = ___

2. Find 7 + 5.

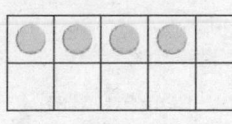

Move ___ counters to make a 10.

7 + 5 is the same as 10 + ___.

7 + 5 = ___   ___ + ___ = ___

Add. Then draw lines to match addition problems with the same sum.

3. 9 + 6 = _____   10 + 2 = _____

4. 7 + 5 = _____   10 + 3 = _____

5. 9 + 5 = _____   10 + 4 = _____

6. 5 + 8 = _____   10 + 5 = _____

Explain how you solved the problem!

7. © MP.3 Explain Blanca wants to add 5 + 8. Describe how she can make a 10 to solve.

5 + 8 = _____

_____

_____

8. Higher Order Thinking
Jay has 14 blocks in all.
He has 6 yellow blocks.
The rest of the blocks are green.
How many green blocks does Jay have?
Make a 10 to solve.
Jay has _____ green blocks.

_____

_____

9. © Assessment Beth has 8 fish and 7 snails. How can Beth make a 10 to find how many fish and snails she has in all?

10 + 9   10 + 8   10 + 7   10 + 5
Ⓐ   Ⓑ   Ⓒ   Ⓓ

10. © Assessment Use the ten-frames.
Show how to find 7 + 6 by making a 10.

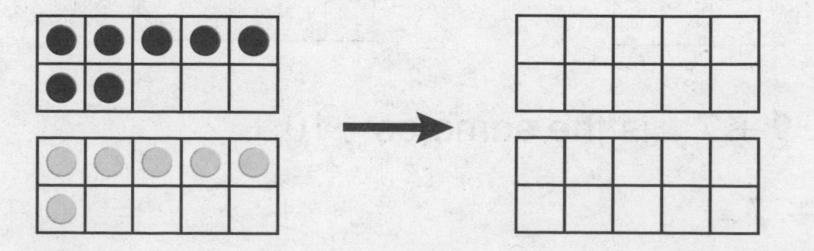

© Pearson Education, Inc. 2

Solve & Share

Look at the sums on an addition facts table for addends 0 to 5. Describe one of the patterns that you see.

Use words, colors, or addition facts to describe the patterns.

+	0	1	2	3	4	5
0	0	1	2	3	4	5
1	1	2	3	4	5	6
2	2	3	4	5	6	7
3	3	4	5	6	7	8
4	4	5	6	7	8	9
5	5	6	7	8	9	10

I can ...
use the patterns on an addition facts table to help me remember the addition facts.

© **Content Standard** 2.OA.B.2
Mathematical Practices MP.2, MP.5, MP.6, MP.7, MP.8

_____

_____

_____

How can you describe a pattern for all the sums of six?

It makes a diagonal pattern.

+	0	1	2	3	4	5	6	7	8	9	10
0	0	1	2	3	4	5	6	7	8	9	10
1	1	2	3	4	5	6	7	8	9	10	11
2	2	3	4	5	6	7	8	9	10	11	12
3	3	4	5	6	7	8	9	10	11	12	13
4	4	5	6	7	8	9	10	11	12	13	14
5	5	6	7	8	9	10	11	12	13	14	15
6	6	7	8	9	10	11	12	13	14	15	16
7	7	8	9	10	11	12	13	14	15	16	17
8	8	9	10	11	12	13	14	15	16	17	18
9	9	10	11	12	13	14	15	16	17	18	19
10	10	11	12	13	14	15	16	17	18	19	20

You can write an addition equation.

$4 + 2 = 6$

4 and 2 are addends for the sum of 6.

+	0	1	2	3	4
0	0	1	2	3	4
1	1	2	3	4	5
2	2	3	4	5	6

Here are all the ways to make a sum of 6.

$6 + 0 = 6$
$5 + 1 = 6$
$4 + 2 = 6$
$3 + 3 = 6$
$2 + 4 = 6$
$1 + 5 = 6$
$0 + 6 = 6$

What pattern do you see?

Do You Understand?

Show Me! How can patterns on an addition facts table help you remember the addition facts?

☆ Guided Practice   Use fact patterns to complete each equation.

1. $10 + \underline{6} = 16$

   $9 + 7 = \underline{16}$

   $\underline{8} + 8 = 16$

   $7 + \underline{9} = 16$

   $6 + \underline{10} = 16$

2. $10 + \underline{} = 14$

   $\underline{} + 5 = 14$

   $8 + 6 = \underline{}$

   $7 + \underline{} = 14$

   $\underline{} + 6 = 14$

   $9 + \underline{} = 14$

   $\underline{} + 4 = 14$

3. $9 + \underline{} = 9$

   $\underline{} + 1 = 9$

   $7 + 2 = \underline{}$

   $6 + \underline{} = 9$

   $\underline{} + 4 = 9$

   $5 + \underline{} = 9$

   $3 + \underline{} = 9$

   $\underline{} + 2 = 9$

   $8 + 1 = \underline{}$

   $\underline{} + 0 = 9$

Topic 1 | Lesson 4

Name _____

Independent Practice ☆   Use fact patterns to complete each equation.

4. 10 + ____ = 12

____ + 3 = 12

8 + 4 = ____

____ + 7 = 12

6 + 6 = ____

7 + ____ = 12

____ + 4 = 12

9 + ____ = 12

5. 7 + ____ = 7

____ + 1 = 7

5 + 2 = ____

____ + 3 = 7

____ + 4 = 7

____ + 5 = 7

____ + 6 = 7

0 + ____ = 7

6. 10 + ____ = 15

____ + 5 = 15

9 + 6 = ____

9 + ____ = 15

7 + ____ = 15

____ + 7 = 15

---

7. Number Sense Find the 8 in the top row of the addition facts table. Complete all of the equations using the 8-column on the table. What pattern do you see?

8 + ____ = 8

8 + ____ = 9

8 + ____ = 10

8 + 3 = ____

8 + ____ = 12

8 + ____ = ____

8 + 6 = ____

8 + ____ = 15

8 + 8 = ____

8 + ____ = ____

8 + 10 = ____

_____

_____

_____

_____

8. © **MP.2 Reasoning** Lucy is sorting items by their texture. She finds 6 items that are bumpy. Lucy finds 5 items that are smooth. How many items does Lucy find in all?

_____ items

9. **A-Z Vocabulary** Look at the **equation** below. Circle the **addends**. Draw a square around the **sum**.

$$9 + 5 = 14$$

10. **Higher Order Thinking** Write 8 addition facts that have a sum of 12. How can patterns help you?

_____

_____

_____

11. © **Assessment** Which have a sum of 17? Choose all that apply.

☐ $10 + 7 = ?$

☐ $7 + 6 = ?$

☐ $9 + 8 = ?$

☐ $8 + 8 = ?$

Think about fact patterns.

Another Look! You can use your addition table to find the addition facts that have 7 as an addend.

Find the 7 in the top row of the table.

Write an equation for each sum in that column.

+	0	1	2	3	4	5	6	7	8	9	10
0	0	1	2	3	4	5	6	7	8	9	10
1	1	2	3	4	5	6	7	8	9	10	11
2	2	3	4	5	6	7	8	9	10	11	12
3	3	4	5	6	7	8	9	10	11	12	13
4	4	5	6	7	8	9	10	11	12	13	14
5	5	6	7	8	9	10	11	12	13	14	15
6	6	7	8	9	10	11	12	13	14	15	16
7	7	8	9	10	11	12	13	14	15	16	17
8	8	9	10	11	12	13	14	15	16	17	18
9	9	10	11	12	13	14	15	16	17	18	19
10	10	11	12	13	14	15	16	17	18	19	20

$0 + 7 = 7$ $5 + 7 = 12$

$1 + 7 = 8$ $6 + 7 = 13$

$2 + 7 = 9$ $7 + 7 = 14$

$3 + 7 = 10$ $8 + 7 = 15$

$4 + 7 = 11$ $9 + 7 = 16$

$10 + 7 = 17$

HOME ACTIVITY Have your child practice using an addition facts table by asking your child to write an equation for each sum that is 16.

You can add in any order. So, complete the list by switching the order of the addends.

Use fact patterns to complete each equation.

1. $9 + 6 = $ _____

_____ $+ 7 = 15$

$7 + $ _____ $= 15$

$6 + $ _____ $= 15$

2. $0 + $ _____ $= 4$

$1 + 3 = $ _____

_____ $+ 2 = 4$

$3 + $ _____ $= 4$

_____ $+ 4 = 4$

3. $5 + $ _____ $= 6$

$4 + $ _____ $= 6$

$3 + 3 = $ _____

_____ $+ 4 = 6$

_____ $+ 5 = 6$

4. $10 + \underline{\quad} = 11$ $5 + \underline{\quad} = 11$ 5. $9 + 9 = \underline{\quad}$ $\underline{\quad} + 4 = 13$

   $\underline{\quad} + 2 = 11$ $4 + \underline{\quad} = 11$ $9 + \underline{\quad} = 17$ $9 + 3 = \underline{\quad}$

   $8 + 3 = \underline{\quad}$ $3 + \underline{\quad} = 11$ $\underline{\quad} + 7 = 16$ $9 + \underline{\quad} = 11$

   $7 + \underline{\quad} = 11$ $\underline{\quad} + 2 = 11$ $9 + 6 = \underline{\quad}$ $\underline{\quad} + 1 = 10$

   $\underline{\quad} + 5 = 11$ $1 + 10 = \underline{\quad}$ $9 + \underline{\quad} = 14$ $9 + 0 = \underline{\quad}$

   $0 + \underline{\quad} = 11$

6. **Higher Order Thinking** Write 8 equations with 2 addends that have a sum of 13. Use patterns to help you.

   _____

   _____

   _____

7. © **Assessment** Which have a sum of 19? Choose all that apply.

   ☐ $10 + 9 = ?$

   ☐ $8 + 8 = ?$

   ☐ $9 + 9 = ?$

   ☐ $9 + 10 = ?$

8. © **Assessment** Which have a sum of 15? Choose all that apply.

   ☐ $7 + 8 = ?$

   ☐ $8 + 7 = ?$

   ☐ $9 + 6 = ?$

   ☐ $5 + 10 = ?$

Solve

Solve & Share

How can counting help you find 12 − 4? Use the number line to show your work.

$$12 - 4 = \underline{\hspace{1.5cm}}$$

Find 10 − 4.

You can count on to subtract.

Start with the lesser number.

Count on to 10 to find the **difference**.

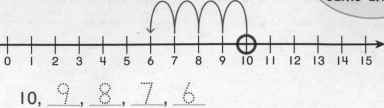

4, _5_, _6_, _7_, _8_, _9_, _10_

It takes 6 moves to count on from 4 to 10.

So, 10 − 4 = 6.

Draw each move as you count.

You can also count back to subtract.

Start with the greater number.

Count back 4 moves.

Counting on and counting back give you the same answer.

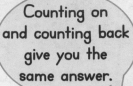

10, _9_, _8_, _7_, _6_

You land on 6. So, 10 − 4 = 6.

Do You Understand?

Show Me! How can you count back on a number line to find 9 − 5?

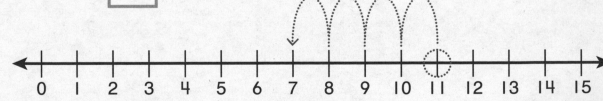

☆ **Guided Practice** ☆ Count on or count back to subtract. Show your work on the number line.

1. 11 − 4 = ☐ 7

2. 14 − 7 = ☐

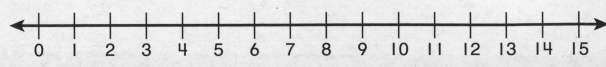

© Pearson Education, Inc. 2

Topic 1 | Lesson 5

Independent Practice ☆ Count on or count back to subtract. Show your work on the number line.

3. $14 - 8 = \boxed{}$

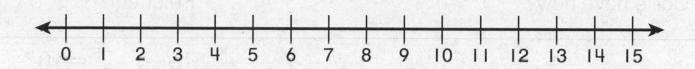

4. $12 - 7 = \boxed{}$

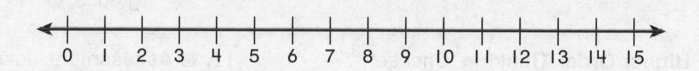

5. $9 - 7 = \boxed{}$

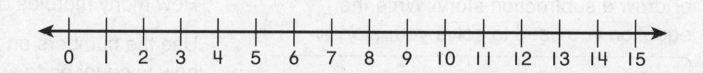

6. $15 - 6 = \boxed{}$

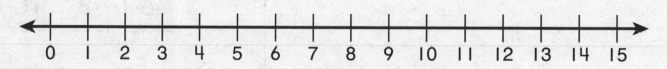

7. Higher Order Thinking How can you count on to find $13 - 4$? Explain.

_____

_____

_____

8. Callie had 8 seeds.
She planted 2 of the seeds.
How many seeds does
Callie have now?

_____ seeds

9. © **MP.1 Make Sense** Peter has 16 grapes.
He eats some of the grapes. Peter has
10 grapes left. How many grapes did
Peter eat?

$16 - \underline{\quad} = 10$

_____ grapes

10. Higher Order Thinking Choose
2 numbers. Use the numbers to write
or draw a subtraction story. Write the
equation you used to solve your story.

_____ − _____ = _____

11. © **Assessment** Jake is playing with
6 marbles. He gives 3 marbles to Sam.
How many marbles does Jake have now?

Use the numbers on the cards to show
how to count on to solve the problem.

| 6 | 3 | 5 | 4 |

Begin with ☐ . Then count on ☐ ,

☐ , ☐ .

Jake has _____ marbles now.

Name _____

Another Look! You can use a number line to count back to subtract.

Find 12 − 5.

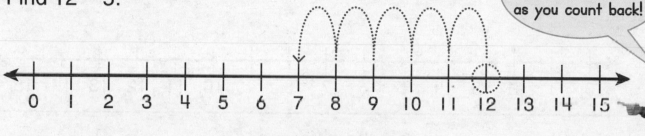

Draw jumps on the number line as you count back!

HOME ACTIVITY Draw a number line from 0 to 15. Have your child show you how to count back from 15 to find 15 − 6 on the line. Then have your child write an equation that includes 9 as the difference.

Start at 12 on the line. Count back 5 moves.

11, 10, 9, 8, 7

So, 12 − 5 = __7__.

Count on or count back to subtract. Show your work on the number line.

1. 6 − 4 = ☐

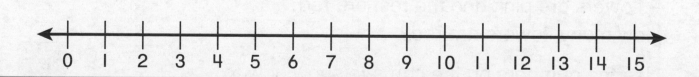

2. 13 − 8 = ☐

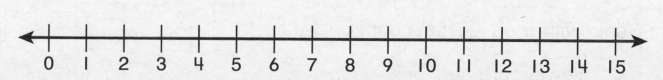

Use Math Practices to Solve Problems ☆ Solve each problem below.

3. © **MP.4 Model** Marta has 15 dinner plates.
She uses 9 of them for a party.
How many of Marta's plates are not used?
Count on or count back to solve.

_____ dinner plates

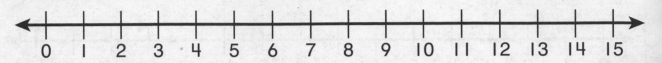

4. **Higher Order Thinking** Complete the squares so that the differences
shown on the outside are correct.

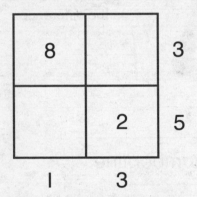

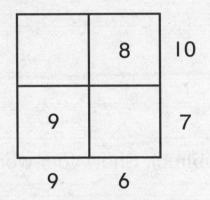

5. © **Assessment** Pat has 12 flowers in his garden.
4 flowers are pink and the rest are red.
How many flowers are red?

Use the numbers on the cards to show how to
count back to solve the problem.

Begin with ☐ . Then count back 11, ☐ , ☐ , ☐ .

_____ flowers are red.

© Pearson Education, Inc. 2

Name _____

Solve & Share

How can you use an addition fact to find 14 − 6?
Use counters to help show how.

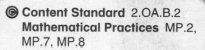

I can ...
use addition to help me
subtract quickly and accurately.

© **Content Standard** 2.OA.B.2
Mathematical Practices MP.2,
MP.7, MP.8

_____ + _____ = _____

So, 14 − 6 = _____.

Find 15 − 7.

One way to subtract is to think about addition.

To find 15 − 7, you can think:

7 plus how many more is 15?
or
7 + ___ = 15

The missing number is the same in both equations.

7 + ___ = 15

15 − 7 = ___

You know the addition fact.

7 + _8_ = 15

You also know the subtraction fact.

15 − 7 = _8_

Do You Understand?

Show Me! How do you know which addition fact to use to complete the subtraction fact?

1. 6 − 4 = ?

4 + _2_ = 6

So, 6 − 4 = _2_.

2. 9 − 3 = ?

3 + ___ = 9

So, 9 − 3 = ___.

3. 14 − 5 = ?

5 + ___ = 14

So, 14 − 5 = ___.

4. 12 − 4 = ?

4 + ___ = 12

So, 12 − 4 = ___.

Tools   Assessment

Independent Practice ☆ Subtract. Write the addition fact that can help you.

5. 8 – 1 = ____

1 + ____ = 8

6. 10 – 2 = ____

2 + ____ = 10

7. 15 – 6 = ____

6 + ____ = 15

8. 17 – 7 = ____

7 + ____ = 17

9. 14 – 8 = ____

8 + ____ = 14

10. 9 – 5 = ____

5 + ____ = 9

11.

```
   18          8
 –  8        + ☐
 ────       ────
  ☐           18
```

12.

```
   16          9
 –  9        + ☐
 ────       ────
  ☐           16
```

13.

```
   19          9
 –  9        + ☐
 ────       ────
  ☐           19
```

Higher Order Thinking Write a related addition fact to complete the subtraction fact.

14. 11 – ____ = 5

____ + ____ = ____

15. 7 – ____ = 2

____ + ____ = ____

16. 12 – ____ = 8

____ + ____ = ____

17. © **MP.2 Reasoning** Kate had 6 pens.
She got 5 more pens from John.
How many pens does
Kate have in all?

_____ + _____ = _____

_____ pens

18. © **MP.2 Reasoning** John had 11 pens.
He gave 5 pens to Kate.
How many pens does
John have now?

_____ − _____ = _____

_____ pens

19. **Higher Order Thinking** Write a
subtraction story using the numbers
18 and 10. Then write an addition fact
that can help you solve the problem in
your story.

_____

_____

_____

_____

_____

_____ + _____ = _____

20. © **Assessment** Pam has 16 cherries.
She eats 7 cherries.
Which addition fact can help you
find how many cherries Pam has left?

$7 + 4 = 11$　　　$7 + 9 = 16$
　Ⓐ　　　　　　　Ⓒ

$7 + 6 = 13$　　　$9 + 9 = 18$
　Ⓑ　　　　　　　Ⓓ

Name _____

Another Look! Addition facts can help you subtract.
Use the pictures to find the missing numbers.

HOME ACTIVITY Make up problems during daily activities such as, "If I have 12 eggs and I use 3 of them, how many eggs do I have left?" Have your child write and solve the subtraction sentence using addition facts.

Addition Fact

Think 6 | _8_ = 14.

Subtraction Fact

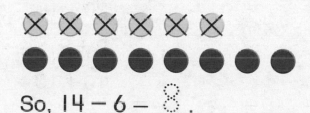

So, 14 − 6 − _8_.

Addition facts can help you subtract.
Use the pictures to find the missing numbers.

1.

Think 9 + ____ = 13.

So, 13 − 9 = ____.

2.

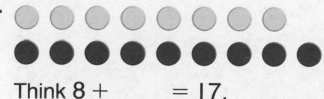

Think 8 + ____ = 17.

So, 17 − 8 = ____.

Higher Order Thinking Circle the addition fact that will help you subtract.
Write an equation to solve each problem.

3. Lucy had 12 books. She gave 3 books to Michael. How many books does Lucy have now?

$3 + 12$

$3 + 9$

$6 + 6$

____ − ____ = ____

____ books

4. Pam has 20 marbles. She puts 10 marbles in a jar. How many marbles are **NOT** in the jar?

$20 + 10$

$9 + 9$

$10 + 10$

____ − ____ = ____

____ marbles

Think about the parts and the whole.

5. © MP.8 **Generalize** Subtract. Write the addition fact that can help you.

$19 - 9 =$ ____

$9 +$ ____ $= 19$

How do addition facts help you subtract?

_____

_____

_____

6. © **Assessment** Maria has 11 rings. She loses 3 rings. Which addition fact can help you find how many rings Maria has left?

$3 + 1 = 4$
Ⓐ

$6 + 5 = 11$
Ⓒ

$3 + 8 = 11$
Ⓑ

$2 + 9 = 11$
Ⓓ

© Pearson Education, Inc. 2

Name _____

Solve & Share

14 ladybugs are on a leaf. 6 ladybugs fly away. How can thinking about 10 help you find how many ladybugs are left? Explain.

I can ...
make a 10 to help me subtract quickly and accurately.

© **Content Standard** 2.OA.B.2
Mathematical Practices MP.3, MP.4, MP.5, MP.7, MP.8

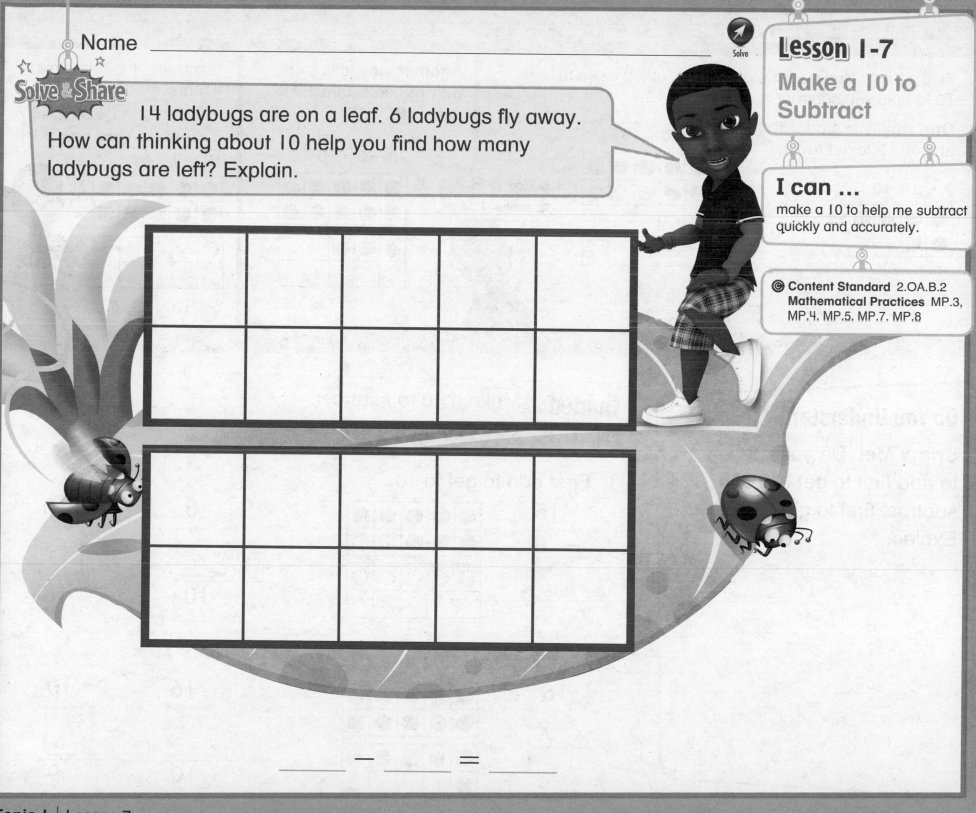

_____ − _____ = _____

Find 13 − 7. You can use 10 to help you subtract.

One way is to start with 7 and add 3 to get to 10.

7 + 3 = 10

Next, add 3 more to make 13.

10 + 3 = 13

7 + 6 = 13,
so 13 − 7 = 6.

I added 6 to 7 to make 13.

Another way is to start with 13 and subtract 3 to get to 10.

13 − 3 = 10

Since 3 + 4 = 7, subtract 4 more.

10 − 4 = 6

I subtracted 7 and have 6 left.

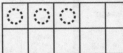

So, 13 − 7 = 6.

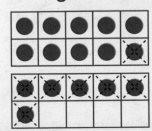

Do You Understand?

Show Me! Do you prefer to add first to get to 10 or subtract first to get to 10? Explain.

☆ Guided Practice ☆

Make a 10 to subtract.
Use counters and your workmat.

1. First add to get to 10.

```
  15
−  8
─────
   7
```

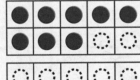

```
   8            10
+  2         +  5
────         ────
  10           15
```

2. First subtract to get to 10.

```
  16
−  7
```

```
  16           10
−            −
────         ────
  10            9
```

© Pearson Education, Inc. 2

Name _____

Independent Practice ☆   Make a 10 to subtract. Use counters and your workmat.

3. 11
   − 4

4. 14
   − 8

5. 12
   − 7

6. 12
   − 4

Think of the ways
you know to make 10.

7. 18
   − 9

8. 17
   − 8

9. 16
   − 8

10. 13
    − 4

11. 15
    − 9

12. 14
    − 7

13. 12
    − 8

14. 16
    − 9

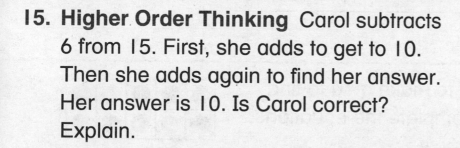

15. **Higher Order Thinking** Carol subtracts
6 from 15. First, she adds to get to 10.
Then she adds again to find her answer.
Her answer is 10. Is Carol correct?
Explain.

_____

_____

_____

_____

16. © **MP.5 Use Tools** Chen had 12 animal stickers. He gave 5 of the stickers away. How many animal stickers does Chen have now?

_____ animal stickers

17. © **MP.5 Use Tools** Angie bought 13 strawberries. She ate 8 of the strawberries. How many strawberries does Angie have now?

_____ strawberries

18. Higher Order Thinking Show how you can make a 10 to find $17 - 9$.

19. © **Assessment** Use the ten-frames. Show how to make a 10 to find $15 - 9$. Start by subtracting to get to 10. Then complete the equations.

$15 - \underline{} = 10$

$10 - \underline{} = \underline{}$

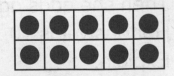

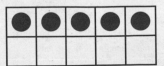

Name _____

Another Look! You can make a 10 to help you subtract. Find $13 - 5$.

One way

Subtract $13 - 3$ to make a 10.

Subtract 2 more to subtract 5 in all.

$10 - 2 = 8$

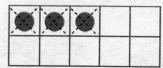

You have 8 left. So, $13 - 5 = 8$.

Another way

Add $5 + 5$ to make a 10.

Add 3 more to make 13.

$10 + 3 = 13$

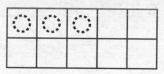

You added $5 + 8 = 13$. So, $13 - 5 = 8$.

HOME ACTIVITY Have your child use 12 small objects to explain how to find $12 - 8$ by first subtracting to get 10

 Use the ten-frames to subtract. Think about the parts and the whole.

1. $11 - 7 =$ _____

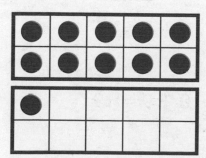

2. $14 - 6 =$ _____

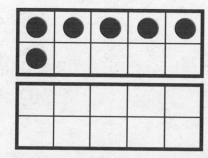

3. $12 - 5 =$ _____

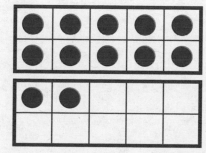

Higher Order Thinking For each problem, pick a bin from each row. Subtract to find how many more bottles are in the bin from the top row than the bin from the bottom row.

A   B   C

D   E   F

4. Bin _____ has _____ more bottles than Bin _____.

5. Bin _____ has _____ more bottles than Bin _____.

6. Bin _____ has _____ more bottles than Bin _____.

7. Bin _____ has _____ more bottles than Bin _____.

8. © **MP.4 Model** Write two subtraction equations to show how to find $15 - 7$.

_____ − _____ = _____

_____ − _____ = _____

9. © **Assessment** Which equations show you how to find $16 - 9$?

Ⓐ $9 + 1 = 10, 10 + 5 = 15$

Ⓑ $9 + 1 = 10, 10 + 6 = 16$

Ⓒ $9 + 2 = 11, 11 + 6 = 17$

Ⓓ $9 + 1 = 10, 10 + 9 = 19$

Name _____

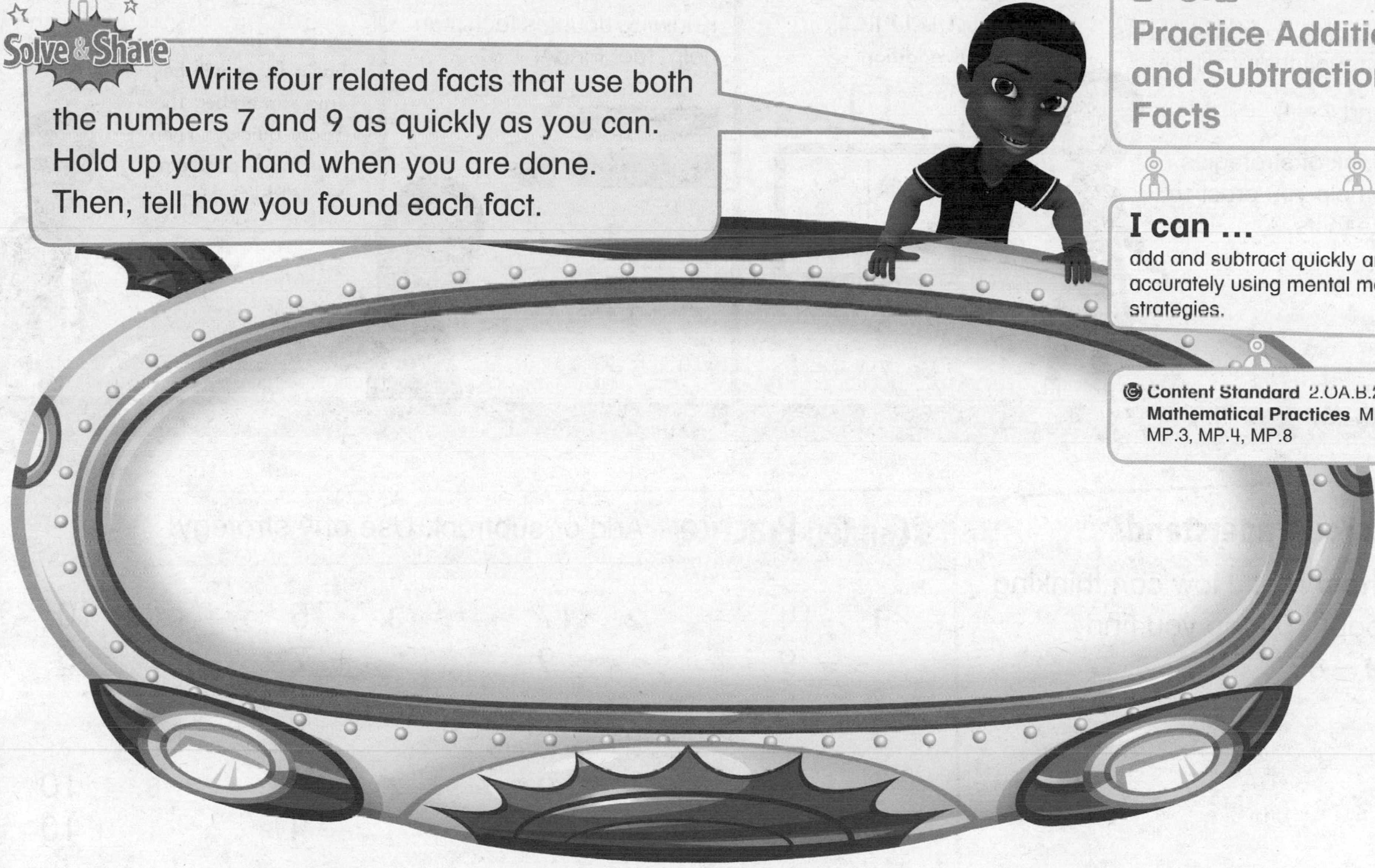

Lesson 1-8

Practice Addition and Subtraction Facts

Solve & Share

Write four related facts that use both the numbers 7 and 9 as quickly as you can. Hold up your hand when you are done. Then, tell how you found each fact.

I can ...

add and subtract quickly and accurately using mental math strategies.

Content Standard 2.OA.B.2
Mathematical Practices MP.2, MP.3, MP.4, MP.8

_____ + _____ = _____   _____ − _____ = _____

_____ + _____ = _____   _____ − _____ = _____

Practice your basic facts to recall them quickly.

Find $7 - 4$.

Think of strategies to help you practice the facts.

One way to subtract is to think about addition.

$$7$$

$4 + \boxed{3} = 7$

So, $7 - 4 = \boxed{3}$.

Knowing doubles facts can help, too! Find $4 + 5$.

$4 + 4$ and 1.

$4 + 5 = \boxed{9}$.

Practicing my basic facts will help me remember the facts quickly. Then my math problems will be easier.

Do You Understand?

Show Me! How can thinking about 10 help you find $14 - 8$?

☆ Guided Practice   Add or subtract. Use any strategy.

1. $\begin{array}{r} 14 \\ -\ 9 \\ \hline 5 \end{array}$

2. $\begin{array}{r} 17 \\ -\ 9 \\ \hline \end{array}$

3. $\begin{array}{r} 5 \\ +\ 7 \\ \hline \end{array}$

4. $\begin{array}{r} 10 \\ -\ 5 \\ \hline \end{array}$

5. $\begin{array}{r} 6 \\ -\ 0 \\ \hline \end{array}$

6. $\begin{array}{r} 9 \\ +\ 9 \\ \hline \end{array}$

7. $\begin{array}{r} 12 \\ -\ 4 \\ \hline \end{array}$

8. $\begin{array}{r} 10 \\ +10 \\ \hline \end{array}$

9. $\begin{array}{r} 11 \\ -\ 4 \\ \hline \end{array}$

10. $\begin{array}{r} 9 \\ +\ 1 \\ \hline \end{array}$

11. $\begin{array}{r} 8 \\ +\ 0 \\ \hline \end{array}$

12. $\begin{array}{r} 16 \\ -\ 8 \\ \hline \end{array}$

© Pearson Education, Inc. 2

Topic I | Lesson 8

Name _____

Independent Practice ☆   Add or subtract. Use any strategy.

13. $14 - 7 =$ _____

14. $3 + 0 =$ _____

15. $8 + 7 =$ _____

16. $13 - 6 =$ _____

17. $10 + 9 =$ _____

18. $17 - 8 =$ _____

19. $18 - 9 =$ _____

20. $9 - 1 =$ _____

21. $7 + 4 =$ _____

22. $6 + 6 =$ _____

23. $16 - 9 =$ _____

24. $20 - 10 =$ _____

25. $16 - 7 =$ _____

26. $15 - 8 =$ _____

27. $7 + 3 =$ _____

28. $2 + 7 =$ _____

29. $9 + 6 =$ _____

30. $10 - 2 =$ _____

Higher Order Thinking   Write the missing number.

31. $6 + \boxed{} = 14 - 5$

32. $12 - 4 = \boxed{} + 2$

33. $14 - \boxed{} = 5 + 4$

34. Math and Science Danielle had 17 pieces of paper. She changed 8 of the pieces by cutting them. How many pieces were not changed? Write an equation to solve.

____ ◯ ____ = ____

____ pieces of paper

35. © MP.4 Model Diego saw 5 frogs on a rock. He also saw 7 frogs in the grass. How many frogs did Diego see in all? Write an equation to solve.

____ ◯ ____ = ____

____ frogs

36. Higher Order Thinking Glen counts on to solve $9 + \boxed{} = 14$. Explain how he can do this. What is the missing addend?

37. © Assessment Deshawn had some shells. He gave 3 shells to his brother. Now Deshawn has 8 shells. How many shells did Deshawn have to begin with? Solve. Explain your solution.

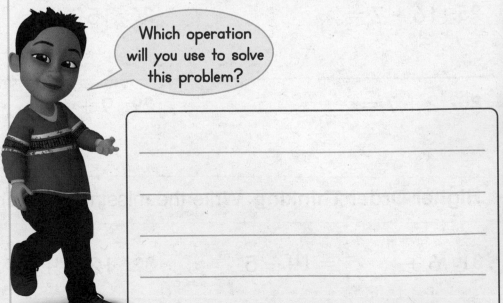

Which operation will you use to solve this problem?

Name _____

Help Tools Games

Homework
& Practice 1-8
Practice Addition
and Subtraction
Facts

Another Look! You can use strategies to help you practice addition and subtraction facts.

Find 12 − 7.

You can think about the relationship between addition and subtraction and use related facts.

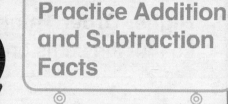

HOME ACTIVITY Give your child the following numbers: 5, 6, and 11. Tell your child to write the fact family for these numbers as quickly as he or she can.

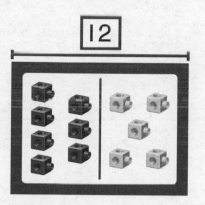

12

7 plus how many more is 12?

or

$7 + \underline{5} = 12$

So, $12 - 7 = 5$.

Add or subtract. Use any strategy.

1.	2.	3.	4.	5.	6.
$\begin{array}{r} 11 \\ -\ 5 \\ \hline 6 \end{array}$	$\begin{array}{r} 12 \\ -\ 6 \\ \hline \end{array}$	$\begin{array}{r} 7 \\ +\ 6 \\ \hline \end{array}$	$\begin{array}{r} 2 \\ +\ 1 \\ \hline \end{array}$	$\begin{array}{r} 12 \\ -\ 3 \\ \hline \end{array}$	$\begin{array}{r} 8 \\ +\ 8 \\ \hline \end{array}$

7. $9 - 3 =$ _____   **8.** $10 + 9 =$ _____   **9.** $10 - 1 =$ _____

Higher Order Thinking Fill in the missing numbers so that the sums on the outside are correct.

10.

	3	11
0		3
8	6	

11.

6		10
	9	18
15		

12.

	7	12
8		17
13	16	

13.

6		14
	10	
	18	

14. © **MP.3 Explain** What addition doubles fact can help you find $4 + 3$? Explain how you know.

_____

_____

_____

15. © **Assessment** Write an addition equation that can help you find $9 - 6$. Explain your answer.

_____

_____

_____

Solve & Share

Diego has 6 apples. Leslie has 9 apples. How many more apples does Leslie have than Diego?

Will you add or subtract to solve this problem? Explain.

Lesson 1-9
Solve Addition and Subtraction Word Problems

I can ...
use addition and subtraction to solve word problems.

© **Content Standards** 2.OA.A.1, 2.OA.B.2
Mathematical Practices MP.1, MP.2, MP.6

add   subtract   ____ ◯ ____ ◯ ____

Leslie has ____ more apples than Diego.

17 books are on a table. 8 books are on a shelf. How many fewer books are on the shelf than on the table?

You can use a bar diagram and an equation to model the problem.

The shelf has fewer books.

books on table

17

8	?

books on shelf   fewer books on shelf

You can write an addition or subtraction equation for the problem.

$17 - 8 = \underline{9}$

$8 + \underline{9} = 17$

17

8	9

So, there are 9 fewer books on the shelf.

Do You Understand?

Show Me! Why can you use addition OR subtraction to solve the problem above?

☆ Guided Practice ☆

Write an equation to solve each problem. Use counters, if needed.

1. Sam has 5 red tomatoes and 3 green tomatoes. How many tomatoes does he have in all?

   $\underline{5} \oplus \underline{3} \ominus \underline{8}$ $\underline{8}$ tomatoes

2. There are 16 party hats in a box. There are 10 party hats in a bag. How many fewer hats are in the bag than in the box?

   ___ ◯ ___ ◯ ___   _____ fewer hats

Independent Practice

Write an equation to solve each problem.
Use counters, if needed.

3. Cho has 3 more toy horses than Hakeem.
Cho has 9 toy horses.
How many toy horses does Hakeem have?

____ ◯ ____ ◯ ____

____ toy horses

4. There are 12 peaches in a bowl.
The children eat some of them.
Now there are 8 peaches.
How many peaches did the children eat?

____ ◯ ____ ◯ ____

____ peaches were eaten.

5. Juan reads 5 books.
Susan reads some books.
They read 11 books in all.
How many books did Susan read?

____ ◯ ____ ◯ ____

____ books

6. Jack has 13 brushes.
Igor has 6 brushes.
How many fewer brushes
does Igor have than Jack?

____ ◯ ____ ◯ ____

____ fewer brushes

7. Number Sense Jen had 3 animal stickers in her collection. Her friend gave her 5 more stickers. Jen bought 7 more stickers. How many stickers does Jen have now? Show your work.

8. Higher Order Thinking Sandy has 8 markers.
Alex has 6 fewer markers than Sandy.
Jill has 2 markers.
How many markers do they have in all?

Show your work. Then explain how you found the answer.

_____

_____

_____

Use counters to solve.

9. © **MP.1 Make Sense** Annika saves
13 dimes. She put some of the dimes in
a box and the rest in a jar.

Write an equation to show one way she
could have sorted the dimes.

____ ◯ ____ ◯ ____

_____ dimes in a jar

_____ dimes in a box

10. © **Assessment** Maria had 5 rings.
She bought some more rings. Now she
has 12 rings.

Choose Yes or No to show if the equation
can be used to find how many more rings
Maria bought.

$12 - 5 = 7$ ◯ Yes   ◯ No

$10 + 2 = 12$ ◯ Yes   ◯ No

$5 + 7 = 12$ ◯ Yes   ◯ No

$12 - 8 = 4$ ◯ Yes   ◯ No

   © Pearson Education, Inc. 2   **Topic 1** | Lesson 9

Name _____

Another Look! You can use counters to solve this problem.

Francine has made 9 wristbands. Jon has made 5 wristbands. How many more wristbands has Francine made than Jon?

You can use an addition or subtraction strategy to help solve the problem.

Compare blue and red wristbands. Count on from 5 and add to find how many more wristbands Francine made.

5 $+$ 4 $=$ 9

You can also subtract. $9 - 5 = 4$

HOME ACTIVITY Make up addition and subtraction word problems. Ask your child to use small objects such as paper clips or pennies to add or subtract to solve the problems. For each problem, have your child write an equation to show how to solve it.

Write an equation to solve each problem. Use counters, if needed.

1. 6 bugs are on a leaf.
   2 bugs join them.
   How many bugs are there in all?

   ____ bugs

2. There are 13 baseballs in a box.
   There are 8 baseballs in a bag.
   How many more baseballs are in a box?

   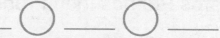

   ____ more baseballs

3. **© MP.6 Be Precise** Devin brought his snail collection to school. He has 10 snails.
How could he put them into 2 tanks so two classes could see them?

Write equations for all the possible ways.
One of the ways is given.

Explain how you know you have found all the ways.

$$10 = 9 + 1$$

_____

_____

_____

Write equations to solve the problem. Use counters, if needed.

4. **Higher Order Thinking** Pat has 9 cards.
Frank has 2 more cards than Steve.
Steve has 3 cards.
How many more cards does Pat have than Frank?

Cards Frank has: ____ ____ ____
More cards Pat has than Frank:

 ____ ____ ____

Pat has ____ more cards than Frank.

5. **© Assessment** Jan has 10 dolls.
Kat has 7 dolls. Choose Yes or No to show if the equation can be used to find how many fewer dolls Kat has than Jan.

$10 - 7 = 3$	○ Yes	○ No
$3 + 7 = 10$	○ Yes	○ No
$10 + 7 = 17$	○ Yes	○ No
$7 + 3 = 10$	○ Yes	○ No

© Pearson Education, Inc. 2

Solve & Share

How can you use the **make a 10** strategy to find 7 + 9?

Explain your thinking and work.
Use pictures, numbers, or words.

Lesson 1-10
Construct Arguments

I can ...
use pictures, numbers, and words to explain why my thinking and work are correct.

© **Mathematical Practices**
MP.3 Also MP.1, MP.2, MP.4
Content Standards 2.OA.A.1, 2.OA.B.2

Thinking Habits
How can I use math to explain why my work is correct?

Is my explanation clear?

Does 1 more than 6 + 6 have the same sum as 6 + 7?

Make a math argument.

How can I make a math argument and show my work?

I can use pictures, words, or numbers to make a math argument and to show my work.

I can draw pictures and write equations.

6 + 6 = 12

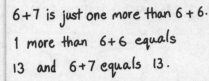

6 + 6 + 1 = 6 + 7

6 + 6 + 1 = 13

6 + 7 = 13

Or I can use words and numbers to make my math argument. My argument is clear and makes sense.

6 + 7 is just one more than 6 + 6.
1 more than 6 + 6 equals 13 and 6 + 7 equals 13.

Do You Understand?

Show Me! Are both math arguments above clear and complete? Explain.

☆ **Guided Practice** ☆   Use the picture to help you solve the problem. Then use words and numbers to make a math argument.

1. Is the sum of 9 + 5 the same as the sum of 10 + 4?

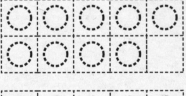

Tools Assessment

Independent Practice

Solve each problem. Use words, pictures, and numbers to make a math argument.

2. Lynn had 14 grapes. She ate 8 of them. She wants to eat 6 more grapes. Will Lynn have enough grapes? Explain.

3. The Lions scored 11 runs in a baseball game. The Tigers scored 7 runs. Did the Tigers score 3 fewer runs than the Lions? Explain.

4. Complete the explanation below for how to find $8 + 9$. Use pictures, words, or numbers to complete the explanation.

I know that $8 + 8 = 16$

© **Performance Assessment**

Puppies Sold

The Sunset Pet Store sells puppies. The table shows how many puppies were sold Monday through Thursday.

Is the total number of puppies sold on Tuesday and Wednesday less than the number of puppies sold on Monday?

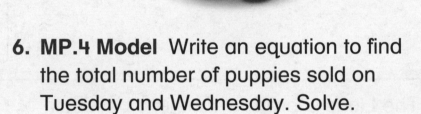

Number of Puppies Sold			
Monday	Tuesday	Wednesday	Thursday
16	10	7	15

5. **MP.1 Make Sense** Will you use all the numbers in the table to solve the problem? Explain.

_____

_____

_____

6. **MP.4 Model** Write an equation to find the total number of puppies sold on Tuesday and Wednesday. Solve.

_____

_____

_____

7. **MP.3 Explain** Solve the problem. Use words, pictures, and numbers to explain your work and thinking.

Name _____

Another Look! Tamra has 8 animal books and 4 sports books. Will she be able to give away 9 of her books?

Solve and explain your work and thinking.

You can use words, pictures, and numbers when you explain.

You can also write 8 + 4 = 12 and 12 − 9 = 3. These equations show that Tamara can give away 9 books.

HOME ACTIVITY Tell your child this story: "Omar has 3 green stickers and 8 blue stickers. If he gives away 5 of these stickers, will Omar have 6 stickers left?" Have your child solve the problem and explain his or her thinking using words, pictures, and numbers.

8 animal *books*   4 *sports books*

Yes, Tamara can give away 9 of her books.

Solve each problem. Use words, pictures, or numbers to make a math argument.

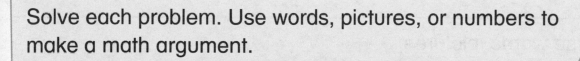

1. Alan has 17 stickers. He wants to give 6 stickers to Jean and 7 stickers to Matt. How many stickers will Alan give away? Explain.

2. Tasha has 12 minutes. She wants to jump rope for 8 minutes and play tag for 5 minutes. Will Tasha have enough time? Explain.

T-shirts

The number of T-shirts that four students own is given in the table.

Are there three students who have a total of 20 T-shirts? If so, which students are they?

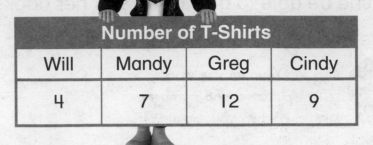

Number of T-Shirts			
Will	Mandy	Greg	Cindy
4	7	12	9

3. **MP.1 Make Sense** What operation will you use to solve the problem? Explain.

_____

_____

_____

4. **MP.2 Reasoning** How will you go about solving the problem? Explain.

_____

_____

_____

5. **MP.3 Explain** Solve the problem. Use words, pictures, and numbers to explain your work and thinking.

☆ Find a Match ☆

Find a partner. Point to a clue. Read the clue.

Look below the clues to find a match. Write the clue letter in the box next to the match.

Find a match for every clue.

I can ...
add and subtract within 20.

© **Content Standard** 2.OA.B.2

Clues

A Near doubles with sums near 8

B Every difference is 6.

C Ways to make 12

D Exactly two differences equal 9.

E Every sum is greater than 14.

F Exactly three differences are equal.

G Near doubles with sums near 6

H Every difference equals 14 − 7.

☐ 5 + 7 6 + 6 8 + 4 9 + 3	☐ 10 − 5 11 − 7 12 − 7 13 − 8	☐ 11 − 5 10 − 4 12 − 6 9 − 3	☐ 4 + 3 3 + 2 2 + 3 3 + 4
☐ 13 − 3 9 − 0 14 − 6 16 − 7	☐ 3 + 4 5 + 4 4 + 3 4 + 5	☐ 8 + 9 7 + 8 8 + 7 6 + 9	☐ 9 − 2 13 − 6 8 − 1 15 − 8

A-Z
Glossary

Word List
- addend
- difference
- doubles
- equation
- near doubles
- sum

Understand Vocabulary

1. Circle a doubles fact.

$7 + 7 = 14$

$6 + 7 = 13$

$7 + 0 = 7$

2. Circle a near doubles fact.

$4 + 4 = 8$

$4 + 1 = 5$

$4 + 5 = 9$

3. Write a subtraction equation using numbers and symbols.

_____

4. Find the sum of $8 + 6$.

_____

5. Find the difference of $12 - 5$.

_____

Use Vocabulary in Writing

6. Describe how you can make a 10 to add $7 + 4$. Use a term from the Word List.

_____

_____

_____

_____

Name _____

Set A

You can count on to find a sum.

4   5   6

2   3   4   5   6

I can add numbers in any order and get the same sum.

$4 + 2 = 6$

$2 + 4 = 6$

$4 + 2 = 2 + 4$

Count on to find the sum. Then change the order of the addends.

1. $9 + 3 =$ ____

   ____ + ____ = ____

   $9 + 3 =$ ____ + ____

2. $6 + 4 =$ ____

   ____ + ____ = ____

   $6 + 4 =$ ____ + ____

Set B

You can use doubles to help you add a near double.

$4 + 4 = 8$

So, $3 + 4 = 7$.

$3 + 4$ is one less than $4 + 4$.

So, $3 + 4 = 7$.

Complete the doubles facts. Use the doubles facts to solve the near doubles.

3. $8 + 8 =$ ____

   So, $7 + 8 =$ ____.

4. $5 + 5 =$ ____

   So, $6 + 5 =$ ____.

You can make a 10 to help you add $8 + 6$.

$8 + 6 = ?$

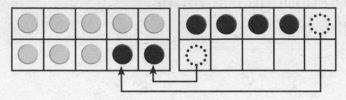

$10 + \underline{4} = \underline{14}$

So, $8 + 6 = \underline{14}$.

Make a 10 to add.

5. $8 + 4 = ?$

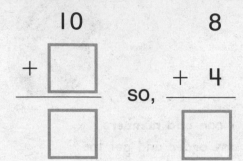

so,

You can count on or count back to find $11 - 4$.

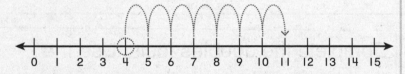

Start at 4 and count on 7 places to 11.

4, 5, 6, 7, 8, 9, 10, 11   So, $11 - 4 = 7$.

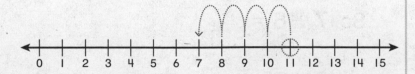

Start at 11 and count back 4 places to get to 7.

11, 10, 9, 8, 7   So, $11 - 4 = \underline{7}$.

Count on or count back to subtract.
Show your work on the number line.

6. $8 - 5 =$ ☐

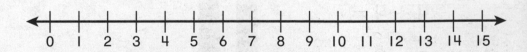

7. $15 - 6 =$ ☐

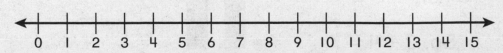

Name _____

Set E

You can think addition to help you subtract.

Find: $16 - 9 = ?$

Think: $9 + \underline{7} = 16$

So, $16 - 9 = \underline{7}$

Subtract. Write the addition fact that helped you.

Reteaching
Continued

8. $13 - 7 = \underline{\hphantom{00}}$

$7 + \underline{\hphantom{00}} = 13$

9. $17 - 9 = \underline{\hphantom{00}}$

$9 + \underline{\hphantom{00}} = 17$

Set F

You can make a 10 to subtract.
Find $17 - 8$.

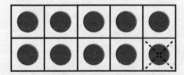

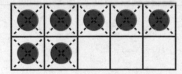

$17 - 7 = 10$

$10 - 1 = 9$

$17 - 8 = \boxed{9}$

Make a 10 to find $13 - 8$.
Draw counters to show your work.

10.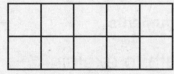

$13 - \underline{\hphantom{00}} = 10$

$10 - \underline{\hphantom{00}} = \underline{\hphantom{00}}$

$13 - 8 = \underline{\hphantom{00}}$

You can use addition or subtraction to solve word problems.

11 grapes are in a bowl.
9 grapes are in a cup.
How many fewer grapes are in the cup?

$$11 - 9 = 2 \qquad 9 + 2 = 11$$

So, 2 fewer grapes are in the cup.

Write an equation to solve each problem.

11. 13 shirts are in a closet.
8 shirts are in a box.
How many more shirts are in the closet?

_____ ◯ _____ ◯ _____ more shirts

12. Drake has 10 more books than Yuri.
Yuri has 10 books.
How many books does Drake have?

_____ ◯ _____ ◯ _____ books

Thinking Habits

Construct Arguments

How can I use math to explain why my work is correct?

Did I use the correct numbers and symbols?

Solve. Use words, pictures, or numbers to construct arguments.

13. Tyler read 15 pages of a book.
Ann read 9 pages of the same book.
Did Tyler read 4 more pages than Ann? Explain.

Name _____

1. Tom draws 7 bugs. Gina draws 4 bugs. How many bugs did they draw in all?

Which shows how to *count on* to solve the problem?

Ⓐ 7, 8, 9, 10, 11

Ⓑ 4, 5, 6, 7

Ⓒ 7 + 4

Ⓓ 4 + 7

2. Lilly has 7 fish. Jack has 1 more fish than Lilly.

Which equations show how many fish in all? Choose all that apply.

☐ 7 + 1 = 8

☐ 7 + 7 + 1 = 15

☐ 7 + 7 = 14

☐ 7 + 8 = 15

3. Use the ten-frames. Show how to find the sum of 8 + 7 by making a 10. Then fill in the gray boxes.

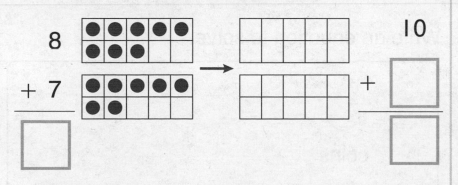

4. Which have a sum of 18? Choose all that apply.

☐ 10 + 8

☐ 9 + 8

☐ 9 + 9

☐ 8 + 10

5. 7 friends go to the movies. They have 4 tickets. How many more tickets do they need?

Draw lines to match each solution to how it was solved.

A. 7, 6, 5, 4   Use an addition fact.

B. 7 − 4 = 3

C. 4, 5, 6, 7   Count back.

                        Count on.

D. 4 + 3 = 7

                        Use a subtraction fact.

6. Nita has 14 grapes. She eats 6 grapes.

Which addition fact can help you find how many grapes Nita has left?

Ⓐ 6 + 6 = 12

Ⓑ 6 + 7 = 13

Ⓒ 6 + 8 = 14

Ⓓ 8 + 8 = 16

7. Show how to make a 10 to find 13 − 7. Then complete the equation.

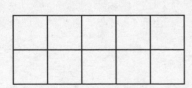
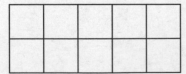

13 − 7 = _____

8. Bruce has some coins.
He gives 4 coins to his brother.
Now Bruce has 9 coins.
How many coins did Bruce have at first?

Write an equation to solve.

_____ 〇 _____ = _____

_____ coins

9. Maria has 4 pears.
She buys some more pears.
Now she has 12 pears.

How many pears does
Maria buy?

Part A
Draw a picture to model
the problem.

Part B
Write an equation to
solve the problem.

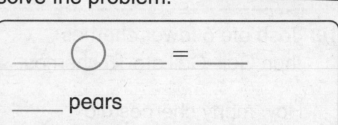

_____ $\bigcirc$ _____ = _____

_____ pears

10. The team has 9 players.
Then 2 players quit.
After that, 5 players join the team.

How many players does the team
have now?

Use the numbers on the cards.
Complete both equations to solve the problem.

2   5

7   12

9 − ☐ = ☐

7 + ☐ = ☐ ☐ players

11. Choose Yes or No to show if 7 will make
each equation true.

8 + ☐ = 16   ○ Yes ○ No

7 + ☐ = 14   ○ Yes ○ No

14 − ☐ = 7   ○ Yes ○ No

15 − 8 = ☐   ○ Yes ○ No

12. Matt finds 9 sticks at the park.
Mabel finds 7 sticks.
How many sticks do they find in all?

_____ sticks in all

13. Choose Yes or No to show if 8 will make each equation true.

$6 + \boxed{} = 14$ $8 + 8 = \boxed{}$ $14 - \boxed{} = 6$ $16 - \boxed{} = 8$

◯ Yes ◯ No   ◯ Yes ◯ No   ◯ Yes ◯ No   ◯ Yes ◯ No

---

14. Josh ate 6 fewer cherries than Gail. Gail ate 15 cherries.

How many cherries did Josh eat?

Part A
Draw a picture to model the problem.

Part B
Write an equation to solve the problem.

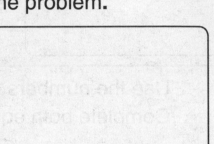

_____ ◯ _____ = _____

_____ cherries

---

15. The table shows how many pictures 3 friends made.

Pictures Made			
	Horses	Cats	Dogs
Brian	9	1	3
Fernando	7	6	2
Laurel	4	0	8

Write an equation to solve the problem.

_____ ◯ _____ ◯ _____ = _____

_____ pictures

Choose one of the friends.
Write the name of the friend you choose.

_____

How many pictures did that friend make?

© Pearson Education, Inc. 2

Topic 1 | Assessment

Name _____

Farm Kittens

Many kittens are born each summer at the Sunshine Farm. The table shows the number of kittens born at the farm from June to August.

Number of Kittens Born		
June	July	August
13	8	7

1. During which two months were a total of 20 kittens born?

2. Write an equation to find the total number of kittens born in July and August. Solve.

_____

_____

_____

_____

3. Joy said 5 more kittens were born in June than in August. Do you agree? Circle Yes or No.

Show your work to explain.

Yes   No

4. Use the clues to complete the table below.

- No kittens were born in December, January, and February.

- In March, 6 kittens were born.

- Three kittens were born in April and in September.

- In May, 4 kittens were born.

- Two kittens were born in October and in November.

Kittens Born at the Sunshine Farm		
Season	Months	Number of Kittens Born
Spring	March, April, and May	
Summer	June, July, and August	28
Fall	September, October, and November	
Winter	December, January, and February	

5. Joy says that more kittens were born in the summer than in all other seasons combined. Is she correct? Explain.

_____

_____

_____

_____

_____

6. How many more kittens were born in the spring than in the fall?

Show how to solve the problem with a subtraction equation.

Work with Equal Groups

Essential Questions: How can you show even and odd numbers? How do arrays relate to repeated addition?

Digital Resources

Solve · Learn · Glossary

Tools · Assessment · Help · Games

Look at these plants and animals!

What plants and animals live in your area?

Wow! Let's do this project and learn more.

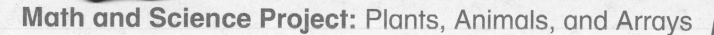

Math and Science Project: Plants, Animals, and Arrays

Find Out Make lists of different types of plants and wild animals that you see. Look in your neighborhood or in a nearby park. Look at how the animals and plants come together.

Journal: Make a Book Show what you find out in a book. In your book, also:

- Tell about plants or animals that you see in groups. Look for patterns.

- Make an array of a group of plants and an array of a group of animals.

Name _____

Review What You Know

A-Z Vocabulary

1. Circle the **addends** in the math below.

$$\begin{array}{r} 5 \\ +8 \\ \hline 13 \end{array} \qquad \begin{array}{r} 8 \\ -5 \\ \hline 3 \end{array}$$

2. Complete the **sum** in the **equation** below.

$$5 + 7 = \underline{\qquad}$$

3. Write the **doubles** fact that the model shows.

Near Doubles

4. Find each sum.

$$\begin{array}{r} 7 \\ +6 \\ \hline \end{array} \qquad \begin{array}{r} 4 \\ +5 \\ \hline \end{array} \qquad \begin{array}{r} 9 \\ +8 \\ \hline \end{array}$$

Adding in Any Order

5. Change the order of the addends and complete both equations.

$$6 + 8 = \underline{\qquad}$$

$$\underline{\qquad} + \underline{\qquad} = \underline{\qquad}$$

Math Story

6. Five brown cows go into the barn. Then 8 black and white cows go into the barn. How many cows are now in the barn?

_____ cows

My Word Cards

Study the words on the front of the card.
Complete the activity on the back.

A-Z
Glossary

even

8 is even.

odd

9 is odd.

array

row

column

bar diagram

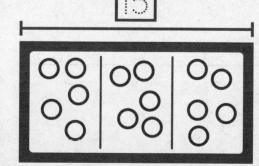

My Word Cards

Use what you know to complete the sentences.
Extend learning by writing your own sentence using each word.

An _____

is a group of objects set in equal rows and columns that forms a rectangle.

An _____

number cannot be shown as pairs of cubes.

An _____

number can be shown as pairs of cubes.

A model for addition and subtraction that shows the parts and the whole is a

_____.

In an array, objects that are shown up and down are in a

_____.

In an array, objects that are shown across are in a

_____.

Name _____

Lesson 2-1
Even and Odd Numbers

Solve & Share

Use cubes to make the numbers below. Shade all the numbers that can be shown as two equal groups of cubes.

What do you notice about the numbers you shaded?

I can ...
tell if a group of objects is even or odd.

© **Content Standards** 2.OA.C.3, 2.OA.B.2
Mathematical Practices MP.1, MP.5, MP.6, MP.7

1	2	3	4	5	6	7	8	9	10
11	12	13	14	15	16	17	18	19	20

How can you tell if a number is **even** or **odd**?

Use cubes to find out.

8

9

An even number can be shown as two equal parts using cubes.

8 is even.
$4 + 4 = 8$

An odd number cannot be shown as two equal parts using cubes.

9 is odd.
$5 + 4 = 9$

The ones digit tells you if a number is even or odd.

18 is even.
19 is odd.

1	2	3	4	5	6	7	8	9	10
11	12	13	14	15	16	17	18	19	20

Do You Understand?

Show Me! You break apart a tower of cubes to make two equal parts, but there is one cube left over.
Is the number of cubes even or odd? Explain.

☆ **Guided Practice** ☆ Look at the number. Circle even or odd. Then write the equation.

1.

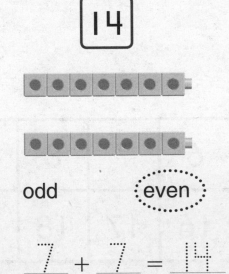

14

odd   (even)

$\underline{7} + \underline{7} = \underline{14}$

2.

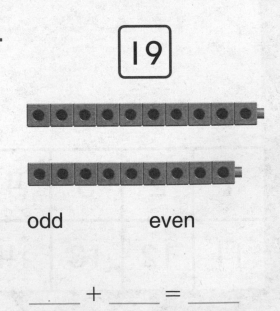

19

odd   even

$\underline{} + \underline{} = \underline{}$

Name _____

Independent Practice   Look at the number. Circle even or odd.
Then write the equation. Use cubes to help.

3. [20]

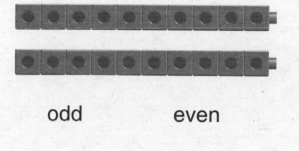

odd   even

___ + ___ = ___

4. [13]

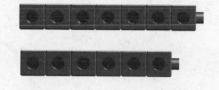

odd   even

___ + ___ = ___

5. [16]

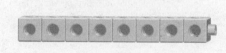

odd   even

___ + ___ = ___

6. [17]

odd   even

___ + ___ = ___

7. [10]

odd   even

___ + ___ = ___

8. [5]

odd   even

___ + ___ = ___

For each number, circle true or false. Then explain your thinking.

9. **Higher Order Thinking**
Dave says 12 is even.
He says 21 is odd.
True or false?

12	21
True	True
or	or
False	False

_____
_____
_____

Topic 2 | Lesson 1

eighty-three **83**

10. © **MP.4 Model** Gemma fills 2 baskets with 9 berries each. She gives both baskets to Alan. Does Alan have an odd or even number of berries? Draw a picture to solve. Then write an equation.

_____ + _____ = _____

Alan has an _____ number of berries.

11. © **MP.4 Model** Tyrone puts 4 marbles in one jar. He puts 3 marbles in another jar. Does Tyrone have an odd or even number of marbles? Draw a picture to solve. Then write an equation.

_____ + _____ = _____

Tyrone has an _____ number of marbles.

12. **Higher Order Thinking** If you add two odd numbers, will the sum be odd or even? Explain. Use numbers, pictures, or words.

13. © **Assessment** Use the numbers on the cards below. Write two different addition equations. The sum in each equation needs to be an odd number.

| 3 | 5 | 4 | 2 |

_____ + _____ = _____   _____ + _____ = _____

© Pearson Education, Inc. 2

Name _____

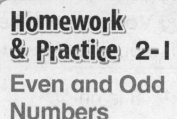

Another Look!

An **even** number can be shown as two equal parts using cubes.
An **odd** number cannot be shown as two equal parts using cubes.

There are 6 cubes.
Is 6 an even or odd number?
Draw lines to match the cubes.

 The cubes can be shown as two equal parts.
$3 + 3 = 6$

6 is an <u>even</u> number.

There are 7 cubes.
Is 7 an even or odd number?
Draw lines to match the cubes.

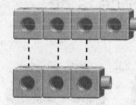 The cubes cannot be shown as two equal parts.
$4 + 3 = 7$

7 is an <u>odd</u> number.

HOME ACTIVITY Choose a number from 2 to 20. Have your child tell if it is even or odd. If needed, he or she can use pennies to help solve.

Draw lines to match the cubes.
Then tell if the number is even or odd.

1.

9 is an _____ number.

2.

12 is an _____ number.

3.

15 is an _____ number.

Vocabulary Tell if the number is **even** or **odd**.
Use objects if needed. Then complete the equation.

4. 8 is an _____ number.

4 + ____ = 8

5. 11 is an _____ number.

6 + ____ = 11

6. 18 is an _____ number.

____ + 9 = 18

Number Sense Look at the pictures. Circle the number you will add or subtract.
Then complete the equation.

7. The sum is an **odd** number.

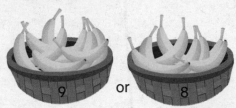

5 + ____ = ____

8. The difference is an **odd** number.

15 − ____ = ____

9. The difference is an **even** number.

19 − ____ = ____

10. Higher Order Thinking Shailen is adding three numbers. He gets a sum that is an even number between 10 and 20. Show two addition equations Shailen could have written.

____ + ____ + ____ = ____

____ + ____ + ____ = ____

11. © Assessment Use the numbers on the cards below. Write two different addition equations. The sum in each equation needs to be an even number.

| 6 | 3 | 8 | 9 |

____ + ____ = ____   ____ + ____ = ____

Solve

Lesson 2-2

Continue Even and Odd Numbers

Is the sum of 3 + 3 even or odd?
Circle **odd** or **even**. Explain. You can use cubes.

Write two more equations where the addends are the same. Is the sum even or odd? What patterns do you see? Use cubes to show each equation.

I can ...
use different ways to tell if a group of objects shows an even or odd number.

© **Content Standards** 2.OA.C.3, 2.OA.B.2
Mathematical Practices MP.2, MP.4, MP.6, MP.7, MP.8

3 + 3 = _____   even   odd

_____ + _____ = _____   even   odd

_____ + _____ = _____   even   odd

What patterns do you see?

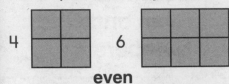
4   6

even

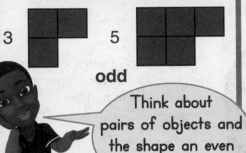
3   5

odd

Think about pairs of objects and the shape an even number makes.

If you can count the squares by 2s the number is even.

2

even

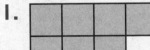
2, 4

even

The sum of two equal addends equals an even number.

$3 + 3 = 6$

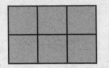
$4 + 4 = 8$

The pattern in the sums is to skip count by 2s.

$$1 + 1 = 2$$
$$2 + 2 = 4$$
$$3 + 3 = 6$$
$$4 + 4 = 8$$

What is the next even number after 8?

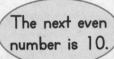

The next even number is 10.

Do You Understand?

Show Me! Is the number 10 even or odd? Draw a picture to show how you know.

✰ **Guided Practice** ✰ Write the number for each model. Circle even or odd. Then write the equation.

1.

___7___   even   (odd)

$4 + 3 = 7$

2.

_____   even   odd

___ + ___ = ___

Topic 2 | Lesson 2

Tools Assessment

Independent Practice Write the number for each model. Circle even or odd. Then write the equation.

3.
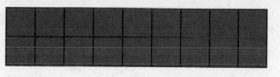

_____ even odd

_____ + _____ = _____

4.
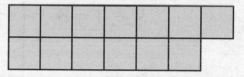

_____ even odd

_____ + _____ = _____

5.

_____ even odd

_____ + _____ = _____

6.
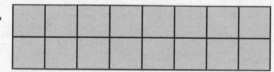

_____ even odd

_____ + _____ = _____

7.

_____ even odd

_____ + _____ = _____

8.

_____ even odd

_____ + _____ = _____

9. **Number Sense** How many squares are shown? Is this an even or odd amount? Draw a picture that shows how you know. Write an equation for your picture.

10. © **MP.7 Look for Patterns** Equations for the first four even numbers are given. What are the next six even numbers? How do you know?

$1 + 1 = 2$
$2 + 2 = 4$
$3 + 3 = 6$
$4 + 4 = 8$

11. **Higher Order Thinking** Mack drew a picture of 5 and 3. He says you can add them to get an even number. Do you agree? Explain and write an equation for the sum.

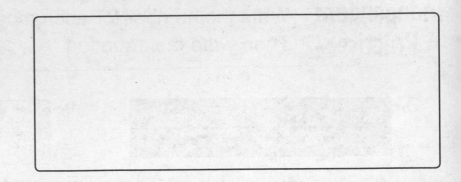

12. **Math and Science** Desert birds are active in the early morning to stay out of the heat. Marcy sees 19 birds. Does Marcy see an odd or even number of birds? Explain with a drawing and equation.

13. © **Assessment** Which equations have a sum that is an odd number? Choose all that apply.

☐ $5 + 7 = 12$

☐ $7 + 7 = 14$

☐ $7 + 6 = 13$

☐ $8 + 7 = 15$

Name _____

Another Look! The pictures show an even and an odd number.

 _10_ (even) odd

2, 4, 6, 8, _10_

Write an equation for each picture.

_5_ + _5_ = _10_

 _7_ even (odd)

The last top square does **NOT** have a pair.

_4_ + _3_ = _7_

HOME ACTIVITY Draw squares to show an even number. Have your child tell if the number is even or odd. Then, ask your child to write an equation that represents the picture and tell why the number is even.

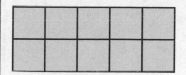

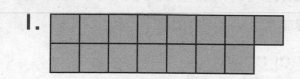
Write the number for the picture. Circle even or odd. Then write the equation.

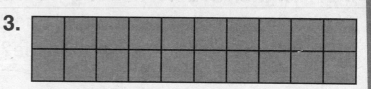
You can count the squares by 2s to tell if the number is even.

1.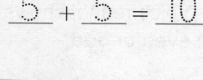

_____ even   odd

____ + ____ = ____

2.

_____ even   odd

____ + ____ = ____

3.

_____ even   odd

____ + ____ = ____

Solve the problems below.

4. © **MP.2 Reasoning** Liam says he has an even number of baseballs. Do you agree? Explain. Draw a picture and write an equation to help.

5. **A-Z Vocabulary** Draw a picture that shows $8 + 8 = 16$. Then circle **even** or **odd**.

even   odd

6. **A-Z Vocabulary** Draw a picture that shows $5 + 6 = 11$. Then circle **even** or **odd**.

even   odd

7. **Higher Order Thinking** Jacob says that an even number plus an odd number equals an odd number. Do you agree? Explain.

8. © **Assessment** Which equations have a sum that is an even number? Choose all that apply.

☐ $5 + 5 = 10$

☐ $2 + 3 = 5$

☐ $6 + 6 = 12$

☐ $9 + 9 = 18$

Name _____

Solve & Share

Show and explain two different ways to find how many circles in all.

I can ...
find the total number of objects in a set of rows and columns.

© **Content Standards** 2.OA.C.4, 2.OA.B.2
Mathematical Practices MP.1, MP.3, MP.4, MP.7

Learn Glossary

You can model repeated addition with an array.

Arrays have equal **rows**. Each row has 3 strawberries.

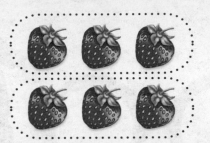

Arrays have equal **columns**. Each column has 2 strawberries.

Write two equations that match the array.

By Rows
$3 + 3 = 6$

By Columns
$2 + 2 + 2 = 6$

Do You Understand?

Show Me! Is this group an array? Explain.

Guided Practice Write two equations that match each array.

1.

By Rows

$4 + 4 = 8$

By Columns

$2 + 2 + 2 + 2 = 8$

2.

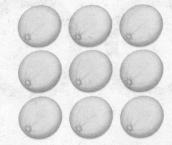

By Rows

___ + ___ + ___ = ___

By Columns

___ + ___ + ___ = ___

© Pearson Education, Inc. 2

Topic 2 | Lesson 3

Tools Assessment

Independent Practice Write two equations that match each array.

3.

By Rows

_____ + _____ + _____ + _____ + _____ = _____

By Columns _____ + _____ + _____ = _____

4.

_____ + _____ + _____ = _____

_____ + _____ + _____ + _____ = _____

5.

By Rows _____ + _____ = _____

By Columns _____ + _____ = _____

6.

_____ + _____ + _____ + _____ + _____ = _____

_____ + _____ + _____ + _____ + _____ = _____

7. Algebra Use the array to find the missing number.

_____ + 5 = 10

8. © **MP.7 Look for Patterns** Ross places the berries in an array. Write two equations that match the array. How many berries are there in all?

Look at the rows and columns.

_____

_____

_____ berries

9. The array shows cars in a parking lot. Can you write two different equations that match the array? Explain. How many cars are in the parking lot in all?

_____

_____

_____ cars

10. **Higher Order Thinking** Draw a garden with up to 5 rows and that has the same number of flowers in each row. Then write two equations that match your array.

11. © **Assessment** Blake sets basketballs in an array. He has 4 rows of basketballs with 3 basketballs in each row. Which equation shows the array Blake made and how many basketballs in all?

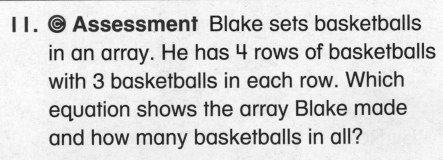

Ⓐ $3 + 3 + 3 + 3 = 12$

Ⓑ $3 + 3 = 6$

Ⓒ $4 + 4 = 8$

Ⓓ $3 + 3 + 3 = 9$

Name _____

Another Look! You can use an array to show equal groups.

There are 3 rows.
There are
3 circles in
each row.

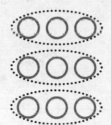 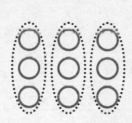

There are 3 columns.
There are
3 circles in
each column.

$\underline{3} + \underline{3} + \underline{3} = \underline{9}$

$\underline{3} + \underline{3} + \underline{3} = \underline{9}$

You can add the objects in an array by rows or columns!

HOME ACTIVITY Gather 12 small objects. Have your child make an array with 4 rows and write an equation that matches their array. Then have your child make an array with 2 columns and write an equation that matches their array.

 Write two equations that match each array.

1.

By Rows ____ + ____ + ____ = ____

By Columns ____ + ____ = ____

2.

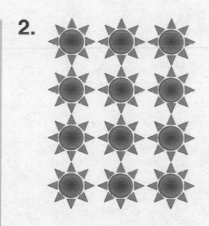

____ + ____ + ____ + ____ = ____

____ + ____ + ____ = ____

3.

_____

_____

Remember to write the sum.

4.

_____

_____

5. **Math and Science** There are 4 rows of plants in the rainforest. Each row has 4 plants. How many plants are in the rainforest in all? Write an equation to solve the problem.

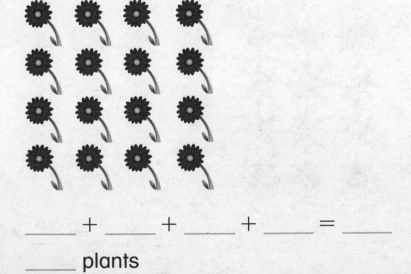

___ + ___ + ___ + ___ = ___

____ plants

6. © **Assessment** Gail puts her crayons in a box. She puts them in 3 rows. 5 crayons are in each row. Which equation shows the array Gail made and how many crayons there are in all?

Ⓐ $3 + 3 + 3 = 9$

Ⓑ $3 + 3 = 6$

Ⓒ $5 + 5 + 5 = 15$

Ⓓ $5 + 5 = 10$

Name _____

Solve & Share

Rusty places his toy trucks in 4 columns. He places 3 trucks in each column. How many trucks does Rusty have in all?

Show how you know with counters and an equation.

Equation

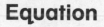

_____

_____ trucks

Jackson's garden has 2 rows with 4 carrots in each row.

How many carrots are in his garden?

You can make an array to show the problem.

Use repeated addition to find out how many carrots are in Jackson's garden.

You can add the number of carrots in each row.

$4 + 4 = \underline{8}$

Repeated addition means adding the same number over and over.

You can also add the number of carrots in each column.

$2 + 2 + 2 + 2 = \underline{8}$

$4 + 4 = \underline{8}$

I have 8 carrots!

Do You Understand?

Show Me! If you have 2 rows with different amounts in each row do you have an array? Explain.

⭐ **Guided Practice** ⭐ Draw an array to show each problem. Use repeated addition to solve.

1. Monica has 2 shelves in her pantry. She puts 3 cans of peas on each shelf. How many cans of peas does she have in all?

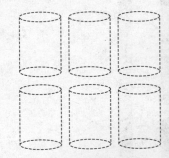

$\underline{3} + \underline{3} = \underline{6}$ cans of peas

2. Dominick is organizing his stickers in columns. He has 4 columns with 4 stickers in each column. How many stickers does he have in all?

$\underline{\quad} + \underline{\quad} + \underline{\quad} + \underline{\quad} = \underline{\quad}$ stickers

© Pearson Education, Inc. 2

Independent Practice Draw an array to show each problem.
Use repeated addition to solve.

3. Sarah bakes loaves of bread. She places them in
3 rows with 5 loaves in each row. How many loaves
of bread does Sarah have in all?

_____ + _____ + _____ = _____ loaves of bread

4. Kristin has 5 shelves in her bookcase.
She puts 4 books on each shelf.
How many books does Kristin have in all?

_____ + _____ + _____ + _____ + _____ = _____ books

5. Malcolm puts his marbles in two columns.
He put 2 marbles in each column.
How many marbles does Malcolm have in all?

_____ + _____ = _____ marbles

6. **Algebra** Find the missing numbers.
Frank has 10 baseball cards. He places them in 2 equal rows.
Show how many baseball cards are in each row.

[ ] + [ ] = 10 baseball cards

Draw an array to show each problem. Use repeated addition to solve.

7. © **MP.2 Reasoning** Jenny has 5 rows on each page in her photo album. She puts 2 pictures in each row. How many pictures does she have on each page?

_____ + _____ + _____ + _____ + _____ = _____ pictures

8. © **MP.2 Reasoning** Nina has a bookcase with 4 shelves. She places 5 dolls on each shelf. How many dolls does Nina have in all?

_____ + _____ + _____ + _____ = _____ dolls

9. **Higher Order Thinking** Write a story problem using repeated addition. Draw an array to match your story.

10. © **Assessment** Whitney has a muffin tin with 2 rows. Each row has 4 muffins. Write an equation that shows how many muffins Whitney has in all.

_____

How can drawing a picture help?

Name _____

Another Look! Make an array and write an equation for the following problem.

Tia places bowls of soup on a tray in 3 columns with 2 bowls in each column. How many bowls of soup are on the tray?

Arrays have equal rows and columns.

First, draw three columns with 2 bowls in each column.

3 columns

2 bowls in each column

HOME ACTIVITY Ask your child to show how they would make an array for the equation 3 + 3 + 3 = 9.

Now, write an equation that matches the array.

_2_ + _2_ + _2_ = _6_ bowls of soup

Draw an array to show each problem. Use repeated addition to solve.

1. Mrs. Smith places the desks in her classroom in 5 columns. She puts 3 desks in each column. How many desks are in her classroom?

____ + ____ + ____ + ____ + ____ = ____ desks

2. **© MP.2 Reasoning** Jim has 4 columns of marbles. He has 3 marbles in each column. How many marbles does he have in all?

3. **© MP.2 Reasoning** Mike has 4 rows of crackers. He has 5 crackers in each row. How many crackers does he have in all?

4. **Higher Order Thinking** Jill has 10 teddy bears in all. If she has 2 columns, how many teddy bears are in each column? Draw an array and complete the equation.

_____ + _____ = 10

5. **© Assessment** Brian has 3 columns of bugs. Each column has 5 bugs. Write an equation that shows how many bugs Brian has in all.

Think about the meaning of the word column.

© Pearson Education, Inc. 2

Topic 2 | **Lesson 4**

Solve

Solve & Share

There are 4 tables in a classroom. 3 children sit at each table. How many children are there in all?

Draw a picture and write an equation to model and solve the problem.

I can ...
model problems using equations, drawings, arrays, and bar diagrams.

© **Mathematical Practices** MP.4
Also MP.1, MP.3, MP.5, MP.6, MP.7, MP.8
Content Standards 2.OA.A.1, 2.OA.C.4

Thinking Habits
How can a picture and an equation help me model problems?

Does my answer make sense?

____ + ____ + ____ + ____ = ____

____ children

Pat has 3 boxes. Each box has 5 marbles inside. How many marbles does Pat have in all?

Use a model to show and solve the problem.

How can I use a model to show and solve the problem?

I can draw an array and write an equation to show how many marbles in all.

$5 + 5 + 5 = 15$

So, Pat has 15 marbles.

Or I can draw a bar diagram and write an equation to show how many marbles in all.

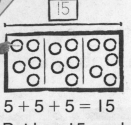

$5 + 5 + 5 = 15$

So, Pat has 15 marbles.

My drawings and equations show that $5 + 5 + 5$ is 15.

Pat has 15 marbles in all.

Do You Understand?

Show Me! How does drawing a picture and writing an equation help you model a problem?

Guided Practice Draw an array and complete the bar diagram to help you solve the problem. Then write an equation.

1. Ray has 2 bookshelves in his room. He has 5 books on each shelf. How many books does Ray have in all?

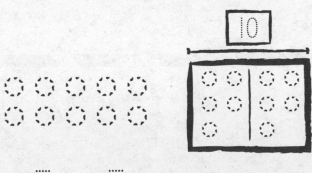

$\underline{5} + \underline{5} = \underline{}$ books

© Pearson Education, Inc. 2

Independent Practice   Draw an array or bar diagram to help you solve each problem. Then write an equation.

2. Mika has 4 groups of playing cards. If there are 4 playing cards in each group, how many cards does Mika have in all?

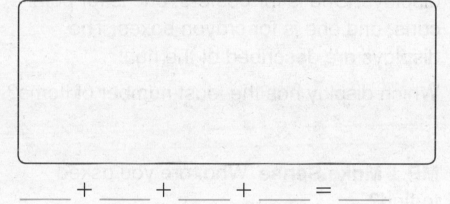

_____ + _____ + _____ + _____ = _____

3. Anita has 3 packs of baseball cards. If there are 6 cards in each pack, how many baseball cards does Anita have in all?

_____ + _____ + _____ = _____

4. **Algebra** Tina drew this bar diagram to show 2 equal groups can make 18. What are the missing numbers? Explain how you know.

18

? | ?

Math Practices and Problem Solving

Window Displays

Mr. Miller's Hobby Shop has 3 window displays. One is for posters, one is for paint cans, and one is for crayon boxes. The displays are described at the right.

Which display has the least number of items?

Posters	Paint Cans	Crayon Boxes
3 rows	4 rows	2 rows
6 posters in each row	3 paint cans in each row	8 crayon boxes in each row

5. **MP.1 Make Sense** What are you asked to find?

_____

_____

_____

6. **MP.3 Explain** Mr. Miller says he will add 3 + 6 to find the total number of posters in the posters display. Do you agree with his plan? Explain.

_____

_____

_____

7. **MP.4 Model** Use a model to help you find which display has the least number of items. Be prepared to explain which model you used and why.

Name _____

Another Look! You can draw an array or bar diagram to model and help solve problems.

Terri has 3 baskets. Each basket has 2 toys.
How many toys does Terri have in all?

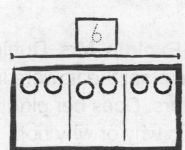

The equation
$2 + 2 + 2 = 6$
also models the problem.

HOME ACTIVITY Have your child draw an array and then write an equation to model this problem: Joel has 2 bags. Each bag has 3 apples. How many apples does Joel have in all?

So, Terri has 6 toys in all.

Draw an array or bar diagram to help you solve each problem. Then write an equation.

1. Beth has 3 rows of sunflowers in her garden. Each row has 5 flowers. How many sunflowers does Beth have in all?

____ + ____ + ____ = ____ sunflowers

2. Curtis makes 2 books.
Each book has 7 pages.
How many pages does Curtis make in all?

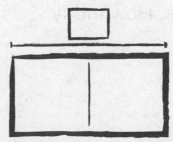

____ + ____ = ____ pages

Topic 2 | Lesson 5   Digital Resources at PearsonRealize.com   one hundred nine **109**

Planting Flowers

Mrs. Dunlap is planting some flowers in her garden. She has 10 tulips, 5 roses, and 10 daffodils. She wants to plant the flowers in an array, where each row has 5 flowers. How many rows of flowers will be in her garden?

Think about what a row means.

3. **MP.1 Make Sense** What do you know? What are you asked to find?

_____

_____

_____

_____

4. **MP.3 Explain** Mrs. Dunlap thinks she should plant the flowers in 4 rows of 5 flowers. Does her plan make sense? Explain why or why not.

_____

_____

_____

_____

5. **MP.4 Model** Draw an array to show how Mrs. Dunlap should plant her flowers. Label the flowers. How many rows are in her garden?

Follow the Path

Color a path from **Start** to **Finish**. Follow the sums and differences that are odd numbers. You can only move up, down, right, or left.

I can ...
add and subtract within 20.

© **Content Standard** 2.OA.B.2

Start

$5 + 6$	$14 - 6$	$13 - 9$	$7 - 3$	$1 + 9$	$10 - 5$	$2 + 9$	$9 + 8$	$16 - 7$
$3 + 4$	$14 - 7$	$2 + 5$	$11 - 6$	$4 + 8$	$8 - 3$	$12 - 6$	$1 + 5$	$11 - 4$
$7 - 1$	$4 + 4$	$12 - 4$	$12 - 7$	$14 - 9$	$4 + 7$	$15 - 7$	$2 + 5$	$1 + 8$
$9 + 9$	$1 + 7$	$6 - 4$	$2 + 8$	$6 + 2$	$1 + 9$	$13 - 9$	$15 - 6$	$2 + 4$
$17 - 9$	$3 + 9$	$7 + 5$	$8 + 8$	$16 - 6$	$9 - 5$	$10 - 6$	$5 + 4$	$10 - 3$

Finish

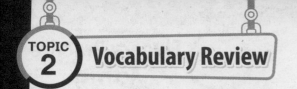

A-Z Glossary

Word List
- addends
- array
- bar diagram
- column
- doubles
- equation
- even
- odd
- row
- sum

Understand Vocabulary

Choose a term from the Word List to complete each sentence.

1. An _____ number cannot be shown as pairs of cubes.

2. An _____ is a group of objects set in equal rows and columns.

3. In an array, objects that are shown across are in a _____.

4. A model for addition and subtraction that shows the parts and the whole is called a _____.

Write T for *true* or F for *false*.

5. _____ 9 is an even number.

6. _____ 13 is an odd number.

7. _____ You can model repeated addition with an array.

8. _____ In an array, objects that are shown up and down are in a column.

Use Vocabulary in Writing

9. Which model could you use to show 4 groups of 5 objects in each group? Use at least 1 term from the Word List.

© Pearson Education, Inc. 2

Name _____

Set A

You can use cubes to tell if a number is even or odd.

12

The number of cubes is even if you can pair or count them by 2s.

odd   (even)

___6___ + ___6___ = ___12___

Circle even or odd. Then write the equation. Use cubes to help.

1.

11

(odd)   even

_____ + _____ = _____

2.

18

odd   even

_____ + _____ = _____

Set B

You can use repeated addition to find the total number of loaves.

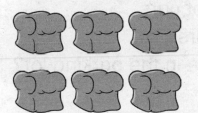

Write two equations that match the array.

Rows: ___3___ + ___3___ = ___6___

Columns: ___2___ + ___2___ + ___2___ = ___6___

Write two equations that match the array.

3.

Rows: _____ + _____ + _____ + _____ = _____

Columns:

_____ + _____ + _____ + _____ + _____ = _____

You can draw arrays and use repeated addition to solve problems.

Alli has 3 shelves in her pantry.
She puts 4 cans of beans on each shelf.
How many cans of beans does Alli have in all?

__4__ + __4__ + __4__ = __12__ cans

Thinking Habits

Model with Math

Can I use a drawing, diagram, table, or graph to model the problem?

Can I write an equation to show the problem?

Draw an array to show the problem. Use repeated addition to solve.

4. Steven puts 3 rows of apples on a table. Each row has 6 apples. How many apples does Steven put on the table?

____ + ____ + ____ = ____ apples

Draw a model and solve the problem.

5. There are 2 rows of cars.
Each row has 8 cars.
How many cars are in the parking lot?

____ + ____ = ____ cars

© Pearson Education, Inc. 2   **Topic 2** | Reteaching

Name _____

© **Assessment**

1. José writes an equation.
   The sum is an even number
   greater than 14.

   Which equation does José write?

   Ⓐ 6 + 6 = ?

   Ⓑ 6 + 7 = ?

   Ⓒ 8 + 8 = ?

   Ⓓ 8 + 7 = ?

2. Jen has 2 rows of apples
   with 4 apples in each row.

   Which equation shows how
   many apples Jen has in all?

   Ⓐ 4 + 2 = 6

   Ⓑ 2 + 2 + 2 = 6

   Ⓒ 4 + 4 = 8

   Ⓓ 4 + 4 + 4 = 12

3. Choose Yes or No to tell if the sum in the equation is an even number.

   3 + 4 = 7   5 + 5 = 10   7 + 6 = 13   9 + 7 = 16
   ○ Yes ○ No   ○ Yes ○ No   ○ Yes ○ No   ○ Yes ○ No

4. Will has 3 rows of trees in his yard.
   Each row has 4 trees.
   How many trees in all?

   Draw a picture to show the array
   of trees.

   Then write an equation for your
   picture.

   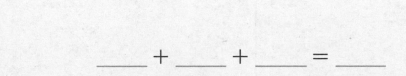

   ____ + ____ + ____ = ____

   There are ____ trees in all.

5. How many squares are shown? Is the number even or odd?

Draw a picture to show how you know.

6. Ben has 8 pennies. Look at each equation. Choose Yes or No to tell if Ben can use the equation to make an array with his pennies.

$2 + 2 + 2 + 2 = 8$ ○ Yes ○ No

$5 + 3 = 8$ ○ Yes ○ No

$4 + 4 = 8$ ○ Yes ○ No

$6 + 2 = 8$ ○ Yes ○ No

---

7. Becky drew this bar diagram to show 2 equal groups can make 14.

Part A
Draw a picture to show what the "?" stands for.

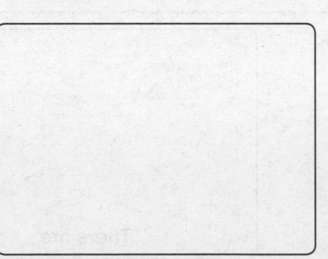

Part B
Change 14 to 16 in the bar diagram. What does the "?" stand for now? Tell how you know.

_____

_____

_____

Name _____

School Garden

Students are planting a garden at school.
The pictures show the number of some plants
in the garden.

Number of Tomato Plants

1. Is there an even or odd
   number of tomato plants
   in the garden?

   Circle your answer.   **even   odd**

   Show or tell how you know.

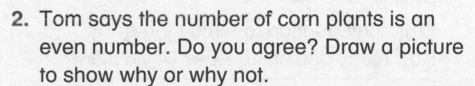

2. Tom says the number of corn plants is an
   even number. Do you agree? Draw a picture
   to show why or why not.

Number of Corn Plants

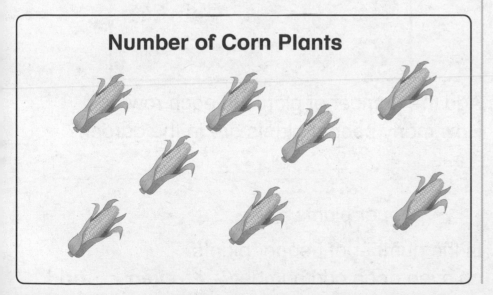

3. David plants peas in the school garden. He plants 4 rows of peas with 3 plants in each row.

Part A

Draw an array to show how David planted the peas.

Part B

Write an equation to match the array. How many pea plants does David plant?

4. Jesse says there are other ways to make an array of 12 plants. Show an array of 12 plants that is different from the array David used.

5. The array below shows the number of pepper plants in the garden.

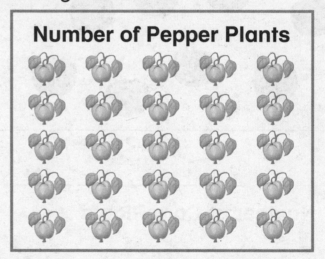

Number of Pepper Plants

Add the number of plants in each row. How many pepper plants are in the garden?

_____ + _____ + _____ + _____ + _____ = _____

_____ pepper plants

Is the number of pepper plants an even or an odd number?   **even**   **odd**

© Pearson Education, Inc. 2

Topic 2 | Performance Assessment

Add Within 100 Using Strategies

Essential Question: What are strategies for adding numbers to 100?

The Earth is always changing!

Some changes can happen quickly. Others take a long time.

Wow! Let's do this project and learn more.

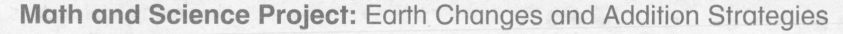

Math and Science Project: Earth Changes and Addition Strategies

Find Out Find and share books about how the Earth changes. Talk about changes that people can see, hear, and feel. Talk about changes that people cannot see happening.

Journal: Make a Book Show what you learn in a book. In your book, also:

• Write new science words you learn. Draw pictures that help show what the words mean.

• Write new math words you learn. Draw pictures that help show what the words mean.

Name _____

Review What You Know

A-Z Vocabulary

1. Draw a circle around each **even** number. Use cubes to help.

15   7   14

2   19   18

2. Draw a square around each **odd** number. Use cubes to help.

12   3   6

17   11   4

3. Complete the **bar diagram** to show the sum of $3 + 5$.

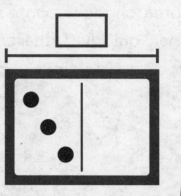

Arrays

Write an equation to show the number of circles in each array.

4.

By rows

_____ + _____ = _____

5.

By columns

_____ + _____ + _____ = _____

Math Story

6. Joe has 5 apples. He picks 3 more apples. How many apples does Joe have now?

_____ apples

Does Joe have an even or an odd number of apples?

_____ number

My Word Cards

Study the words on the front of the card.
Complete the activity on the back.

A-Z
Glossary

tens

$$54 + 14 = 68$$

↑ ↑ ↑

ones

$$54 + 14 - 68$$

↑ ↑ ↑

open number line

+10   +10

26   36   46

$$26 + 20 = 46$$

mental math

Start at 23. Count on 2 tens. 33, 43

$$23 + 20 = 43$$

break apart

$$27 + 35 = ?$$

Tens: 20   30

Ones: 7   5

compensation

$$38 + 24 = ?$$
$$+ 2 \quad - 2$$

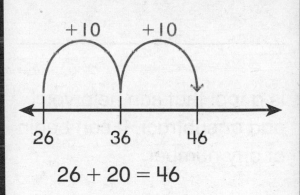

You add 2 to 38 to make 40. Then subtract 2 from 24 to get 22. 40 + 22 = 62.

So, 38 + 24 = 62.

My Word Cards

Use what you know to complete the sentences.
Extend learning by writing your own sentence using each word.

An _____

_____

is a tool that can help you add or subtract. It can begin at any number.

The digit that shows how many ones are in a number is called the

_____ digit.

The digit that shows how many groups of 10 are in a number is called the

_____ digit.

_____

is a mental math strategy you can use when you add or subtract.

You can _____

a number into its place value parts.

_____

is math you do in your head.

© Pearson Education, Inc. 2

Name _____

Solve & Share

How can you use the hundred chart to help you find 32 + 43? Explain.

Write an equation to show the sum.

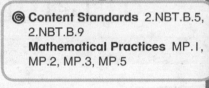

I can ...
add within 100 using place-value strategies.

Ⓒ **Content Standards** 2.NBT.B.5, 2.NBT.B.9
Mathematical Practices MP.1, MP.2, MP.3, MP.5

1	2	3	4	5	6	7	8	9	10
11	12	13	14	15	16	17	18	19	20
21	22	23	24	25	26	27	28	29	30
31	32	33	34	35	36	37	38	39	40
41	42	43	44	45	46	47	48	49	50
51	52	53	54	55	56	57	58	59	60
61	62	63	64	65	66	67	68	69	70
71	72	73	74	75	76	77	78	79	80
81	82	83	84	85	86	87	88	89	90
91	92	93	94	95	96	97	98	99	100

_____ + _____ = _____

You can add on a hundred chart. Find 54 + 18.

Start at 54. You need to add the tens from 18. Move down 1 row to show 1 ten.

51	52	53	54	55	56	57	58	59	60
61	62	63	64	65	66	67	68	69	70
71	72	73	74	75	76	77	78	79	80

Now add the **ones.**

You are already at 64. Now move ahead 8 to show 8 ones. You need to go to the next row to add them all. So, 54 + 18 = 72.

51	52	53	54	55	56	57	58	59	60
61	62	63	64	65	66	67	68	69	70
71	72	73	74	75	76	77	78	79	80

Do You Understand?

Show Me! How can you use a hundred chart to find 53 + 24?

☆ Guided Practice ☆

Add using the hundred chart. Draw arrows on the chart if needed.

11	12	13	14	15	16	17	18	19	20
21	22	23	24	25	26	27	28	29	30
31	32	33	34	35	36	37	38	39	40
41	42	43	44	45	46	47	48	49	50

1. 17 + 32 = 49

2. 28 + 21 = _____

3. _____ = 19 + 20

4. 18 + 8 = _____

Independent Practice ⭐ Add using the hundred chart.

1	2	3	4	5	6	7	8	9	10
11	12	13	14	15	16	17	18	19	20
21	22	23	24	25	26	27	28	29	30
31	32	33	34	35	36	37	38	39	40
41	42	43	44	45	46	47	48	49	50
51	52	53	54	55	56	57	58	59	60
61	62	63	64	65	66	67	68	69	70
71	72	73	74	75	76	77	78	79	80
81	82	83	84	85	86	87	88	89	90
91	92	93	94	95	96	97	98	99	100

5. $33 + 9 =$ _____

6. _____ $= 12 + 73$

7. $38 + 21 =$ _____

8. $56 + 42 =$ _____

9. $47 + 28 =$ _____

10. $39 + 17 =$ _____

11. _____ $= 61 + 19$

12. **Higher Order Thinking** Write the digit that makes each equation true.

☐ $+ 83 = 90$ $34 + 2$☐ $= 57$ 1☐ $+ 51 = 67$ $62 +$ ☐$1 = 83$

© **MP.5 Use Tools** Use the hundred chart to solve the problems.

13. Sara has 48 buttons. Luis has 32 buttons. How many buttons do they have in all?

_____ buttons

14. Mika had 70 buttons. Then she found 19 more buttons. How many buttons does Mika have now?

_____ buttons

31	32	33	34	35	36	37	38	39	40
41	42	43	44	45	46	47	48	49	50
51	52	53	54	55	56	57	58	59	60
61	62	63	64	65	66	67	68	69	70
71	72	73	74	75	76	77	78	79	80
81	82	83	84	85	86	87	88	89	90
91	92	93	94	95	96	97	98	99	100

15. **Higher Order Thinking** Write the steps you take to add 43 and 39 on a hundred chart.

16. © **Assessment** Which weights will balance the weights already on the scale? Use a hundred chart to help.

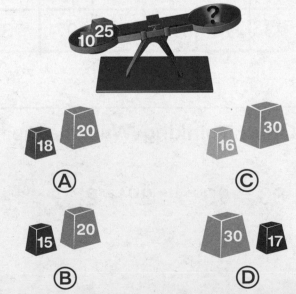

Ⓐ 18 20

Ⓑ 15 20

Ⓒ 16 30

Ⓓ 30 17

Help   Tools   Games

Another Look!

Find 16 + 23.

1	2	3	4	5	6	7	8	9	10
11	12	13	14	15	16	17	18	19	20
21	22	23	24	25	26	27	28	29	30
31	32	33	34	35	36	37	38	39	40
41	42	43	44	45	46	47	48	49	50
51	52	53	54	55	56	57	58	59	60
61	62	63	64	65	66	67	68	69	70
71	72	73	74	75	76	77	78	79	80
81	82	83	84	85	86	87	88	89	90
91	92	93	94	95	96	97	98	99	100

1. Start on square 16.

2. Move down 2 rows to show the tens in $\boxed{2}$ 3.

3. Move 3 squares to the right to add the ones in 2 $\boxed{3}$.

4. Where did you stop? ___39___

So, __16__ + __23__ = __39__.

HOME ACTIVITY Ask your child to describe how to add 37 and 16 on a hundred chart.

The numbers increase by 10 as you move down each row.

Add using the hundred chart.

1. 12 + 11 = _____

2. 31 + 45 = _____

3. 81 + 14 = _____

Write the digits that make each equation true.

4. $\boxed{}4 + 1\boxed{} = 39$

5. $4\boxed{} + \boxed{}9 = 82$

6. $74 + \boxed{}4 = 8\boxed{}$

---

7. **Math and Science** There are 21 active volcanoes in California and 17 active volcanoes in Hawaii. How many active volcanoes are in California and Hawaii?

_____ active volcanoes

8. © **MP.1 Make Sense** Kenji threw two bean bags at the target. He scored 79 points. One bean bag landed on 61. Which number did the other bean bag land on?

| 53 | 28 |
| 61 | 18 |

The other bean bag landed on _____.

---

9. **Higher Order Thinking** Explain how you could use a hundred chart to find the missing number.

$63 + \boxed{?} = 87$

The missing number is _____.

10. © **Assessment** Which weights can you put on the scale to make it balance? Use a hundred chart to help.

Ⓐ   29   32

Ⓒ   34   29

Ⓑ   30   29

Ⓓ   30   34

© Pearson Education, Inc. 2

Name _____

Solve & Share

How can you use the number line to help you find 30 + 40? Explain.

Write an equation to show the sum.

Solve

I can ...
add tens on an open number line.

© **Content Standards** 2.NBT.B.5, 2.NBT.B.9
Mathematical Practices MP.1, MP.3, MP.4, MP.5, MP.6

_____ + _____ = _____

Find 36 + 30.

You can add tens on an **open number line**.

First, place 36 on the number line.

36

You need to add the tens in 30.

30 is 3 tens. So, count on by 10 three times. Show each 10 on the number line.

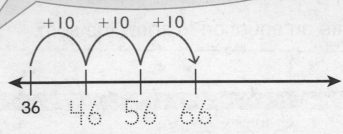

+10   +10   +10

36   46   56   66

You land on 66. So, 36 + 30 = _66_.

Do You Understand?

Show Me! How could you use an open number line to find 10 + 40?

⭐ Guided Practice   Use an open number line to find each sum.

1. 53 + 40 = _____

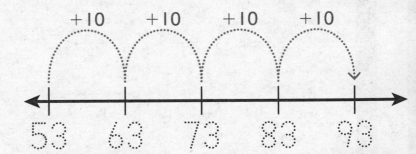

+10   +10   +10   +10

53   63   73   83   93

2. 35 + 20 = _____

© Pearson Education, Inc. 2

Name _____

Independent Practice ☆ Use an open number line to find each sum.

3. 30 + 10 = _____

4. 55 + 30 = _____

5. 23 + 20 = _____

6. 46 + 40 = _____

7. Higher Order Thinking Susan found 50 + 20 using this open number line. She said that 20 + 50 = 70, too. Is she correct? Explain.

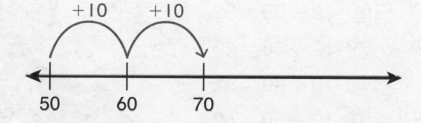

8. **© MP.5 Use Tools** Sam has 38 golf balls. He gets 20 more golf balls. How many golf balls does Sam have now? Use the open number line to solve.

_____ golf balls

9. **A-Z Vocabulary** Complete each sentence using one of the terms below.

equation   open number line   addend

Numbers are written in order from left to right on an _____.

$34 + 60 = 94$ is an _____.

34 and 60 are _____.

10. **Higher Order Thinking** Geno used the open number line below to solve a problem. What is the missing number in the equation?

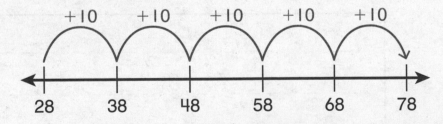

$28 + \underline{\hspace{1cm}} = 78$

11. **© Assessment** Which equation does this open number line show?

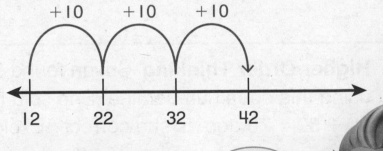

Ⓐ $12 + 20 = 32$

Ⓑ $12 + 30 = 42$

Ⓒ $12 + 40 = 52$

Ⓓ $12 + 50 = 62$

Count the jumps!

Topic 3 | Lesson 2

Name _____

Another Look! Find 64 + 20 using an open number line.

Place 64 on the number line. Then count on by 10 twice.

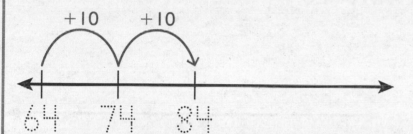

+10   +10

64   74   84

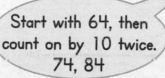
Start with 64, then count on by 10 twice. 74, 84

$\underline{64} + \underline{20} = \underline{84}$

HOME ACTIVITY Ask your child to find 45 + 30 on an open number line.

Use an open number line to find each sum.

1. 63 + 30 = _____

2. 47 + 20 = _____

3. © **MP.5 Use Tools** Bridget has 34 books. She gets 30 more books. How many books does Bridget have now?

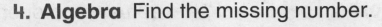

$$\boxed{} + \boxed{} = \boxed{}$$

4. **Algebra** Find the missing number.

$$57 + 20 = \boxed{}$$

5. **Higher Order Thinking** Mary did 20 jumping jacks on Monday, 30 jumping jacks on Tuesday, and 20 jumping jacks on Wednesday.

How many jumping jacks did she do on all three days?

_____ jumping jacks

6. © **Assessment** Which equation does this number line show?

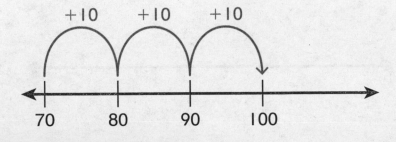

Ⓐ 70 + 10 = 80

Ⓑ 70 + 20 = 90

Ⓒ 70 + 30 = 100

Ⓓ 70 + 40 = 110

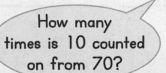

How many times is 10 counted on from 70?

Solve & Share

How can you use the open number line to find 35 + 24?

Write an equation to show the sum. Explain your work.

I can ...
use an open number line to add tens and ones within 100.

© **Content Standards** 2.NBT.B.5, 2.NBT.B.9
Mathematical Practices MP.2, MP.3, MP.4, MP.5, MP.6

_____ + _____ = _____

Find 48 + 23. Use an open number line.

One Way

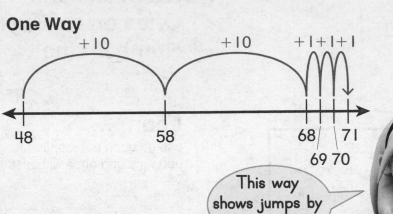

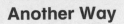

This way shows jumps by 10s and 1s.

Another Way

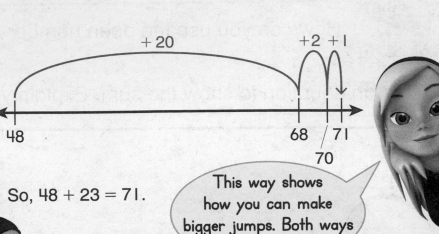

So, 48 + 23 = 71.

This way shows how you can make bigger jumps. Both ways are correct.

Do You Understand?

Show Me! Explain how you can use an open number line to find 56 + 35.

☆**Guided Practice** Use an open number line to find each sum.

1. 59 + 24 = _____

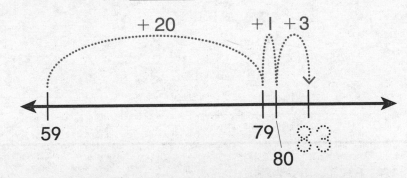

2. 47 + 25 = _____

© Pearson Education, Inc. 2

Name _____

Independent Practice   Use an open number line to find each sum.

3. 34 + 15 = _____

4. 46 + 34 = _____

5. 28 + 16 = _____

6. 59 + 26 = _____

7. Number Sense Matt found 55 + 28 using the open number line below. Is his work correct? Explain.

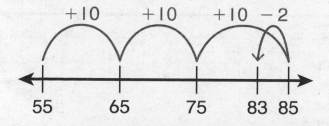

+10   +10   +10 − 2

55   65   75   83 85

_____

_____

_____

_____

_____

_____

Use the open number line to solve each problem below.

8. © **MP.5 Use Tools** There are 24 apples in a basket. There are 19 apples on a tray. How many apples are there in all?

_____ apples

9. © **MP.5 Use Tools** Jamie has 27 more berries than Lisa. Lisa has 37 berries. How many berries does Jamie have?

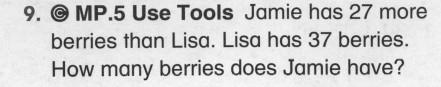

_____ berries

10. **Higher Order Thinking** Use two different number lines to show that $34 + 23$ has the same value as $23 + 34$.

11. © **Assessment** Use the numbers on the cards. Write the missing numbers under the number line to show how to find the sum.

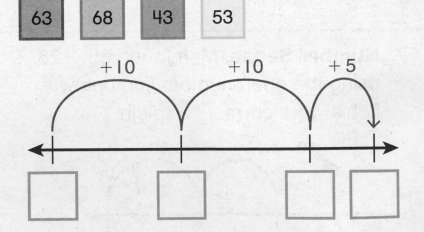

| 63 | 68 | 43 | 53 |

$43 + 25 =$ _____

© Pearson Education, Inc. 2

Another Look! You can add two-digit numbers by counting on an open number line. 46 + 27 = ?

Place 46 on an open number line.

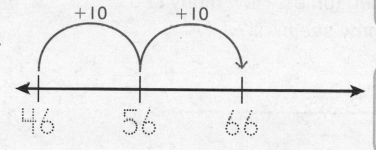

Count on 2 tens from 46.

46   56   66

I can use this strategy to add any numbers.

Count on 7 ones from 66.

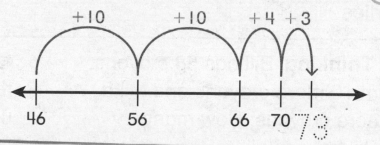

So, 46 + 27 = 73.

46   56   66 70 73

HOME ACTIVITY Ask your child to show how he or she would find 28 + 13 using an open number line.

Use an open number line to find each sum.

I. 34 + 25 = _____

2. 57 + 18 = _____

Use an open number line to solve each problem.

3. © MP.5 Use Tools Jimmy sees 10 baby sea turtles on the shore. He then sees 23 more baby sea turtles. How many sea turtles does Jimmy see in all?

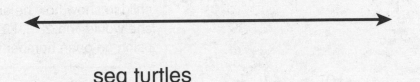

_____ sea turtles

4. © MP.5 Use Tools Ebony has 45 beads. Ivory gives her 26 more beads. How many beads does Ebony have in all?

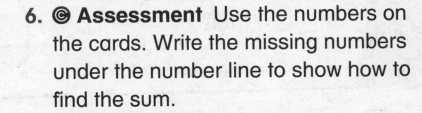

_____ beads

5. Higher Order Thinking Bill has 58 crayons. Steve gives him 10 more crayons and Mika gives him 14 more crayons. How many crayons does Bill have in all?

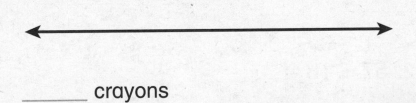

_____ crayons

An open number line can show more than two addends.

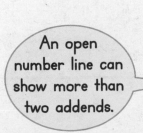

6. © Assessment Use the numbers on the cards. Write the missing numbers under the number line to show how to find the sum.

| 86 | 60 | 80 | 70 |

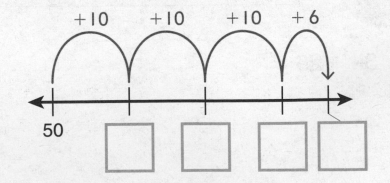

+10   +10   +10   +6

50

$50 + 36 =$ _____

© Pearson Education, Inc. 2

Solve & Share

Monica has 24 crayons. Paul has 64 crayons. How many crayons do they have in all?

Solve any way you choose. Explain your work.

Lesson 3-4
Break Apart Numbers to Add

I can ...
add within 100 using place-value strategies.

© **Content Standards** 2.NBT.B.5, 2.NBT.B.9
Mathematical Practices MP.2, MP.4, MP.5, MP.7, MP.8

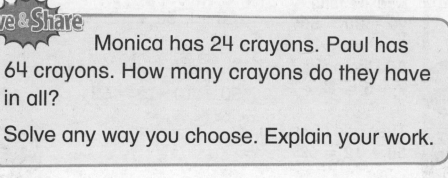

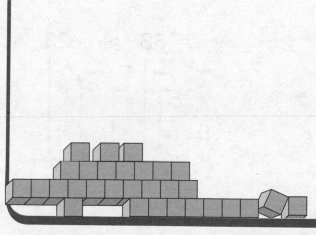
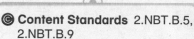

$24 + 64 =$ _____

_____ **crayons**

$27 + 35 = ?$

You can use place value to **break apart** numbers into **tens** and **ones**.

27   +   35   =   ?

20   30

7   5

I can then use mental math to find the sum.

Add the tens.
20 + 30 = 50

Add the ones.
7 + 5 = 12

Think: 50 + 12
       /\
      10 2

50 + 10 + 2 = 62

Then add the sums.
50 + 12 = 62

So, $27 + 35 = \underline{62}$.

Do You Understand?

Show Me! Explain how you can break apart numbers to find $14 + 32$.

☆ Guided Practice ☆   Break apart numbers to find each sum. Use blocks to help, if needed.

1.   17   +   42   = __59__

10   40

7   2

50
+ 9
___
59

2. ____ = 53 + 23

□   □

□   □

© Pearson Education, Inc. 2

Independent Practice

Break apart numbers to find each sum.
Use blocks to help, if needed.

3.   23   +   26 = _____

☐
☐

4.   9   +   42 = _____

☐
☐

5. _____ = 51   +   16

☐
☐

---

6. 56 + 15 = _____

7. _____ = 76 + 11

8. 33 + 49 = _____

Add tens and ones to solve.

9. Algebra One number makes both equations true.
Find the missing number.

$17 + \boxed{} = 28$

$\boxed{} + 28 = 39$

10. Billy puts 34 skateboard wheels in a pile. He puts 34 more wheels in another pile. How many wheels does Billy have in all?

_____ wheels

11. **Math and Science** A new office and house was built after a hurricane. 24 windows are needed for the office. 18 windows are needed for the house. How many windows are needed in all?

_____ windows

12. **Higher Order Thinking** Write a story problem about $14 + 41$. Then solve the problem.

$$14 + 41 = \_\_\_\_\_$$

13. © **Assessment** Cindy has 15 more toy planes than Julie. Julie has 12 toy planes. How many toy planes does Cindy have?

Ⓐ 3

Ⓑ 15

Ⓒ 25

Ⓓ 27

Name _____

Homework & Practice 3-4

Break Apart Numbers to Add

Another Look!

Find $34 + 24$.

You can draw a picture to show the tens and ones.

$$34 \quad + \quad 24$$

30   20

4   4

Add the tens.

$30 + 20 = \underline{50}$

Add the ones.

$4 + 4 = \underline{8}$

Add the sums.

$50 + 8 = \underline{58}$

So, $34 + 24 = \underline{58}$.

HOME ACTIVITY Ask your child to show how he or she would break apart tens and ones to find $23 + 46$.

Break apart numbers to find each sum.
Show your work. Draw pictures, if needed.

1. $34 + 6 = $ _____

2. $35 + 48 = $ _____

3. $67 + 28 = $ _____

4. $57 + 19 = $ _____

5. $32 + 12 =$ _____

6. $54 + 7 =$ _____

7. $37 + 43 =$ _____

8. **Higher Order Thinking** Carla buys two packages of pens. She buys 49 pens in all. Which color pens does Carla buy? Show how you found the answer.

Pen Packages	
Pen Color	Number of Pens
Blue	25
Black	12
Red	24
Green	33

9. Toby has 63 grapes. There are 33 red grapes and the rest are green grapes. How many of Toby's grapes are green?

10. © **Assessment** Tad has 72 seashells. He finds 15 more seashells. How many seashells does Tad have in all?

    77   87   88   97

    Ⓐ   Ⓑ   Ⓒ   Ⓓ

_____ grapes

Name _____

Solve & Share

Josh has 34 cans to recycle. Jill has 27 cans. How many cans do they have in all?

Solve any way you choose. Use drawings and equations to explain your work.

I can ...
break apart numbers into tens and ones to find their sum.

© **Content Standards** 2.NBT.B.5, 2.NBT.B.9
Mathematical Practices MP.1, MP.4, MP.7

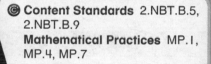

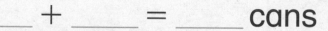

_____ + _____ = _____ cans

$37 + 25 = ?$

You can break apart just the second addend into **tens** and **ones**.

$$37 \quad + \quad 25 \quad = \quad ?$$

| 37 | | 20 | 5 |

37 + 25 = 37 + 20 + 5

Add the tens of the second addend.

$37 + \mathbf{20} = 57$

Add the ones of the second addend.

$57 + \mathbf{5} = 62$

So, $27 + 35 = \underline{62}$.

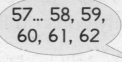
57... 58, 59, 60, 61, 62

Do You Understand?

Show Me! Explain how you can break apart 28 to find $33 + 28$.

Guided Practice Break apart the second addend to find the sum. Show your work. Use blocks to help, if needed.

1. $57 \quad + \quad 32 = \underline{}$

| 57 | | 30 | 2 |

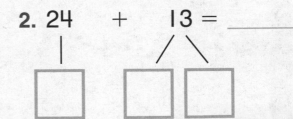

$\underline{57} + \underline{30} = \underline{87}$

$\underline{87} + \underline{2} = \underline{89}$

2. $24 \quad + \quad 13 = \underline{}$

| | | | | |

© Pearson Education, Inc. 2
Topic 3 | Lesson 5

Tools   Assessment

Independent Practice   Break apart the second addend to find the sum. Show your work. Use blocks, if needed.

3. 42   +   16 = _____

□   □ □

4. 36   +   44 = _____

□   □ □

5. 41   +   37 = _____

□   □ □

6. 35 + 47 = _____

7. 32 + 28 = _____

8. 48 + 27 = _____

9. **Number Sense** Write the digit that makes each equation true.

3 □ + 58 = 94

28 + 4 □ = 75

1 □ + 43 = 61

53 + 2 □ = 82

It helps to break apart the numbers.

10. Amir planted 35 trees.
    Juan planted 27 trees.
    How many trees did they plant in all?

    _____ trees

11. Carmen has 18 pennies.
    Patrick has 12 more pennies than Carmen.
    How many pennies does Patrick have?

    _____ pennies

12. **Higher Order Thinking** Use the numbers on the cards. Use each number once to write a true equation.

    5 ☐ + ☐ 4 = ☐ 6

13. © **Assessment** Which has a sum of 67? Choose all that apply.

    ☐ 15 + 52

    ☐ 15 + 62

    ☐ 38 + 29

    ☐ 11 + 55

    Remember, you can add numbers in any order.

© Pearson Education, Inc. 2

Name _____

Another Look!

Find $25 + 34$.

Think 25 plus 3 tens and 4 ones.

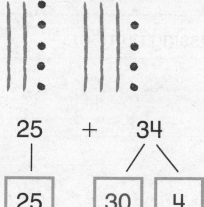

$$25 \quad + \quad 34$$

| 25 | | 30 | 4 |

Count on by tens to add 3 tens.

25, <u>35</u>, <u>45</u>, <u>55</u>

Then count on by ones to add 4 ones.

55, <u>56</u>, <u>57</u>, <u>58</u>, <u>59</u>

So, $25 + 34 = 59$.

You can break apart the second addend to find the sum.

HOME ACTIVITY Ask your child to explain how to add $43 + 26$ in his or her head.

Break apart numbers to find the sums. Show your work. Draw pictures, if needed.

1. $16 + 22 =$ _____

2. $47 + 29 =$ _____

3. $56 + 35 =$ _____

4. $14 + 28 =$ _____

5. $26 + 48 =$ _____

6. $43 + 17 =$ _____

7. © **MP.7 Look for Patterns** Break apart numbers to solve. Show your work.

Lily has 46 songs on her music player. Tonya has 53 songs on her music player. How many songs do they have in all?

_____ songs

8. **Algebra** Write the missing number.

$50 + \blacktriangle = 75$

$\blacktriangle + 25 = 50$

$\blacktriangle =$ _____

$\blacksquare + 38 = 80$

$30 + \blacksquare = 72$

$\blacksquare =$ _____

9. **Higher Order Thinking** Use the numbers on the cards. Use each number once to write a true equation.

6 7 8

1 ☐ $+$ ☐ 5 $=$ ☐ 2

10. © **Assessment** Which has a sum of 60? Choose all that apply.

☐ $30 + 30$

☐ $35 + 35$

☐ $45 + 15$

☐ $50 + 10$

Solve

Solve & Share

35 + 8 = _____

Solve the problem by changing the 8 so that it is easier to find the sum of 35 + 8.

Explain your work.

I can ...
break apart addends and combine them in different ways to make numbers that are easy to add mentally.

 **Content Standard** 2.NBT.B.5
Mathematical Practices MP.2, MP.3, MP.8

35 + 8 = _____

Find 38 + 23.

You can use compensation to make numbers that are easier to add.

40   **21**

38 is close to 40. It's easier to add 40 than 38.

So, take 2 from 23 and give it to 38 to make 40.

38	+	23
+ 2		− 2
40	+	21 = ?

Add mentally.

$40 + 21 = ?$

$40 + 21$

20	1

$40 + 20 + 1 = 60 + 1 = 61$

So, $40 + 21 = 61$.

If you give an amount to one addend, you must take away the same amount from the other addend, so the sum stays the same.

$40 + 21 = 38 + 23$

So, $38 + 23 = 61$.

Do You Understand?

Show Me! Solve.

$19 + 26 = \boxed{}$

Explain how you can change the addends to make them easier to add.

☆ **Guided Practice** ☆   Use compensation to make numbers that are easier to add. Then solve. Show your work.

1. $17 + 9 = \underline{\hspace{1cm}}$
    $+3 \quad -3$
    $20 + 6 = 26$

2. $23 \quad + \quad 12 \quad = \underline{\hspace{1cm}}$
    $\bigcirc \qquad \bigcirc$
    $\underline{\hspace{1cm}} \quad + \underline{\hspace{1cm}} = \underline{\hspace{1cm}}$

3. $25 \quad + \quad 47 \quad = \underline{\hspace{1cm}}$
    $\bigcirc \qquad \bigcirc$
    $\underline{\hspace{1cm}} \quad + \underline{\hspace{1cm}} = \underline{\hspace{1cm}}$

Topic 3 | **Lesson 6**

Independent Practice

Use compensation to make numbers that are easier to add. Then solve. Show your work.

4. 33 + 19 = _____
    ◯ _____   ◯ _____

    _____ + _____ = _____

5. 28 + 8 = _____
    ◯ _____   ◯ _____

    _____ + _____ = _____

6. 27 + 36 = _____
    ◯ _____   ◯ _____

    _____ + _____ = _____

7. **Number Sense** Explain how you can use compensation to make numbers that are easy to add. Solve. Show your work.

28 + 37 = ☐

_____ + _____ = ☐

8. **Higher Order Thinking** Show two different ways you could use compensation to make numbers that are easy to add. Solve. Show your work.

17 + 26 = ☐

Use compensation to make numbers that are easier to add. Then solve. Show your work.

9. © **MP.3 Explain** Bella said there is only one way to rewrite this problem to make the numbers easier to add. Is she correct? Explain. Then solve.

$42 + 29 = \boxed{}$

_____

_____

_____

10. **A-Z Vocabulary** Show two different ways to use **compensation** to find the sum. Then solve.

$46 + 47 = \boxed{}$

What number is close to 46 or 47?

11. **Higher Order Thinking** Show two different ways to use compensation to find the sum. Then solve.

$37 + 16 + 5 = \boxed{}$

12. © **Assessment** Is the amount equal to $42 + 4 + 8$? Choose Yes or No.

$50 + 4$	○ Yes	○ No
$40 + 4 + 10$	○ Yes	○ No
54	○ Yes	○ No
$40 + 12$	○ Yes	○ No

Name _____

Another Look! You can use compensation to make numbers that are easy to add mentally.

Use compensation to find 47 + 28.

- Give 3 to 47 to make 50.
  Give 2 to 28 to make 30.

- Then it is easy to add in your head.

- You added 3 + 2 = 5. So subtract 5 from 80 to find the answer.
  You can count back 5 from 80 to check your answer.

So, 47 + 28 = 75.

$47 + 28$
$+3 \ +2$

$50 + 30 = 80$

$80 - 5 = 75$

$80, \underline{79}, \underline{78}, \underline{77}, \underline{76}, \underline{75}$

Compensation is a way to make numbers that are easy to add in your head!

HOME ACTIVITY Ask your child to oxplain how to use compensation to add 17 + 38 mentally.

Use compensation to make numbers that are easier to add. Then solve. Show your work.

1. 26 + 6 = _____
   ◯ ◯
   _____ + _____ = _____

2. 17 + 19 = _____
   ◯ ◯
   _____ + _____ = _____

3. 39 + 54 = _____
   ◯ ◯
   _____ + _____ = _____

Use compensation to make numbers that are easier to add.
Then solve. Show your work.

4. $24 + 18 =$ _____

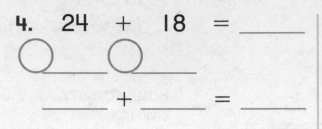

_____ + _____ = _____

5. $25 + 27 =$ _____

_____ + _____ = _____

6. $43 + 32 =$ _____

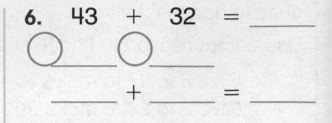

_____ + _____ = _____

7. **© MP.2 Reasoning** Use compensation to solve. Show your work.

Wendy found 13 bugs and Wally found 27 bugs. How many bugs did they find in all?

_____ bugs

8. **Higher Order Thinking** Use compensation to write 3 different equations with the same sum as $38 + 16$. Then solve.

$38 + 16 =$ _____

A. _____ + _____ = _____

B. _____ + _____ = _____

C. _____ + _____ + _____ = _____

9. **© Assessment** Which is equal to $14 + 8$? Choose all that apply.

☐ $12 + 6$

☐ $12 + 10$

☐ $10 + 12$

☐ $10 + 4 + 8$

10. **© Assessment** Is the amount equal to $26 + 16$? Choose Yes or No.

$30 + 10 + 2$ ◯ Yes ◯ No

$30 + 12$ ◯ Yes ◯ No

$25 + 20$ ◯ Yes ◯ No

$20 + 22$ ◯ Yes ◯ No

Name _____

Solve & Share

Tameka has 39 blocks. Kim has 43 blocks. How many blocks do they have in all?

Choose any strategy. Solve. Show and explain your work.

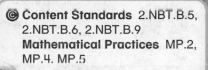

I can ...
choose a strategy to help me add two-digit numbers.

© **Content Standards** 2.NBT.B.5, 2.NBT.B.6, 2.NBT.B.9 **Mathematical Practices** MP.2, MP.4. MP.5

$43 + 39 =$ _____

_____ blocks

Find 66 + 25.

You can break apart numbers or use compensation.

One Way

Break apart 25 into 20 + 5.

66 + 25

66 + 20 + 5

86 + 5 = 91

Another Way

You can use compensation.

66 + 25

− 5   + 5

61 + 30 = 91

You get the same answer both ways!

So, 66 + 25 = 91.

Do You Understand?

Show Me! In 66 + 25 above, why was 5 subtracted from 66 and then added to 25?

☆ **Guided Practice** ☆ Find each sum. Use any strategy. Show your work.

1.   14 + 32 = _____

14 + 30 + 2

44 + 2 = 46

2. 67 + 26 = _____

Name _____

Tools Assessment

Independent Practice ☆ Find each sum. Use any strategy. Show your work.

3. 33 + 52 = _____

4. 27 + 6 = _____

5. _____ = 49 + 45

6. 57 + 12 = _____

7. _____ = 63 + 20

8. 14 + 58 = _____

9. 45 + 55 = _____

10. 87 + 9 = _____

11. 19 + 61 = _____

Number Sense Write the digit that makes each equation true.

12. 45 + 1 ☐ = 61

13. 84 = ☐ 8 + 56

14. 3 ☐ + 19 = 56

Topic 3 | Lesson 7

one hundred sixty-one **161**

15. ©️ MP.2 Reasoning Martin has 44 marbles. Carol has 39 marbles. Steve has 90 marbles. How many marbles do Martin and Carol have in all? Do they have more or fewer marbles than Steve?

_____ marbles

Circle: more   fewer

31	32	33	34	35	36	37	38	39	40
41	42	43	44	45	46	47	48	49	50
51	52	53	54	55	56	57	58	59	60
61	62	63	64	65	66	67	68	69	70
71	72	73	74	75	76	77	78	79	80
81	82	83	84	85	86	87	88	89	90
91	92	93	94	95	96	97	98	99	100

16. Higher Order Thinking José collected 32 leaves on Saturday. On Sunday, he collected 14 more leaves than he did on Saturday. How many leaves did José collect in all?

_____ leaves

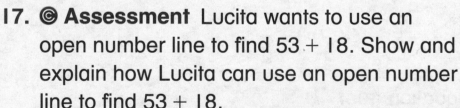

Move down one row to show adding tens. Move ahead to show adding ones.

17. ©️ Assessment Lucita wants to use an open number line to find $53 + 18$. Show and explain how Lucita can use an open number line to find $53 + 18$.

© Pearson Education, Inc. 2

Topic 3 | Lesson 7

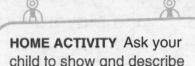

Another Look!

Find 24 + 56.

Step 1: Remember, 24 + 56 = 56 + 24.

Step 2: Place ___56___ on an open number line.

Step 3: Count on ___2___ tens from 56 to get to ___76___ .

Step 4: Then, count on ___4___ ones from 76 to get to ___80___ .

So, 24 + 56 = ___80___ .

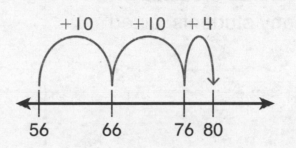

56   66   76 80

You can add numbers in any order and get the same sum.

HOME ACTIVITY Ask your child to show and describe how to find 46 + 27 using an open number line.

Add using an open number line or another strategy. Show your work.

1. 38 + 6 = _____

2. 29 + 67 = _____

3. 48 + 34 = _____

Use any strategy to solve each problem. Show your work.

4. © **MP.2 Reasoning** There were 43 students on the playground. Some more students joined them. Now there are 63 students on the playground. How many students joined?

_____ students

5. Roger has 14 grapes. Lisa has 49 grapes. How many grapes do Roger and Lisa have in all?

_____ grapes

6. Higher Order Thinking Two teams collected cans for a food drive. How many cans did they collect in all? Show your work.

Red Team		Blue Team	
Boys	**Girls**	**Boys**	**Girls**
23	28	12	30

7. © **Assessment** Ali wrote this first step in how to add 27 + 12 on a hundred chart.

> Start at 27 on the chart.

Write the other steps.

© Pearson Education, Inc. 2

Name _____

Solve & Share

The Red Team has 15 more points than the Blue team. The Blue Team has 36 points. How many points does the Red Team have?

Solve and explain your answer using counters, drawings, or equations.

I can ...
use drawings and equations to solve one-step and two-step problems.

Red Team
?

Period
3

Blue Team
36

10:00

© **Content Standard** 2.OA.A.1
Mathematical Practices MP.1, MP.2, MP.4, MP.6

Matt sold 17 tickets.
Jenn sold 8 fewer tickets than Matt.
Amy sold 3 more tickets than Jenn.

How many tickets did each person sell?

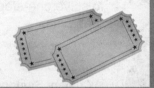

Step 1

tickets Matt sold

17

8	9

fewer tickets   tickets Jenn sold

$17 - 8 = 9$
Jenn sold 9 tickets.

Step 2

tickets Amy sold

12

9	3

tickets Jenn sold   more tickets

$9 + 3 = 12$
Amy sold 12 tickets.

Matt: 17 tickets
Jenn: 9 tickets
Amy: 12 tickets

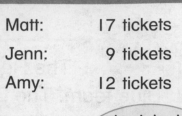

Look back! Does your answer make sense?

Do You Understand?

Show Me! What steps did you take to find the number of tickets Amy sold? Explain.

☆ **Guided Practice**   Solve the two-step problem. Show your work.

1. Steve read 15 books. Sam read 9 fewer books than Steve. Dixon read 8 more books than Sam.

How many books did Sam read?

$\underline{15} - \underline{9} = \underline{\hspace{1cm}}$

How many books did Dixon read?

$\underline{6} + \underline{8} = \underline{\hspace{1cm}}$

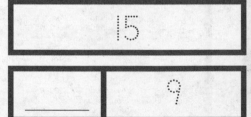

15

	9

Sam read _____ books.

____

6	8

Dixon read _____ books.

© Pearson Education, Inc. 2

Topic 3 | **Lesson 8**

Name _____

Independent Practice ☆ Solve the problems below. Show your work.

2. Brian has 17 fewer marbles than Kyle. Brian has 21 marbles. How many marbles does Kyle have?

_____ marbles

3. Clint catches 7 frogs. 3 frogs hop away. Then Clint catches 6 more frogs. How many frogs does Clint have now?

_____ frogs

4. Erwin sees 23 birds in a tree. Then 18 more birds come. How many birds does Erwin see now?

_____ birds

5. There are 31 blue fish in a pond. There are also 8 gold fish and 3 red fish in the pond. How many fish are in the pond?

_____ fish

6. Higher Order Thinking Mr. Leu buys 6 bananas. Then he buys 8 more bananas. He gives some bananas to Mr. Shen. Now Mr. Leu has 5 bananas. How many bananas did Mr. Leu give to Mr. Shen?

_____ bananas

7. There are 21 more green crayons than blue crayons. There are 14 blue crayons. How many green crayons are there?

_____ green crayons

8. © MP.1 Make Sense Dan swims 4 laps on Monday. He swims 5 laps on Tuesday. Then he swims 9 laps on Wednesday. How many laps does Dan swim in all?

_____ + _____ = _____

_____ + _____ = _____

_____ laps

9. Higher Order Thinking Robert has 20 blueberries. He has 10 more blueberries than Janessa. He has 14 fewer blueberries than Amari. How many blueberries does Janessa have? How many blueberries does Amari have?

_____ − _____ = _____

_____ + _____ = _____

Janessa has _____ blueberries.

Amari has _____ blueberries.

10. © Assessment Billy saw 19 animals at Grayson Zoo in the morning. He saw 17 more animals after lunch. How many animals did Billy see in all?

_____ + _____ = _____ animals

Taylor saw 41 animals at Richmond Zoo. How many animals did Billy and Taylor see in all?

_____ + _____ = _____

Billy and Taylor saw _____ animals in all.

Name _____

Another Look! Write equations to solve two-step problems.

Allison collected 23 rocks.
Jason collected 15 more rocks than Allison.
Phil collected 3 fewer rocks than Allison.

How many rocks does Jason have?
How many rocks does Phil have?

Number of Rocks Jason has: $23 + 15 = ?$

$23 + 10 = 33$ and $33 + 5 = 38$

So, Jason has ___38___ rocks.

You can count back 3 from 23 to find the number of rocks Phil has.

23, __22__, __21__, __20__ So, Phil has __20__ rocks.

Be sure to solve each part of the problem!

HOME ACTIVITY Make up story problems that take two questions, or steps, to solve. Ask your child to solve both steps of each problem.

Write equations to solve the problems.

1. There are 4 fewer students in Ms. Jagger's class than Mr. Curley's class. Mr. Curley's class has 20 students. How many students are in Ms. Jagger's class?

   _____ − _____ = _____

   _____ students

2. There are 13 green grapes and 7 red grapes in a bowl. Joe ate 5 of the grapes. How many grapes are in the bowl now?

   _____ + _____ = _____

   _____ − _____ = _____

   _____ grapes

Algebra Find the missing numbers.

3. ■ + 42 = 58

   ■ = _____

4. 33 + 49 = ▲

   ▲ = _____

5. 76 + ● = 89

   ● = _____

Write equations to solve each problem.

6. © **MP.1 Make Sense** There are 6 girls at a park. 6 boys join them. Then 4 girls go home. How many children are at the park now?

_____ + _____ = _____

_____ − _____ = _____

_____ children.

7. **Higher Order Thinking** Mr. Villa's class has 23 students. Ms. Anderson's class has 3 more students than Mr. Villa's class. How many students are there in all?

Check your work. Does your answer make sense?

_____ students

8. © **Assessment** Mike used 27 nails to build a chair. He used 14 more nails to build a table than he used to build the chair. How many nails did Mike use to build the table? Use any strategy to solve. Explain your solution.

_____ nails

© Pearson Education, Inc. 2

Name _____

Solve & Share

There are 23 red balloons in a bag. There are 38 blue balloons in the same bag. How many balloons are in the bag?

Use a tool to solve the problem. Be ready to explain which tool you used and why.

I can ...
choose a tool and use it to solve a problem.

© **Mathematical Practices** MP.5 Also MP.1, MP.2, MP.3 **Content Standards** 2.OA.A.1, 2.NBT.B.5

Thinking Habits

Which of these tools can I use?

Tools

Cubes	Paper and
Counters	pencil
Hundred chart	Place-value
Technology	blocks

Is there a different tool I can use?

Learn   Glossary

Ted's puzzle has 37 more pieces than Mia's puzzle. Mia's puzzle has 48 pieces. How many pieces does Ted's puzzle have?

Which tool can I use?

Tools
• cubes
• counters
• hundred chart
• technology
• paper and pencil
• place-value blocks

Which tool is a good choice?

Ted has 37 more pieces than Mia. I can use place-value blocks to find 48 + 37.

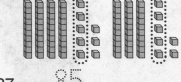

48 + 37 = __85__
Ted's puzzle has 85 pieces.

If I used counters, I'd need to count each one.

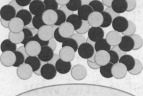

With place-value blocks, I can add the tens quicker.

I can break apart 37 and add each part to 48 to check.

48 + 30 = 78

78 + 7 =
78 + 2 + 5 = 85
My answer makes sense.

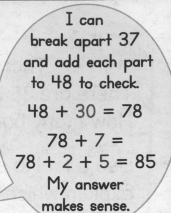

Do You Understand?

Show Me! Explain why a ten-frame is not the best tool to use to solve the problem above.

Guided Practice Choose a tool to help you solve the problem. Show your work. Explain why you chose that tool and how you solved the problem.

1. There are 16 chickens in the yard. There are 19 chickens in the barn. How many chickens are there in all?

Will you use place-value blocks or counters to solve the problem? Explain.

16 ⊕ 19 ⊜ ___

___ chickens

© Pearson Education, Inc. 2   **Topic 3 | Lesson 9**

Tools   Assessment

Independent Practice

Choose a tool to help solve each problem. Show your work. Explain your tool choice and how you solved the problem.

2. Greg had 45 sports cards. Jamal gives him 26 more cards. How many sports cards does Greg have now?

AWESOME MAVERICKS
P. LOVE

_____
_____
_____
_____

_____ ◯ _____ ◯ _____

_____ sports cards

3. Denise drew 8 stars with crayons. Then she drew 6 more stars. Trina drew 5 stars. How many fewer stars did Trina draw than Denise?

_____
_____
_____
_____

_____ ◯ _____ ◯ _____
       ◯   ◯
_____   _____

_____ fewer stars

Math Practices and Problem Solving

Performance Assessment

Bean Bag Toss

Evan and Pam want to choose the best tool to solve this problem.

Evan and Pam each throw two bean bags. Points are added for a score. Pam's total score is 100. Which two numbers did Pam's bean bags land on?

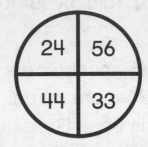

Bean Bag Toss Game Board

4. © **MP.1 Make Sense** What information is given? What do you need to find?

_____

_____

_____

_____

5. © **MP.3 Explain** Which numbers did Pam's bags land on? Explain how you know.

_____

_____

_____

_____

6. © **MP.5 Use Tools** Which tool did you use? How could you use a hundred chart to solve the problem? Explain.

_____

_____

1	2	3	4	5	6	7	8	9	10
11	12	13	14	15	16	17	18	19	20
21	22	23	24	25	26	27	28	29	30
31	32	33	34	35	36	37	38	39	40
41	42	43	44	45	46	47	48	49	50
51	52	53	54	55	56	57	58	59	60
61	62	63	64	65	66	67	68	69	70
71	72	73	74	75	76	77	78	79	80
81	82	83	84	85	86	87	88	89	90
91	92	93	94	95	96	97	98	99	100

© Pearson Education, Inc. 2

Name _____

Another Look! What tool would you use to solve this problem?

Jamie read 23 pages of a book last week.

This week, she read 26 more pages.

How many pages did Jamie read in all?

23	24	25	26	27	28	29
33	34	35	36	37	38	39
43	44	45	46	47	48	49

A hundred chart is a good tool to use. You can start at 23 and count on 2 tens, and then 6 ones. You land on 49. So, 23 + 26 = 49.

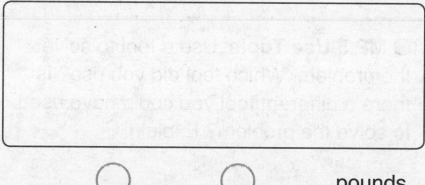

HOME ACTIVITY Take turns adding two 2-digit numbers. Use drawings of tens and ones to show how you found each sum.

23 + 26 = 49 pages. Jamie read 49 pages in all.

Choose a tool to help you solve the problem. Show your work.
Explain your tool choice and how you solved the problem.

1. A year ago, Maggie's puppy weighed 16 pounds. Now her puppy weighs 37 pounds more. How much does Maggie's puppy weigh now?

____ ◯ ____ ◯ ____ pounds

Rubber Bands

Juan is trying to find the best tool to solve this problem.

Juan wants to buy 1 large bag and 1 small bag of rubber bands. How many rubber bands will he buy?

Number of Rubber Bands		
Small	**Medium**	**Large**
25	45	70

2. © **MP.1 Make Sense** What information is given? What do you need to find?

_____

_____

_____

3. © **MP.3 Reasoning** Juan wants to use counters to solve the problem. Do you think Juan's tool choice is a good one? Why or why not?

_____

_____

_____

_____

4. © **MP.5 Use Tools** Use a tool to solve the problem. Which tool did you use? Is there a different tool you could have used to solve the problem? Explain.

_____

_____

_____

_____

_____

© Pearson Education, Inc. 2

TOPIC 3 **Fluency Practice Activity**

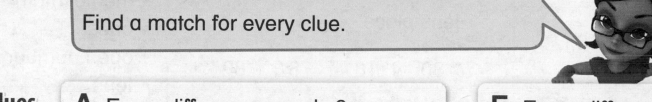

Find a partner. Point to a clue. Read the clue.

Look below the clues to find a match. Write the clue letter in the box next to the match.

Find a match for every clue.

Find a Match

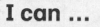
I can ...
subtract within 20.

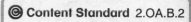
© Content Standard 2.OA.B.2

Clues

A Every difference equals 3.

B Every difference is less than 2.

C Every difference equals 11 − 5.

D Exactly two differences are equal.

E Every difference is greater than 8.

F Exactly three differences are odd.

G Every difference equals 16 − 8.

H Exactly three differences are even.

☐ 6 − 5 8 − 8 10 − 10 9 − 9	☐ 8 − 6 12 − 8 15 − 8 4 − 0	☐ 18 − 9 16 − 7 11 − 2 10 − 1	☐ 10 − 8 9 − 4 6 − 2 14 − 9
☐ 17 − 9 9 − 1 13 − 5 12 − 4	☐ 14 − 8 12 − 6 8 − 2 13 − 7	☐ 11 − 6 5 − 3 14 − 7 12 − 3	☐ 12 − 9 9 − 6 11 − 8 10 − 7

Vocabulary Review

TOPIC 3 **Vocabulary Review**

Understand Vocabulary

1. Circle the numbers that have a 3 in the ones place.

33   45   13   38

2. Cross out the numbers that do **NOT** have an 8 in the tens place.

80   18   78   89

Glossary

Word List
- bar diagram
- break apart
- compensation
- mental math
- ones
- open number line
- tens

---

3. Write an equation to show how to break apart 54 by place value.

_____

4. Use the open number line to find 38 + 23. Add the tens and then add the ones.

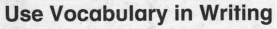

Use Vocabulary in Writing

5. Describe a way to find 47 + 18. Use terms from the Word List.

© Pearson Education, Inc. 2

Name _____

Set A

You can use a hundred chart to help you add. Find 62 + 12.

Start at 62.
Move down
1 row to add
the one ten
in 12.

51	52	53	54	55	56	57	58	59	60
61	62	63	64	65	66	67	68	69	70
71	72	73	74	75	76	77	78	79	80
81	82	83	84	85	86	87	88	89	90
91	92	93	94	95	96	97	98	99	100

Then move over
2 columns to add
the 2 ones in 12. So, 62 + 12 = __74__.

Reteaching

Use a hundred chart to find each sum.

1. 85 + 15 = _____

2. 60 + 23 = _____

Set B

You can use an open number line to find 64 + 20.

Place 64 on the number line.

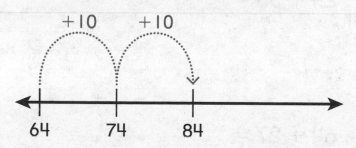

Count on by 10 two times from 64.

So, 64 + 20 = __84__.

Use an open number line to find each sum.

3. 50 + 30 = _____

4. 16 + 40 = _____

You can use an open number line to find 49 + 32.

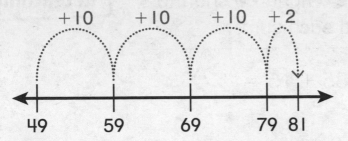

+10   +10   +10   +2

49   59   69   79 81

Place 49 on the number line. There are 3 tens in 33. So, count on by 10 three times. There are 2 ones in 32. So, count on 2 from 79.

So, 49 + 32 = __81__.

Find 32 + 19.
Break apart the tens and ones.

32   +   19   =   __51__

Tens | 30 | | 10 |
Ones | | 2 | | 9 |

Add the tens: __30__ + __10__ = __40__

Add the ones: __2__ + __9__ = __11__

Add the sums: 40 + 11 = __51__

Use an open number line to find each sum.

5. 35 + 13 = _____

6. 47 + 26 = _____

Break apart numbers to find each sum.
Show your work.

7. 24 + 55 = _____

8. 64 + 27 = _____

© Pearson Education, Inc. 2

TOPIC
3

Set E

Find 55 + 17.
Break apart 17 into 10 + 7.

55 + 17 = ?

| 55 | | 10 | 7 |

Add tens: 55 + 10 = 65

Add ones: 65 + 7 = 72

So, 55 + 17 = _72_.

Break apart the second
addend to find the sum.
Show your work.

Reteaching

9. 53 + 28 = _____

10. 78 + 19 = _____

Set F

Find 48 + 27.

48 is close to 50. So, take 2 from 27
and give it to 48 to make 50.

48 + 27 = ?

+ 2   − 2

50 + 25 = ?

| 20 | 5 |

_50_ + _20_ + _5_ = _75_

So, 48 + 27 = _75_

Use compensation to make numbers
that are easier to add. Then solve.
Show your work.

11. 17 + 46 = _____

12. 29 + 57 = _____

Marla walks 12 blocks on Monday.
On Tuesday she walks 4 fewer blocks.
How many blocks does Marla walk in all?

Blocks Marla walks on Tuesday:

$$\underline{12} - \underline{4} = \underline{8}$$

Blocks Marla walks on Monday and Tuesday:

$$\underline{12} + \underline{8} = \underline{20}$$

$\underline{20}$ blocks

Solve the two-step problem.

13. Wyatt has 16 crayons.
His father buys him 24 new crayons.
Then Wyatt's sister gives him 7 more crayons.
How many crayons does Wyatt have now?

$$\underline{\hspace{2em}} + \underline{\hspace{2em}} = \underline{\hspace{2em}}$$

$$\underline{\hspace{2em}} + \underline{\hspace{2em}} = \underline{\hspace{2em}}$$

$\underline{\hspace{2em}}$ crayons

Thinking Habits

Use Tools

Which of these tools can I use?

Cubes   Paper and
Counters   pencil
Hundred chart   Place-value
Technology   blocks

Is there a different tool
I can use?

Choose a tool to help solve the problem. Show your work.
Explain your tool choice.

14. 42 people are at a park before lunch. 29 people join those people after lunch.
How many people are at the park in all?

© Pearson Education, Inc. 2

Name _____

1. Use mental math. Which weights can you put on the scale to make it balance?

Ⓐ 10 40

Ⓒ 40 33

Ⓑ 10 21

Ⓓ 33 10

2. Terry has 63 crayons.
She gets 25 more crayons.
How many crayons does Terry have in all? Show your work.

Ⓔ **Assessment**

_____ crayons

---

3. Which equation does this number line show?

Ⓐ 50 + 30 = 80   Ⓒ 50 + 50 = 100

Ⓑ 50 + 40 = 90   Ⓓ 50 + 90 = 140

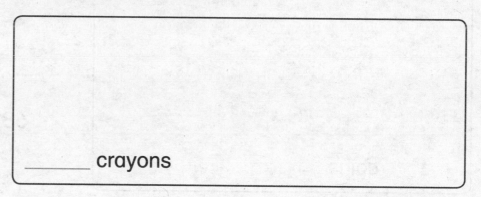

---

4. Use the numbers on the cards. Write the missing numbers under the number line to show how to find the sum of 40 + 35.

| 75 | 60 | 50 | 70 |

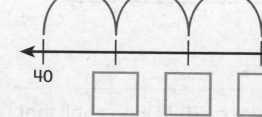

5. Colin has 54 pennies and 28 nickels. How many coins does Colin have?

Break apart the numbers to solve. Show your work.

_____ coins

6. Show how to add 68 + 16 using the open number line.

68 + 16 = _____

7. Part A Show how you can use an open number line to find 44 + 27.

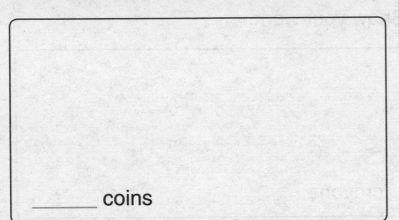

44 + 27 = _____

Part B In words, tell how you used the open number line to find the sum.

_____
_____
_____
_____

8. Which has a sum of 70? Choose all that apply.

☐ 35 + 35   ☐ 40 + 30   ☐ 45 + 45   ☐ 50 + 20

Name _____

9. Lisa has 18 markers.
Adam has 22 markers.
How many markers are there in all?

Choose a tool to solve the problem.

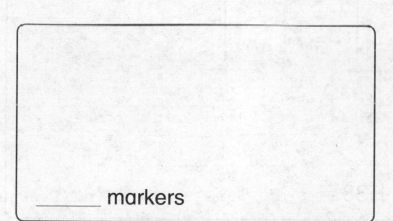

_____ markers

10. Ted has 52 cards in a box.
Tyrone has 48 more cards
than Ted. How many cards
does Tyrone have?

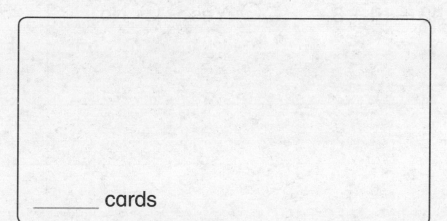

_____ cards

---

11. Which is equal to 47 + 25? Choose all that apply.

☐ 40 + 20 + 7 + 5   ☐ 40 + 20 + 12   ☐ 50 + 12   ☐ 50 + 22

---

12. Emma has 46 rocks.
She gets 25 more rocks from Gus.
How many rocks does Emma
have now?

_____ ◯ _____ = _____

_____ rocks

41	42	43	44	45	46	47	48	49	50
51	52	53	54	55	56	57	58	59	60
61	62	63	64	65	66	67	68	69	70
71	72	73	74	75	76	77	78	79	80

13. Is each sum 64? Choose Yes or No.

22 + 34 + 8   ◯ Yes   ◯ No

32 + 32   ◯ Yes   ◯ No

28 + 34 + 2   ◯ Yes   ◯ No

42 + 14 + 8   ◯ Yes   ◯ No

14. Break apart numbers to find 56 + 38.
Show your work.

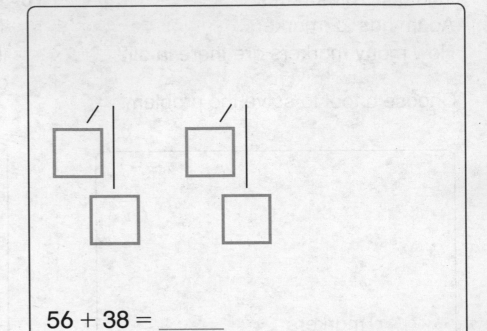

56 + 38 = _____

15. Write an equation to solve each part
of the two-step problem.

Ken has 45 stamps.
He uses 20 stamps.
Then he buys 7 more stamps.
How many stamps does he have now?

Ken has _____ stamps.

16. Show two different ways
to find 28 + 49.

Way 1

Way 2

Topic 3 | Assessment

Name _____

Popcorn Sales

A second-grade class is selling popcorn to help pay for a field trip.
This table shows how many boxes some students have sold.

Number of Popcorn Boxes Sold	
Ted	21
Nancy	19
Darnell	28
Mary	34
Elena	43

© Performance Assessment

1. How many boxes of popcorn did Ted and Mary sell in all? Use the open number line to solve. Show your work.

⟵─────────────────────⟶

_____ boxes

2. James says that Mary and Nancy sold more boxes in all than Darnell and Ted sold in all. Do you agree with him?

Circle   **yes**   **no**

Explain your answer.

_____

_____

_____

_____

3. Which two students sold a total of 55 boxes? Use any strategy to solve. Show your work.

Circle the names of the two students.

Ted   Nancy   Darnell

Mary   Elena

Which tool can I use?

Tools
- cubes
- counters
- hundred chart
- technology
- paper and pencil
- place-value blocks

4. Nancy sold 18 fewer boxes than Lucas. How many boxes did Lucas sell?

Part A Solve the problem. Show your work and explain your thinking.

_____ boxes

Part B Emily wants to use a tool to solve the problem. Look at the list of tools at the left. Which tool would be a good choice? Which tool would **NOT** be a good choice? Explain.

Fluently Add Within 100

Essential Question: What are strategies for adding numbers to 100?

Digital Resources

Solve Learn Glossary

Tools Assessment Help Games

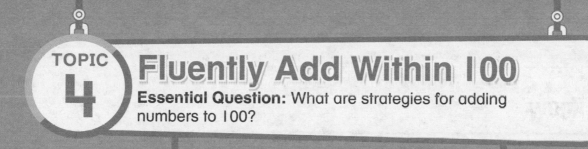

The islands of Hawaii began as volcanoes!

You can still see some volcanoes if you visit Hawaii.

Wow! Let's do this project and learn more.

Math and Science Project: Making and Using Models

Find Out Find and share books about Hawaii and volcanoes. Make a model of a volcano that becomes an island. Tell about how the island can change over a long time.

Journal: Make a Book Show what you learn in a book. In your book, also:

• Draw pictures to show how volcanoes can become islands.

• Show how you can use models to help you add numbers to 100.

Name _____

Review What You Know

A-Z Vocabulary

1. Circle the **tens** digit in each number.

73

53

82

2. Circle the **ones** digit in each number.

34

43

97

3. **Break apart** 23 into tens and ones.

23 = _____ tens and

_____ ones

Mental Math

4. Use mental math to find each sum.

$34 + 10 =$ _____

$50 + 5 =$ _____

$20 + 40 =$ _____

Open Number Line

5. Use the open number line to find $39 + 15$.

$39 + 15 =$ _____

Math Story

6. Stacy has 17 marbles. Diana gives her 22 marbles. How many marbles does Stacy have now?

_____ marbles

My Word Cards

Study the words on the front of the card.
Complete the activity on the back.

A-Z
Glossary

partial sum

Tens	Ones	
5	7	
+ 2	8	
7	0	← partial sum
+ 1	5	← partial sum
8	5	← sum

regroup

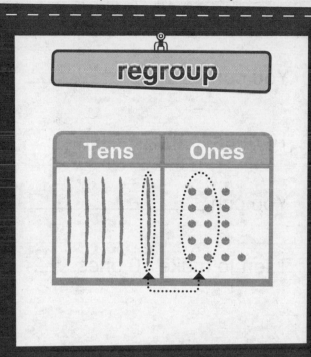

Tens	Ones

compatible numbers

8 + 2
20 + 7
53 + 10

My Word Cards

Use what you know to complete the sentences.
Extend learning by writing your own sentence using each word.

_____

_____

are numbers that are easy
to add or subtract using
mental math.

You can _____

10 ones to make 1 ten.

You can _____

1 ten to make 10 ones.

When you add numbers,
the sum of one of the place
values is called a

_____ .

© Pearson Education, Inc. 2

Solve

Solve & Share

Use place-value blocks to find 47 + 22.
Then draw a picture to show your work.

I can ...
add using place value and partial sums.

© **Content Standards** 2.NBT.B.5, 2.NBT.B.9
Mathematical Practices MP.1, MP.4, MP.5, MP.6, MP.7

47 + 22 = _____

Find 57 + 28.

	Tens	Ones
	5	7
+	2	8

I can use place-value blocks to check my work.

First, add the tens.

That's one **partial sum**.

	Tens	Ones
	5	7
+	2	8

50 + 20 = | 7 | 0 |

Then add the ones.

That's another partial sum.

	Tens	Ones
	5	7
+	2	8

50 + 20 = | 7 | 0 |
7 + 8 = | 1 | 5 |

Then add the partial sums to find the sum.

	Tens	Ones
	5	7
+	2	8

50 + 20 = | 7 | 0 |
7 + 8 = | 1 | 5 |
Sum = | 8 | 5 |

So, 57 + 28 = 85.

Do You Understand?

Show Me! How can you use partial sums to add 23 + 8? Explain.

☆ Guided Practice ☆

Add. Use partial sums. Show your work. Use place-value blocks, if needed.

1. 24 + 13

	Tens	Ones
	2	4
+	1	3
20 + 10 =	3	0
4 + 3 =		7
Sum =		

2. 68 + 7

	Tens	Ones
	6	8
+		7
60 + 0 =		
8 + 7 =		
Sum =		

© Pearson Education, Inc. 2

Tools   Assessment

Independent Practice Add. Use partial sums. Use place-value blocks, if needed.

3. 34 + 25

Tens	Ones
3	4
+ 2	5
___ + ___ =		
___ + ___ =		
Sum =		

4. 68 + 18

Tens	Ones
6	8
+ 1	8
___ + ___ =		
___ + ___ =		
Sum =		

5. 37 + 8

Tens	Ones
3	7
+	8
___ + ___ =		
___ + ___ =		
Sum =		

6. 52 + 38

Tens	Ones
5	2
+ 3	8
___ + ___ =		
___ + ___ =		
Sum =		

7. 45 + 29

Tens	Ones
4	5
+ 2	9
___ + ___ =		
___ + ___ =		
Sum =		

8. 28 + 39

Tens	Ones
2	8
+ 3	9
___ + ___ =		
___ + ___ =		
Sum =		

Number Sense Write each missing tens or ones digit.

9. $23 + 1\boxed{} = 37$

10. $59 = \boxed{}8 + 31$

Solve each problem. Use place-value blocks, if needed. Show your work.

11. © **MP.4 Model** 34 students are on the playground. 17 students are in the gym. How many students are there in all?

12. Sarah put 8 white roses in a vase. Then she added 7 red roses and 12 yellow roses to the vase. How many roses are in the vase now?

Why does the partial sums method work? Think about it!

_____ students

_____ roses

13. **Higher Order Thinking** Write each missing tens or ones digit. What strategy did you use?

$$\begin{array}{r} 12 \\ +3\,\square \\ \hline 50 \end{array}$$

$$\begin{array}{r} 24 \\ +3\,\square \\ \hline 60 \end{array}$$

$$\begin{array}{r} 35 \\ +3\,\square \\ \hline 70 \end{array}$$

14. © **Assessment** Sasha has 28 pennies. Her sister gives her 36 more pennies. How many pennies does she have now? Use partial sums to solve.

(A) 8

(B) 12

(C) 54

(D) 64

© Pearson Education, Inc. 2

Name _____

Another Look! Use partial sums to find $32 + 45$.

Write the problem this way. $32 + 45 = ?$

Step 1: Add the tens $30 + 40 = 70$

Step 2: Add the ones. $2 + 5 = 7$

Step 3: Add the
         partial sums. $70 + 7 = 77$

So, $32 + 45 = \underline{77}$.

> Break apart the numbers into tens and ones.

HOME ACTIVITY Ask your child to show you how to add $24 + 33$ using partial sums.

> Add. Use partial sums. Show your work.

1. $23 + 16 = \underline{\hspace{2em}}$

Add the tens.

$\underline{\hspace{2em}} + \underline{\hspace{2em}} = \underline{\hspace{2em}}$

Add the ones.

$\underline{\hspace{2em}} + \underline{\hspace{2em}} = \underline{\hspace{2em}}$

Add the partial sums.

$\underline{\hspace{2em}} + \underline{\hspace{2em}} = \underline{\hspace{2em}}$

2. $37 + 61 = \underline{\hspace{2em}}$

Add the tens.

$\underline{\hspace{2em}} + \underline{\hspace{2em}} = \underline{\hspace{2em}}$

Add the ones.

$\underline{\hspace{2em}} + \underline{\hspace{2em}} = \underline{\hspace{2em}}$

Add the partial sums.

$\underline{\hspace{2em}} + \underline{\hspace{2em}} = \underline{\hspace{2em}}$

3. $35 + 29 = \underline{\hspace{2em}}$

Add the tens.

$\underline{\hspace{2em}} + \underline{\hspace{2em}} = \underline{\hspace{2em}}$

Add the ones.

$\underline{\hspace{2em}} + \underline{\hspace{2em}} = \underline{\hspace{2em}}$

Add the partial sums.

$\underline{\hspace{2em}} + \underline{\hspace{2em}} = \underline{\hspace{2em}}$

Solve each problem. Show your work.

4. © MP.I **Make Sense** 28 leaves fell from a tree. Then 32 more leaves fell. How many leaves fell in all?

_____ leaves

5. Liam put 6 cars on his empty toy racetrack. Then Joe put 8 cars on the track. Then Kim put 4 cars on the track. How many cars are on the track now?

_____ cars

6. **Higher Order Thinking** Write each missing number. What pattern do you see?

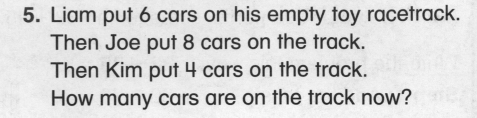

7. © **Assessment** Amir had 37 stamps. Then Tim gave him 16 more stamps. How many stamps does Amir have now? Use partial sums to solve.

Ⓐ 16

Ⓑ 21

Ⓒ 43

Ⓓ 53

© Pearson Education, Inc. 2

Name _____

Solve & Share

Wendy picked 37 pears. Toni picked 46 pears. How many pears did they pick in all?

Solve the problem using partial sums.
Draw place-value blocks to help explain your work.

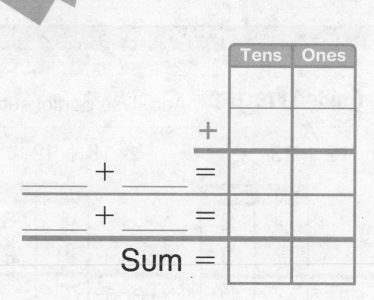

	Tens	Ones
+		
____ + ____ =		
____ + ____ =		
Sum =		

_____ pears

Find 38 + 59.

Tens	Ones
3	8
+ 5	9

You can use mental math to find partial sums.

First, add the tens.

Tens	Ones
3	8
+ 5	9
Tens: 8	0

Then, add the ones.

Tens	Ones
3	8
+ 5	9
Tens: 8	0
Ones: 1	7

Last, add the partial sums.

Tens	Ones
3	8
+ 5	9
Tens: 8	0
Ones: 1	7
Sum: 9	7

So, 38 + 59 = 97.

Do You Understand?

Show Me! Ken adds 43 + 27. His sum is 60. Is he correct? Explain.

Guided Practice Add. Use partial sums. Show your work.

1. 12 + 23

Tens	Ones
1	2
+ 2	3
Tens: 3	0
Ones:	5
Sum:	

2. 18 + 42

Tens	Ones
1	8
+ 4	2
Tens:	
Ones:	
Sum:	

3. 33 + 48

Tens	Ones
3	3
+ 4	8
Tens:	
Ones:	
Sum:	

Name _____

Tools Assessment

Independent Practice ☆ Add. Use partial sums. Show your work.

4. 18 + 24

Tens	Ones
1	8
+ 2	4

Tens: ___

Ones: ___

Sum: ___

5. 47 + 38

Tens	Ones
4	7
+ 3	8

Tens: ___

Ones: ___

Sum: ___

6. 26 + 47

Tens	Ones
2	6
+ 4	7

Tens: ___

Ones: ___

Sum: ___

7. 34 + 58

Tens	Ones
3	4
+ 5	8

Tens: ___

Ones: ___

Sum: ___

Higher Order Thinking Read the sum above each box.
Circle all the pairs of numbers in the box that match the sum.

8.   Sum 33

13	21	12
20	27	11
13	6	22

9.   Sum 48

28	40	22
20	8	38
23	25	10

10.   Sum 64

48	15	49
16	40	24
42	26	38

11. Toby planted 28 trees.
Juan planted 36 trees.
How many trees did they
plant in all?

	Tens	Ones
+		
Tens:		
Ones:		
Sum:		

_____ trees

12. © MP. I Make Sense Jenny has
13 tennis balls. Sal had 19 tennis balls,
but he gave 7 of them to Joe. How many
tennis balls do Jenny and Sal have now?

_____ tennis balls

13. Higher Order Thinking Write an addition
story using two 2-digit numbers.
Then solve the problem for your story.

14. © Assessment Which is the same amount
as $28 + 16$? Choose all that apply.

☐ $20 + 10 + 8 + 6$

☐ $30 + 14$

☐ 34

☐ 44

Is there more
than one correct
answer?

© Pearson Education, Inc. 2

Name _____

Another Look! Find 36 + 28.

Step 1
Add the tens.
3 tens + 2 tens
30 + 20 = 50

Tens	Ones

Step 2
Add the ones.
6 + 8 = 14

Tens	Ones

Make 1 ten with 10 ones.

Step 3
Add the partial sums.

	Tens	Ones
	3	6
+	2	8
Tens:	5	0
Ones:	1	4
Sum:	6	4

So, 36 + 28 = 64.

HOME ACTIVITY Write 27 + 44 on a sheet of paper. Ask your child to use partial sums to find the total.

Add. Use partial sums. Show your work.

1. 24 + 35

	Tens	Ones
	2	4
+	3	5
Tens:		
Ones:		
Sum:		

2. 17 + 44

	Tens	Ones
	1	7
+	4	4
Tens:		
Ones:		
Sum:		

3. 58 + 24

	Tens	Ones
	5	8
+	2	4
Tens:		
Ones:		
Sum:		

4. 25 + 65

	Tens	Ones
	2	5
+	6	5
Tens:		
Ones:		
Sum:		

5. 53 + 23

Tens	Ones
5	3
+ 2	3

Tens:

Ones:

Sum:

6. 35 + 28

Tens	Ones
3	5
+ 2	8

Tens:

Ones:

Sum:

7. 39 + 48

Tens	Ones
3	9
+ 4	8

Tens:

Ones:

Sum:

8. 69 + 27

Tens	Ones
6	9
+ 2	7

Tens:

Ones:

Sum:

9. Higher Order Thinking Draw the second addend. Write the number.

First Addend

Second Addend

Sum

There is more than one correct answer!

10. Algebra Write each missing number.

28 + ■ = 48

■ = _____

▲ + 18 = 68

▲ = _____

11. © **Assessment** Which is the same amount as 12 + 9 + 8? Choose all that apply.

☐ 20 + 9

☐ 12 + 10 + 7

☐ 29

☐ 39

Name _____

Solve & Share

Leslie collects 36 rocks. Her brother collects 27 rocks. How many rocks do they collect in all?

Use place-value blocks to help you solve. Draw your place-value blocks.

I can ...
use models to add 2-digit numbers and then explain my work.

© **Content Standards** 2.NBT.B.5, 2.NBT.B.9
Mathematical Practices MP.2, MP.3, MP.4, MP.5, MP.6

Tens	Ones
+	

_____ rocks

Let's add!

37 + 19 = ?

Show 37.
Then show 19.

Tens	Ones
☐	
3	7
1	9

Add the ones.

7 ones + 9 ones = 16 ones

Tens	Ones
☐	
3	7
1	9

There are 16 ones.
Regroup 16 ones as
1 ten and 6 ones.

Tens	Ones
1	
3	7
1	9
	6

Write **6** ones.
Write **1** to show 1 ten.

Add the tens.

3 tens + 1 ten = 4 tens
4 tens + 1 ten = 5 tens

Tens	Ones
1	
3	7
1	9
5	6

Write **5** to show 5 tens.

Do You Understand?

Show Me! When do you have to regroup when adding?

☆ Guided Practice ☆

Add. Draw place-value blocks to show your work. Regroup if needed.

1.

Tens	Ones
☐	
3	2
2	9
6	1

Tens	Ones

2.

Tens	Ones
☐	
2	4
5	2

Tens	Ones

3.

Tens	Ones
☐	
1	5
3	8

Tens	Ones

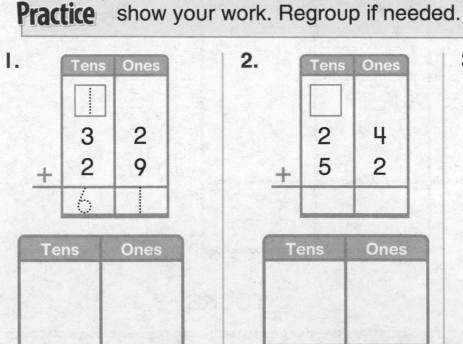
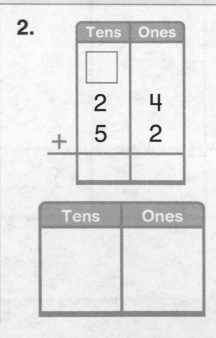
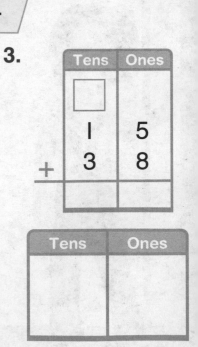

© Pearson Education, Inc. 2

Name _____

Independent Practice ✰ Add. Draw place-value blocks to show your work. Regroup if needed.

4.

Tens	Ones
□	
3	6
+ 2	9

Tens	Ones

5.

Tens	Ones
□	
2	7
+ 2	3

Tens	Ones

6.

Tens	Ones
□	
5	9
+ 1	3

Tens	Ones

7.

Tens	Ones
□	
2	4
+ 3	5

Tens	Ones

8. Higher Order Thinking Draw the second addend.

First Addend	Second Addend	Sum

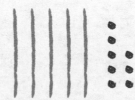

Math Practices and Problem Solving

Solve the problems below. Draw place-value blocks to show your work.

9. **© MP.4 Model** Chen counts 47 buttons. Then he counts 20 more buttons. How many buttons does Chen count in all?

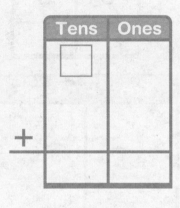

_____ buttons

10. **Math and Science** There were 24 earthquakes in the U.S. one year. There were 23 earthquakes the next year. How many earthquakes were there in those two years?

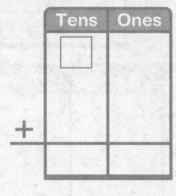

_____ earthquakes

11. **Higher Order Thinking** Write an addition story about the desks and chairs in your classroom. Use pictures, numbers, or words.

12. **© Assessment** Do you have to regroup to find each sum? Choose Yes or No.

$62 + 34 = ?$ ○ Yes   ○ No

$72 + 19 = ?$ ○ Yes   ○ No

$43 + 49 = ?$ ○ Yes   ○ No

$26 + 60 = ?$ ○ Yes   ○ No

© Pearson Education, Inc. 2

Name _____

Another Look! You can use these steps to add. Add $46 + 18$.

Way 1:

Step 1: Draw the tens and ones.
Make 1 ten with 10 ones.

Tens	Ones
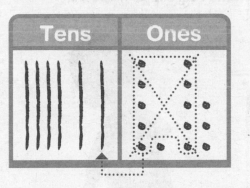

Step 2: Count the tens. Count the ones.

Tens	Ones

Way 2:

	Tens	Ones
	1	
	4	6
+	1	8
	6	4

$46 + 18 = \underline{64}$

HOME ACTIVITY Ask your child to show you how to add $27 + 34$. Have your child explain each step of the addition.

 Follow the steps to add. Draw place-value blocks to show your work. Regroup if needed.

1.

	Tens	Ones
	☐	
	2	4
+	2	9

2.

	Tens	Ones
	☐	
	3	8
+	4	5

Higher Order Thinking Write the missing numbers.
Draw place-value blocks if you need to.

3.

Tens	Ones
☐	
5	7
2	7
+	

4.

Tens	Ones
☐	
6	2
1	5
+	

5.

Tens	Ones
☐	
1	9
3	3
+	

Remember to write the regrouped numbers.

6.

Tens	Ones
☐	
2	7
◯	8
+	
4	5

7.

Tens	Ones
☐	
2	◯
5	7
+	
8	0

8.

Tens	Ones
☐	
3	8
◯	4
+	
6	2

9. © MP.2 Reasoning Lia has 38 red cups.
She has 25 blue cups.
How many cups does Lia have in all?

_____ cups

10. © Assessment Do you have to regroup to find each sum? Choose Yes or No.

$22 + 41 = ?$ ◯ Yes   ◯ No

$19 + 60 = ?$ ◯ Yes   ◯ No

$64 + 28 = ?$ ◯ Yes   ◯ No

$39 + 52 = ?$ ◯ Yes   ◯ No

© Pearson Education, Inc. 2

Topic 4 | Lesson 3

Name _____

Solve & Share

Add 46 + 26.

Draw place-value blocks, if needed.
Explain how you solved the problem.

I can ...
add 2-digit numbers and then explain my work.

Content Standards 2.NBT.B.5, 2.NBT.B.9
Mathematical Practices MP.1, MP.2, MP.3, MP.4, MP.6

Tens	Ones

☐

+

_____

_____

_____

Find 56 + 17.
Show 56. Then show 17.
Start by adding the ones.

Tens	Ones

Tens	Ones
5	6
1	7

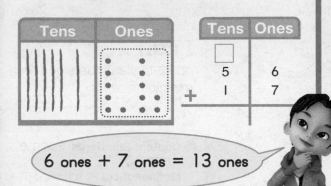

6 ones + 7 ones = 13 ones

Regroup 13 ones
as 1 ten and 3 ones.

Tens	Ones

Tens	Ones
5	6
1	7
	3

Write **3** ones.
Write **1** to show
1 ten.

5 tens + 1 ten = 6 tens
6 tens + 1 ten = 7 tens

Add the tens.

Tens	Ones

Tens	Ones
1	
5	6
1	7
7	3

Write **7** to show 7 tens.

So, 56 + 17 = 73.

Do You Understand?

Show Me! Roger found
54 + 27. His sum was 71. Is
he correct? Why or why not?
Draw place-value blocks to
check.

 **Guided Practice** Write the addition problem. Find the sum.
Use drawings if you need to.

1. 34 + 17

Tens	Ones
3	4
1	7
5	1

2. 52 + 31

Tens	Ones

3. 35 + 26

Tens	Ones

© Pearson Education, Inc. 2
Topic 4 | Lesson 4

Independent Practice

Write the addition problem. Find the sum.
Use drawings if you need to.

4. 15 + 28

Tens	Ones
☐	

+

5. 29 + 20

Tens	Ones
☐	

+

6. 63 + 29

Tens	Ones
☐	

+

7. 37 + 48

Tens	Ones
☐	

+

8. 67 + 17

Tens	Ones
☐	

+

9. 15 + 18

Tens	Ones
☐	

+

10. 43 + 49

Tens	Ones
☐	

+

11. 62 + 28

Tens	Ones
☐	

+

Higher Order Thinking Write the missing ones or tens digits.

12. $27 + 2\boxed{} = 50$

13. $3\boxed{} + 16 = 48$

14. $\boxed{}4 + 49 = 93$

15. © **MP.1 Make Sense**
Amir plants 25 trees.
Juan plants 27 trees.
How many trees do
they plant in all?

Tens	Ones

+

_____ trees

16. On Monday, Sasha
puts 32 pennies in her
bank. On Tuesday, she
puts 57 more pennies
in her bank. How many
pennies does she put in
her bank on both days?

Tens	Ones

+

_____ pennies

17. Higher Order Thinking Write an addition
story using 2 two-digit numbers. Then
solve the problem for your story.

_____

_____

Tens	Ones

_____

+

_____

_____

18. © **Assessment** 52 acorns fall from a
tree. Then 37 more acorns fall. How
many acorns in all fall from the tree?
Show how you solved the problem.

_____ acorns

© Pearson Education, Inc. 2
Topic 4 | Lesson 4

Name _____

Another Look! Remember these steps for adding.

Step 1: Add the ones.　　**Step 2:** Regroup if you need to.　　**Step 3:** Add the tens.

$34 + 27 = ?$
Regroup
11 ones as
1 ten and
1 one.

Tens	Ones
1	
3	4
+ 2	7
6	1

$12 + 36 = ?$
You do
not need
to regroup
8 ones.

Tens	Ones
1	2
+ 3	6
4	8

HOME ACTIVITY Write $28 + 45$ on a sheet of paper. Have your child find the sum using paper and pencil. Once finished, have your child explain why regrouping was needed.

Write the addition problem. Find the sum. Use drawings, if needed.

1. $15 + 26$
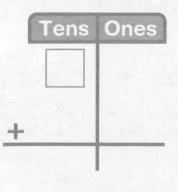

Tens	Ones
+	

2. $32 + 24$
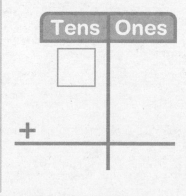

Tens	Ones
+	

3. $28 + 15$
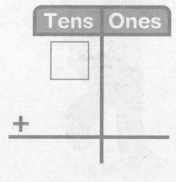

Tens	Ones
+	

4. $49 + 13$
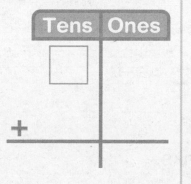

Tens	Ones
+	

5. $75 + 13$
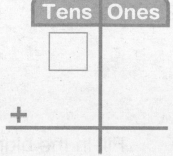

Tens	Ones
+	

Higher Order Thinking Read the sum. Circle all of the number pairs in the box that match that sum.

6. Sum 22

10	4	18
12	15	14
20	21	13

7. Sum 55

25	30	14
18	14	45
15	21	10

8. Sum 83

30	45	30
56	19	64
27	29	20

9. **A-Z Vocabulary** Paul has a stack of 47 cards. He also has a stack of 36 cards. How many cards does Paul have in all?

_____ cards

 Be precise.

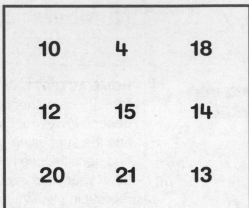

10. © Assessment
One box has 38 blue paper clips.
Another box has 43 green paper clips.
A third box has 6 red paper clips.
How many paper clips are in all the boxes?
Show how you solved the problem.

Fill in the blanks.

I **regrouped** _____ ones for _____ ten.

_____ paper clips

© Pearson Education, Inc. 2

Topic 4 | Lesson 4

Name _____

Solve & Share

Make three 2-digit numbers. The tens digit for each number is shown below. Toss a number cube three times to find the ones digit for each number.

How can you add your three numbers? Explain.

I can …
add three or four 2-digit numbers.

© **Content Standards** 2.NBT.B.6, 2.NBT.B.9
Mathematical Practices MP.2, MP.3, MP.4, MP.6, MP.8

Tens	Ones
2	
+ 2	

_____

_____

_____

Start by adding the ones.
Add in any order.

```
  2 4
  1 6
  1 4
+ 1 5
```

You can use doubles.

```
  2 ④
  1 6
  1 ④
+ 1 5
     9
```

4 + 4 = 8
6 + 5 = 11
11 + 8 = 19

Or you can make 10.

```
  2 4
  1 ⑥
  1 ④
+ 1 5
     9
```

6 + 4 = 10
4 + 5 = 9
10 + 9 = 19

Then add the tens.

```
  2 4
  1 6
  1 4
+ 1 5
  6 9
```

The sum
is 69!

Do You Understand?

Show Me! When you add more than three numbers, can you always make 10 to help you add the ones digits? Explain.

☆ Guided Practice   Add. Circle the two digits you added first.

1.
```
  1⑧
  1②
+ 15
  45
```

2.
```
  14
  11
+  9
```

3.
```
  21
  14
  41
+  2
```

4.
```
  21
  15
  32
+ 25
```

Remember, you can add numbers in any order.

Tools Assessment

Independent Practice ⭐ Add. Circle the two digits you added first.

5.
```
   22
   14
+  22
```

6.
```
   16
   23
+  26
```

7.
```
   27
   13
+  21
```

8.
```
   13
   33
+  25
```

9.
```
   25
   21
+  32
```

10.
```
   55
    7
   24
+   2
```

11.
```
   32
   16
   18
+  31
```

12.
```
   16
   42
   12
+  22
```

13.
```
   17
   41
   27
+  13
```

14.
```
   37
   11
   15
+  28
```

Algebra Find the missing numbers.

15. $8 + 3 + \boxed{} + 2 = 18$

16. $5 + \boxed{} + 6 + 5 = 19$

17. $7 + 27 + 23 + \boxed{} = 61$

18. $\boxed{} + 24 + 18 + 4 = 52$

19. © **MP.8 Generalize**

28 trucks are blue.

32 trucks are yellow.

17 trucks are green.

11 trucks are pink.

How many trucks are there in all?

Are there shortcuts you can take to solve the problems?

_____ trucks

---

20. Higher Order Thinking Henry is adding the numbers 24, 36, and 18. He makes a ten to add. Which ones digits does Henry add first? Explain.

_____

_____

21. © **Assessment** Find the sum. Explain your work.

$$\begin{array}{r} 25 \\ 16 \\ 15 \\ +\ 8 \\ \hline \end{array}$$

© Pearson Education, Inc. 2

Name _____

Another Look! You can add three or four numbers in any order. Remember to add the ones first. Then, add the tens.

Look for doubles.

```
 14    4 + 4 = 8
 35    8 + 5 = 13
+24
 73
```

Make a ten.

```
 13
 26
 24    6 + 4 = 10
+12    3 + 2 = 5
 75    10 + 5 = 15
```

Count on.

```
 53
 19
+22    Count on from 12.
 94    13, 14
```

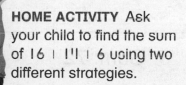

9 + 3 = 12

HOME ACTIVITY Ask your child to find the sum of 16 + 14 + 6 using two different strategies.

Add. Circle the two digits you added first.

1. Look for doubles.

```
  21
  10
  34
+ 24
```

2. Count on.

```
  12
  17
+ 24
```

3. Make a ten.

```
  15
  28
+ 22
```

4. Choose a way to add.

```
  26
  22
+ 36
```

© **MP.4 Model** Look at the sum. Read the clues. Circle the three numbers that add up to that sum. Show the addition you used to find the sum.

5. Sum: 83

5   44   12   19   10   20

One number is the sum of 22 + 22.
One number is one less than 20.
One number is greater than 19 and less than 44.

---

6. Sum: 72

36   12   25   7   33   14

One number has two of the same digits.
One number is greater than 12 and less than 25.
One number is 20 more than 5.

---

7. Higher Order Thinking Mac's family donates clothes to charity. Mac donates 16 shirts. His brother donates 14 shirts, and his mother donates 9 more shirts than Mac. How many shirts does Mac's family give to charity?

_____ shirts

8. © **Assessment** There are 37 ants, 39 worms, 12 moths, and 11 beetles living in a big garden. Find the sum. Explain your work.

$$
\begin{array}{r}
37 \\
39 \\
12 \\
+\ 11 \\
\end{array}
$$

© Pearson Education, Inc. 2

Solve & Share

Maria has 39 stickers. Sally has 28 stickers. They found 14 more stickers. How many stickers do they have in all?

Show your work. Explain how you found the answer.

_____ stickers

I can …
use mental math strategies and models to add more than two numbers.

© **Content Standards** 2.NBT.D.5, 2.NBT.B.6, 2.NBT.B.9
Mathematical Practices MP.2, MP.3, MP.4, MP.6, MP.7

Find 27 + 38 + 12 + 3.
One Way: Use partial sums.

Tens	Ones
2	(7)
3	8
1	2
+	(3)

Tens: 6 0
Ones: 2 0
Sum: 8 0

Look for compatible numbers to make tens.
7 + 3 = 10
8 + 2 = 10
10 + 10 = 20

Another Way: Add the ones. Regroup, if needed. Then add the tens.

I get the same sum either way!

Tens	Ones
2	
2	(7)
3	8
1	2
	(3)
8	0

Check your work.

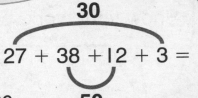

You can add the numbers in a different order to check your work.

30

27 + 38 + 12 + 3 =

30 + 50 = 80   **50**
So, 27 + 38 + 12 + 3 = 80.

Do You Understand?

Show Me! Find the sum of
14 + 28 + 33 + 22. Explain.

How can you check your work?

☆ Guided Practice Add.

1.
```
  18
  43
+ 12
―――
  73
```

2.
```
  29
+ 47
```

3.
```
   9
  34
+ 21
```

4.
```
  33
  27
  18
+ 13
```

Topic 4 | Lesson 6

Independent Practice ⭑ Add.

5.   28
       + 8

6.   8
       + 17

7.   5
         31
       + 29

8.   36
          4
       + 28

9.   20
         16
       + 16

10.   27
          13
          12
        + 5

11.   9
          29
           5
        + 35

12.   18
          23
           7
        + 42

13.   27
          15
          33
        + 24

14.   13
           7
          20
        + 55

Number Sense Solve each problem. In which order did you add the numbers? Explain.

15. 22 + 17 + 8 + 3 = _____

16. 5 + 12 + 15 + 3 = _____

_____

_____

_____

_____

_____

_____

17. © MP.4 Model Kim has 38 seashells. Mike has 27 seashells. Use **partial sums** to find how many shells they have in all. Then check your answer by adding another way.

_____ seashells

18. Math and Science Fossils form slowly over millions of years. Many fossils come from the sea. Kyle has 9 fossils, Jorie has 12 fossils, Leah has 6 fossils, and Joshua has 8 fossils. How many fossils did they have in all?

_____ fossils

19. Higher Order Thinking Find the sum. Explain why your strategy works.

```
  22
  13
  18
+  7
```

20. © Assessment Kate has 7 balloons. Claire has 9 balloons. Billy has 6 balloons. How many balloons do they have in all? Show your work.

_____ balloons

Another Look! Find the sum.

```
 34
 29
 18
+ 6
 60
+27
 87
```

Step 1: Add the tens in any order.
$30 + 20 + 10 = 50 + 10 = 60$

Step 2: Add the ones in any order.

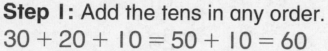
$(4) + 9 + 8 + (6) = ?$

$10 + 17 = 27$

Step 3: Add the partial sums.
Think: $60 + 27 = ?$
$60 + 20 + 7 = 87$
So, $34 + 29 + 18 + 6 = 87.$

HOME ACTIVITY Write $22 + 33 + 18 + 7$ on a sheet of paper. Ask your child to show you how to find the sum.

Add in any order. It helps to make a 10. $4 + 6 = 10$

Add using partial sums.

1.

Tens	Ones
2	8
1	(3)
+	(7)

Tens: | 3 | 0 |
Ones: | 1 | 8 |
Sum: | | |

2.

Tens	Ones
3	4
2	6
+	7

Tens: | | |
Ones: | | |
Sum: | | |

3.

Tens	Ones
3	1
2	4
1	1
+	9

Tens: | | |
Ones: | | |
Sum: | | |

4.

Tens	Ones
2	3
3	7
	8
+ 2	8

Tens: | | |
Ones: | | |
Sum: | | |

© MP.6 Be Precise Add any way you choose. Show your work.

5.
```
   26
+ 48
```

6.
```
    8
   13
+ 22
```

7.
```
    5
   11
+ 59
```

8.
```
   16
    4
   28
+ 48
```

9.
```
   20
    6
   17
+ 46
```

Number Sense Find each missing number.

10. $6 + 13 + 4 + 7 =$ ☐

11. $5 + 15 + 12 +$ ☐ $= 38$

12. **Higher Order Thinking** Write an addition story problem with 3 or more addends. Then solve the problem. Show your work.

13. **© Assessment** Ricky is building a toy. He uses 27 red blocks. He uses 10 blue blocks and 36 brown blocks. How many blocks in all? Show your work.

_____ blocks

© Pearson Education, Inc. 2

Topic 4 | Lesson 6

Name _____

Solve

Solve & Share

The second graders take a trip to a nature center. The Green Class sees 23 animals. The Blue Class sees 14 animals. The Yellow Class sees 32 animals. How many animals do they see in all?

Solve using drawings, models, or an equation.
Be prepared to explain your work.

I can ...
use drawings, models, and equations to solve one- and two-step problems.

© **Content Standard** 2.OA.A.1
Mathematical Practices MP.1, MP.4, MP.5, MP.8

_____ animals

Aimee and Devin count 36 butterflies. Suddenly, more butterflies join them. Now, there are 53 butterflies.

How many new butterflies join them?

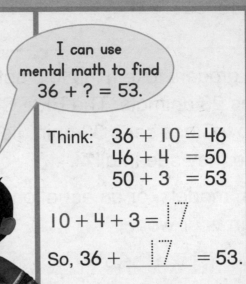

53

| 36 | ? |

36 + ? = 53

The total is 53. The first group has 36 butterflies. I will use a bar diagram to model the problem.

I can use mental math to find 36 + ? = 53.

Think: 36 + 10 = 46
          46 + 4 = 50
          50 + 3 = 53

10 + 4 + 3 = 17

So, 36 + ___17___ = 53.

So, 17 butterfiles join them.

Check your work.

```
    1
    3  6
 +  1  7
    5  3
```

The answer makes sense.

36 + 17 = 53

Do You Understand?

Show Me! Suppose you count 28 butterflies. Then suddenly there are 54. How could you use mental math to find how many join?

☆ **Guided Practice** ☆   Use the bar diagram and mental math to solve each problem. Then check your work.

1. There are 29 red marbles, 7 green marbles, and 11 blue marbles in a bag.

   How many marbles are in the bag?

   __29__ + __7__ + __11__ = ____

   ____ marbles

   ☐

   | 29 | 7 | 11 |

   ```
     1
     2  9
        7
  +  1  1
  ```

© Pearson Education, Inc. 2

Name _____

Independent Practice

Use the bar diagram and mental math to solve each problem. Then check your work.

2. 29 students are on the bus.
Then some more students get on the bus.
Now, there are 46 students on the bus.
How many students got on the bus?

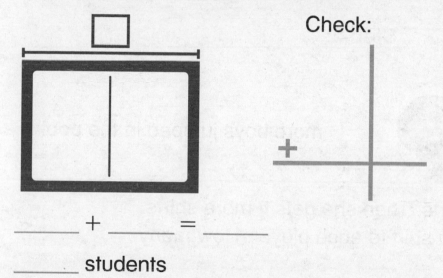

Check:

_____ + _____ = _____

_____ students

3. Ella has 34 more buttons than Julio.
Julio has 49 buttons. How many buttons does Ella have?

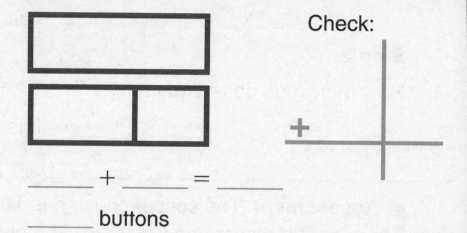

Check:

_____ + _____ = _____

_____ buttons

4. Wendy has 14 more crayons than Oscar.
Oscar has 54 crayons.
How many crayons does Wendy have?

The bar diagram helps you see how the numbers are related.

Check:

_____ + _____ = _____

_____ crayons

5. © **MP.1 Make Sense** Mariah has 17 figs. Kendra has 20 more figs than Mariah. Toby has 33 more figs than Kendra. How many figs do Kendra and Toby each have?

Step 1:

How many figs does Kendra have?

_____ ◯ _____ = _____ _____ figs

Step 2:

How many figs does Toby have?

_____ ◯ _____ = _____ _____ figs

Solve one step at a time.

6. **Higher Order Thinking** 8 girls and some boys are in the pool. In all, 17 children are in the pool. Then some more boys jump in the pool. Now there are 13 boys in the pool. How many more boys jumped in the pool?

Step 1:

_____ ◯ _____ = _____

Step 2:

_____ ◯ _____ = _____

_____ more boys jumped in the pool

7. © **Assessment** The soccer coach has 18 shirts. Then she gets 9 more shirts. There are 22 players on her team. She gives a shirt to each player. How many shirts does the coach have left?

Use the numbers on the cards. Complete both equations to solve the problem.

| 5 | 27 | 9 | 22 |

Step 1:

$18 + \boxed{} = \boxed{}$

Step 2:

$27 - \boxed{} = \boxed{}$

The coach has _____ shirts left.

Another Look! You can write the numbers in a chart to solve the problem.

There are 33 red cars, 27 gray cars, and 25 tan cars in the parking lot.
How many cars in all?

Tens	Ones
3	3
2	7
+ 2	5
Tens: 7	0
Ones: 1	5
Sum: 8	5

85

33	27	25

_____ cars

Add in any order.
It helps to make a 10.
$3 + 7 = 10$
$10 + 5 = 15$

HOME ACTIVITY Write $39 + 14 + 11$ on a sheet of paper. Ask your child to show you how to find the sum.

Solve the problem. Show your work.

1. On Monday, Matt puts 32 cents in his bank. On Tuesday, he puts in 25 cents. On Wednesday, he puts in 18 cents. How much money does Matt put in his bank on those three days?

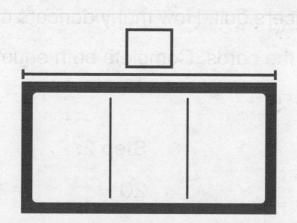

Tens	Ones
+	
Tens:	
Ones:	
Sum:	

_____ cents

Solve each problem. Show your work.

2. © **MP.8 Generalize** Alexis has 16 peaches, 18 apples, and 12 pears to bring to school for the class snack. How many pieces of fruit does Alexis have in all?

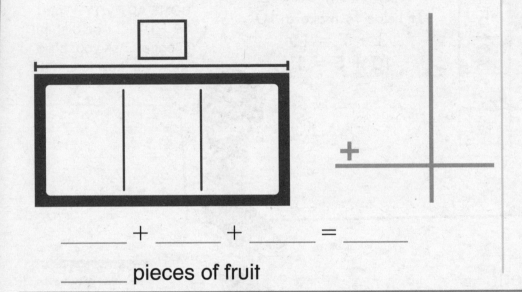

_____ + _____ + _____ = _____

_____ pieces of fruit

3. **Higher Order Thinking** Chris has 16 party hats. Then he gets 27 more hats. He gives away 20 hats at his birthday party. How many hats are left?

Step 1:

_____ ◯ _____ = _____

Step 2:

_____ ◯ _____ = _____

_____ hats

4. © **Assessment** The dance team has 13 dancers. Then 7 more dancers join. The next week 5 dancers quit. How many dancers are now on the team?

Use the numbers on the cards. Complete both equations to solve the problem.

| 20 | 15 | 13 | 5 |

Step 1:

☐ + 7 = ☐

Step 2:

20 − ☐ = ☐

The team now has _____ dancers.

© Pearson Education, Inc. 2

Name _____

Solve & Share

Kim puts 25 toys into an empty toy box.
Then she puts 17 more toys in the toy box.
How many toys are in the box in all?

Use a model to show the problem. Be ready to explain
how your model helps you solve the problem.

I can ...
make models to help solve
math problems.

ⓒ **Mathematical Practices**
MP.4 Also MP.1, MP.2, MP.3
Content Standards 2.OA.A.1,
2.NBT.B.5

Thinking Habits

Can I use a drawing,
diagram, table,
graph, or objects to
show the problem?

Can I write an
equation to show
the problem?

_____ toys

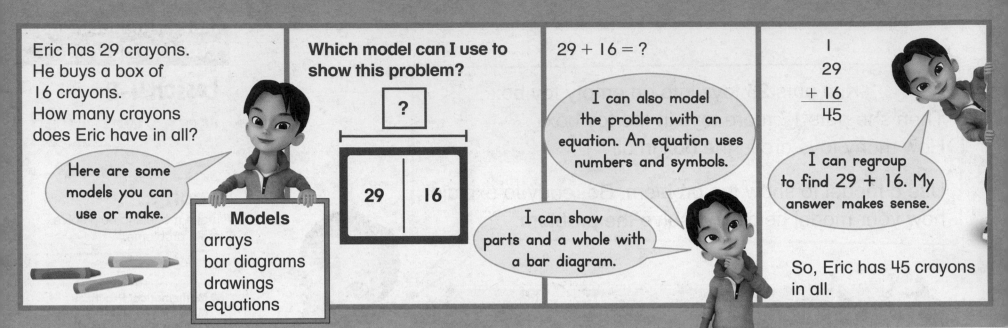

Eric has 29 crayons. He buys a box of 16 crayons. How many crayons does Eric have in all?

Here are some models you can use or make.

Models
arrays
bar diagrams
drawings
equations

Which model can I use to show this problem?

?

| 29 | 16 |

$29 + 16 = ?$

I can also model the problem with an equation. An equation uses numbers and symbols.

I can show parts and a whole with a bar diagram.

$$\begin{array}{r} 1 \\ 29 \\ + 16 \\ \hline 45 \end{array}$$

I can regroup to find $29 + 16$. My answer makes sense.

So, Eric has 45 crayons in all.

Do You Understand?

Show Me! How does drawing a bar diagram or writing an equation model a problem? Is there another way to model the problem?

☆ **Guided Practice** ☆ Complete the bar diagram and write an equation to model and solve each problem.

1. Flora has 24 books about birds. She has 18 books about bugs. How many books is that?

   <u>24</u> + <u>18</u> = <u>?</u> books

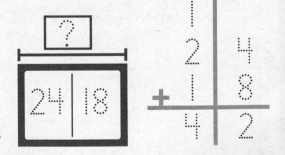

2. Barb saw 14 cars on one street. She saw 15 cars on another street. How many cars did Barb see on both streets?

   _____ + _____ = _____ cars

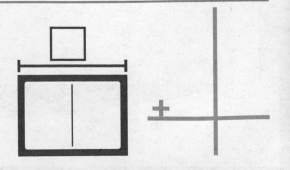

Tools Assessment

Independent Practice

Make a model to show each problem. Then use the model to solve. Show your work.

3. Avi takes 16 pictures.
   Then he takes 17 more pictures.
   How many pictures does Avi take?

Remember, you can use different models. Be ready to explain how your model shows the problem!

4. Tina picks 55 blueberries.
   Then she picks 27 more.
   How many blueberries does Tina pick?

5. Raj finds 47 acorns in his front yard.
   He finds 29 acorns in his back yard.
   How many acorns does Raj find in all?

Math Practices and Problem Solving

Performance Assessment

African Safari
The Santos family are on an African safari. The chart at the right shows the number of animals they see.

How many animals do they see?

Number of Animals	
Giraffes	15
Elephants	9
Lions	16
Zebras	11

6. **MP.1 Make Sense** What do you know? What are you asked to find?

7. **MP.2 Reasoning** Make a model to help you find the number of animals they see. Be ready to explain why you chose the model you did.

8. **MP.4 Model** What other model could you use to show the problem? Make another model. Explain which model you think is better.

Name _____

Another Look! Complete the bar diagram and equation to model and solve the problem.

Paul has 23 counters.
He gets 27 more counters.
How many counters does Paul have in all?

You can show pictures or numbers in a bar diagram.

HOME ACTIVITY Ask your child to model and find 14 + 19 by drawing a bar diagram and writing an equation.

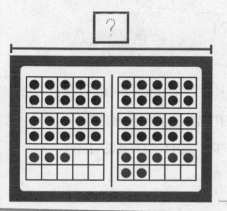

23 + 27 = ?

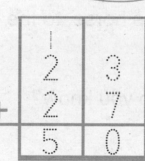

```
    2 3
  + 2 7
  -----
    5 0
```

Paul has 50 counters in all.

Make a model to show the problem. Then use the model to solve.
Show your work.

Be ready to explain how your model shows the problem!

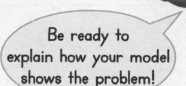

1. There were 38 yo-yos at a toy store.
   Then the store got 12 more yo-yos.
   How many yo-yos are at the store now?

Math Practices and Problem Solving

On the Path

The diagram shows the distances, in feet, of paths between each farm animal. What is the total distance of the paths from the cow to the chicken, to the horse, to the pig, to the cow?

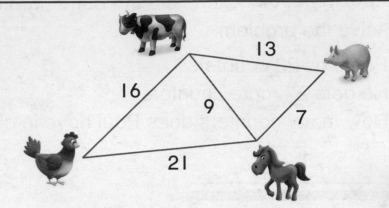

2. **MP.1 Make Sense** What do you know? What are you asked to find?

_____

_____

_____

_____

3. **MP.2 Reasoning** Make a model to help you find the total distance in the problem. Be ready to explain why you chose the model you did.

4. **MP.4 Model** What other model could you use to show the problem? Make another model. Explain which model you think is better.

© Pearson Education, Inc. 2

Name _____

Point & Tally

Find a partner. Get paper and a pencil.
Each partner chooses a different color: light blue or dark blue.

Partner 1 and Partner 2 each point to a black number at the same time. Both partners add those numbers.

If the answer is on your color, you get a tally mark.
Work until one partner gets twelve tally marks.

I can ...
add within 20.

© Content Standard 2.OA.B.2

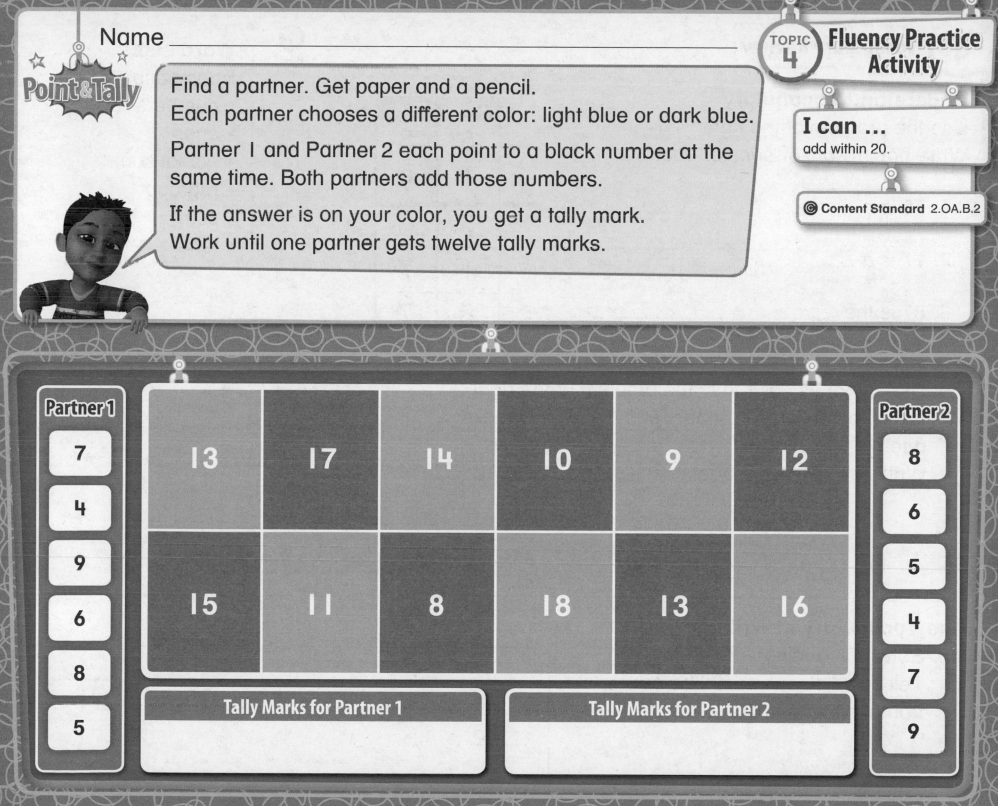

Partner 1

7
4
9
6
8
5

| 13 | 17 | 14 | 10 | 9 | 12 |
| 15 | 11 | 8 | 18 | 13 | 16 |

Partner 2

8
6
5
4
7
9

Tally Marks for Partner 1

Tally Marks for Partner 2

A-Z
Glossary

Word List
- compatible numbers
- ones
- partial sum
- regroup
- sum
- tens

Understand Vocabulary

Use the problem at the right.
Write *partial sum* or *sum* for each.

Tens	Ones
6	8
+ 1	9
7	0
1	7
8	7

1. 70 is a _____.

2. 17 is a _____.

3. 87 is the _____.

---

4. Use the ones column in the problem at the right.
   Which compatible numbers can you add to make
   a ten?
   Write two different equations.

Tens	Ones
3	8
1	4
2	2
+	6

Use Vocabulary in Writing

5. Solve the addition problem.
   Tell how you solved it. Use terms
   from the Word List.

   27
   + 35
   _____
   _____
   _____

© Pearson Education, Inc. 1

Name _____

Set A

You can use partial sums to find the sum. Find $46 + 37$.

	Tens	Ones	
	4	6	
+	3	7	
$\underline{40} + \underline{30} =$	7	0	Add the tens.
$\underline{6} + \underline{7} =$	1	3	Add the ones.
Sum =	8	3	Add the partial sums.

Reteaching

Add. Use partial sums. Use place-value blocks, if needed.

1.

	Tens	Ones
	3	3
+	5	7
___ + ___ =		
___ + ___ =		
Sum =		

Set B

You can show partial sums another way. Find $29 + 63$.

	Tens	Ones	
	2	9	
+	6	3	
Tens:	8	0	Add the tens.
Ones:	1	2	Add the ones.
Sum:	9	2	Add the partial sums.

Add. Use partial sums. Show your work.

2.

	Tens	Ones
	1	4
+	4	5
Tens:		
Ones:		
Sum:		

3.

	Tens	Ones
	1	7
+	7	7
Tens:		
Ones:		
Sum:		

You can regroup to find a sum.
Find 28 + 34.

8 ones + 4 ones = 12 ones.
So regroup 12 as 1 ten and 2 ones.

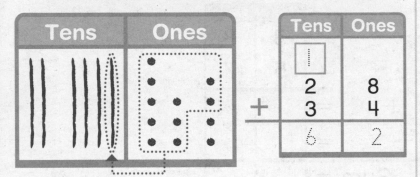

Tens	Ones
1	
2	8
+ 3	4
6	2

Add. Draw place-value blocks to
show your work. Regroup if needed.

4.

Tens	Ones
☐	
3	2
+ 4	8

Tens	Ones

Line up the tens and the ones to add.
45 + 29 = ?

Tens	Ones
1	
4	5
+ 2	9
7	4

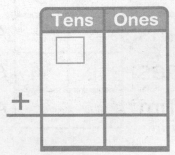

Regroup 14 ones
as 1 ten and 4 ones.

Write each addition problem. Find each sum.
Use drawings, if needed.

5.   67 + 26

Tens	Ones
☐	
+	

6.   38 + 25

Tens	Ones
☐	
+	

Set E

You can add more than two
2-digit numbers. Add the ones in
any order. Make a 10 to help.

Then add the tens.

```
  5
3 7
2 2
+ 2 3
─────
8 7
```

Add. Circle the two digits you
added first.

Reteaching
Continued

7.
```
  15
   9
+ 21
```

8.
```
  33
  46
   2
+ 14
```

Set F

Use partial sums to find
$45 + 7 + 21 + 13$.

Tens	Ones
4	5
	7
2	1
+ 1	3
Tens: 7	0
Ones: 1	6
Sum: 8	6

Look for
compatible
numbers
to make tens.
$7 + 3 = 10$

So, $45 + 7 + 21 + 13 = \underline{86}$

Add using partial sums.

9.

Tens	Ones
2	2
2	1
	9
+ 1	8
Tens:	
Ones:	
Sum:	

27 students are eating lunch.
More students join them.
Now 63 students are eating lunch.
How many students joined them?

Write an equation: $27 + ? = 63$
Count on to find the missing addend:

$27 + 30 = 57$ | $30 + 3 + 3 = \underline{36}$

$57 + 3 = 60$ | $27 + \underline{36} = 63$

$60 + 3 = 63$

So, 36 students joined them.

Complete the bar diagram and solve.

10. Lana has 24 crayons.
Then she gets some
more crayons.
Now she has 42 crayons.
How many crayons does
Lana get?

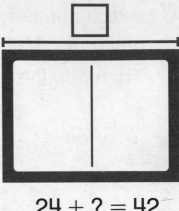

$24 + ? = 42$

Thinking Habits

Model with Math

Can I use a drawing,
diagram, table, graph, or
objects to show the problem?

Can I write an equation to
show the problem?

Make a model and solve the problem.

11. Students ride buses to the museum.
28 students ride in Bus A.
27 students ride in Bus B.
How many students ride in both buses?

© Pearson Education, Inc. 2

Topic 4 | Reteaching

Name _____

1. Kelly has 46 beads.
   Her sister gives her 28 more beads.
   How many beads does Kelly have now?

   Ⓐ 18

   Ⓑ 22

   Ⓒ 64

   Ⓓ 74

2. Which is the same amount as 45 + 38? Choose all that apply.

   ☐ 40 + 30 + 5 + 8

   ☐ 70 + 13

   ☐ 83

   ☐ 93

3. Do you have to regroup to find each sum? Choose Yes or No.

   42 + 56 = ?   ○ Yes ○ No

   52 + 29 = ?   ○ Yes ○ No

   37 + 50 = ?   ○ Yes ○ No

   63 + 19 = ?   ○ Yes ○ No

4. Circle the addition problem that you can use regrouping to solve.
   Then explain how you know.

   30 + 29   54 + 38   43 + 44

   _____

   _____

   _____

   _____

5. Ryan has 57 stones in his collection.
Joy gives him 15 more stones.
How many stones does Ryan
have now?

Ⓐ 82

Ⓑ 72

Ⓒ 62

Ⓓ 42

6. Which is the same amount as
$13 + 8 + 7$? Choose all that apply.

☐ $20 + 8$

☐ $10 + 10 + 8$

☐ 18

☐ 28

7. One zoo has 26 dolphins.
Another zoo has 53 dolphins.
A third zoo has 7 dolphins.
How many dolphins in all?

Show your work.

_____ dolphins

8. Faith has 23 shells.
Then she finds 19 more shells.
Faith gives 10 of the shells to a friend.
How many shells does Faith have now?

Show your work.

_____ shells

Topic 4 | Assessment

9. Part A Find the sum.
Show your work.

```
   25
   37
   15
 +  8
```

Part B

Tell how you found the sum.

_____
_____
_____
_____
_____

---

10. Ms. Wise has 12 tablets.
Then she gets 9 more tablets.
Ms. Wise has 20 students in her class.
She gives each student one tablet.
How many tablets does she have left?

Use the numbers on the cards below.
Complete both equations to solve the problem.

| 1 | 9 | 20 | 21 |

Step 1: 12 + ☐ = ☐

Step 2: 21 − ☐ = ☐

_____ tablet

11. Pearl has 8 medals.

Grace has 9 medals.

Timmy has 6 medals.

How many medals do they have in all?

Solve and show your work in the blue box at the right.

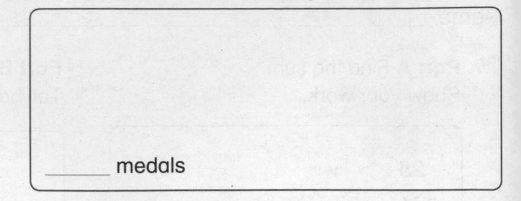

_____ medals

---

12. Match each number card to an equation to find the missing addend.
Draw lines to match. Then write the missing addend in the gray box.

5   ○ 6 + 14 + [ ] + 3 = 30

6   ○ 3 + 32 + 7 + [ ] = 50

7   ○ 25 + 25 + [ ] + 5 = 60

8   ○ 5 + [ ] + 15 + 14 = 40

---

13. Corey has 17 more marbles than Tony.
Tony has 64 marbles.
How many marbles does Corey have?

Use the bar diagram to model and solve the problem. Show your work.

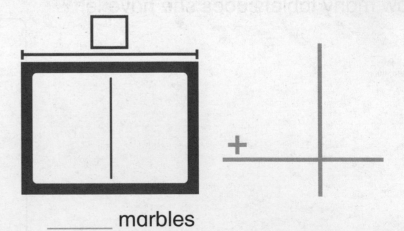

_____ marbles

© Pearson Education, Inc. 2

Name _____

Our Pets

Students draw pictures of their pets. The chart shows the number of pets the students have.

Number of Pets	
Dogs	41
Cats	29
Rabbits	6
Fish	24

1. How many dogs and cats do the students have?
Show your work.

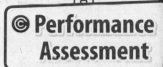
Performance Assessment

_____ dogs and cats

2. How many cats and fish do the students have?
Show your work.

_____ cats and fish

3. Use partial sums to find how many cats, rabbits, and fish the students have.

Then use regrouping to check your work.

Check:

Tens	Ones
+	
Tens:	
Ones:	
Sum:	

Tens	Ones
☐	

How many cats, rabbits, and fish in all?

_____ cats, rabbits, and fish

4. Explain why you can use regrouping when you add.

_____

_____

_____

5. The students also draw pictures of 10 hamsters, 19 birds, and 5 mice.

Part A

Complete the model to show how to find the total number of hamsters, birds, and mice.

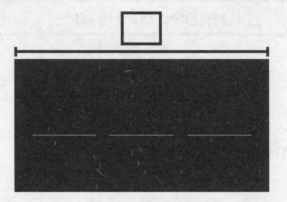

Part B

Complete the equation to show how many hamsters, birds and mice they draw. Then write the total.

_____ ◯ _____ ◯ _____ = _____

_____ hamsters, birds, and mice

© Pearson Education, Inc. 2

Topic 4 | Performance Assessment

Subtract Within 100 Using Strategies

Essential Question: What are strategies for subtracting numbers to 100?

Look at the big pieces of ice in the water!

How can heating and cooling change water and ice?

Wow! Let's do this project and learn more.

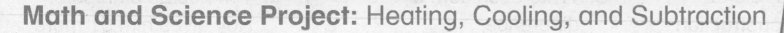

Math and Science Project: Heating, Cooling, and Subtraction

Find Out Have an adult help you heat and cool water and other materials. Find out if water and ice can change back and forth. Find out if heating and cooling an egg can change it back and forth.

Journal: Make a Book Show what you learn in a book. In your book, also:

• Tell about how heating and cooling are related.

• Tell about how addition and subtraction are related.

Review What You Know

A-Z Vocabulary

1. Circle each **difference** in the math problems shown below.

$15 - 5 = 10$

$$\begin{array}{r} 23 \\ + 32 \\ \hline 55 \end{array} \qquad \begin{array}{r} 14 \\ - 7 \\ \hline 7 \end{array}$$

2. Circle the statement if it describes **mental math**.

Math that is done with paper and pencil.

Math that you can do in your head.

3. Circle the statement if it describes **compatible numbers**.

Numbers that are close to numbers that you want to add or subtract.

Numbers that you can add or subtract using mental math.

Addition and Subtraction Facts

4. Complete the related addition and subtraction facts below.

$6 + \boxed{} = 13$

$13 - \boxed{} = 6$

5. Write each sum or difference.

$$\begin{array}{r} 4 \\ + 7 \\ \hline \end{array} \quad \begin{array}{r} 12 \\ - 3 \\ \hline \end{array} \quad \begin{array}{r} 9 \\ + 6 \\ \hline \end{array} \quad \begin{array}{r} 16 \\ - 8 \\ \hline \end{array}$$

You can use addition facts to help you subtract.

Math Story

6. Tim has 25 stamps. Roy gives him 51 more stamps. How many stamps does Tim have now?

_____ stamps

Name _____

Solve & Share

How can you use the hundred chart to help you find 57 − 23? Explain. Write an equation.

Lesson 5-1
Subtract Tens and Ones on a Hundred Chart

I can ...
use a hundred chart to subtract tens and ones.

© **Content Standards** 2.NBT.B.5, 2.NBT.B.9
Mathematical Practices MP.1, MP.3, MP.5, MP.6, MP.7

1	2	3	4	5	6	7	8	9	10
11	12	13	14	15	16	17	18	19	20
21	22	23	24	25	26	27	28	29	30
31	32	33	34	35	36	37	38	39	40
41	42	43	44	45	46	47	48	49	50
51	52	53	54	55	56	57	58	59	60
61	62	63	64	65	66	67	68	69	70
71	72	73	74	75	76	77	78	79	80
81	82	83	84	85	86	87	88	89	90
91	92	93	94	95	96	97	98	99	100

_____ ◯ _____ = _____

Topic 5 | Lesson 1
Digital Resources at PearsonRealize.com
two hundred fifty-five **255**

Find 43 − 28 using a hundred chart.

I need to find the difference between 28 and 43.

Start at 28. Count to the next number that matches the ones in 43.

21	22	23	24	25	26	27	28	29	30
31	32	33	34	35	36	37	38	39	40
41	42	43	44	45	46	47	48	49	50

Count by ones! I counted 5 ones to get from 28 to 33.

Count by tens to 43.

21	22	23	24	25	26	27	28	29	30
31	32	33	34	35	36	37	38	39	40
41	42	43	44	45	46	47	48	49	50

That's 1 ten, or 10 more.

I added 5 and 10. That makes 15.

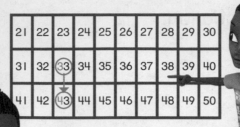

$28 + 15 = 43$
So, $43 − 28 = 15$.

Do You Understand?

Show Me! How can you use a hundred chart to find $60 − 18$?

☆ **Guided Practice** ☆ Subtract using the hundred chart. Draw arrows if you need to.

21	22	23	24	25	26	27	28	29	30
31	32	33	34	35	36	37	38	39	40
41	42	43	44	45	46	47	48	49	50
51	52	53	54	55	56	57	58	59	60
61	62	63	64	65	66	67	68	69	70

1. $69 − 36 = \underline{33}$

2. $54 − 24 = \underline{}$

3. $\underline{} = 65 − 34$

4. $47 − 22 = \underline{}$

© Pearson Education, Inc. 2

Name _____

Independent Practice ☆ Subtract using the hundred chart. Draw arrows if you need to.

1	2	3	4	5	6	7	8	9	10
11	12	13	14	15	16	17	18	19	20
21	22	23	24	25	26	27	28	29	30
31	32	33	34	35	36	37	38	39	40
41	42	43	44	45	46	47	48	49	50
51	52	53	54	55	56	57	58	59	60
61	62	63	64	65	66	67	68	69	70
71	72	73	74	75	76	77	78	79	80
81	82	83	84	85	86	87	88	89	90
91	92	93	94	95	96	97	98	99	100

5. $54 - 7 =$ _____

6. _____ $= 96 - 63$

7. $45 - 22 =$ _____

8. $82 - 61 =$ _____

9. $65 - 21 =$ _____

10. _____ $= 79 - 47$

11. $84 - 6 =$ _____

Algebra Write the digit that makes each equation true.

12. $73 - \boxed{}2 = 41$

$5\boxed{} - 32 = 26$

13. $46 - \boxed{}1 = 15$

$78 - 36 = \boxed{}2$

14. $53 - \boxed{}2 = 31$

$99 - \boxed{}3 = 16$

15. Darren's puzzle has 98 pieces. Darren fits 55 pieces together. How many more pieces does Darren still need to fit to complete the puzzle?

_____ – _____ = _____ pieces

The hundred chart is a good tool to use. Count by ones and tens to subtract.

41	42	43	44	45	46	47	48	49	50
51	52	53	54	55	56	57	58	59	60
61	62	63	64	65	66	67	68	69	70
71	72	73	74	75	76	77	78	79	80
81	82	83	84	85	86	87	88	89	90
91	92	93	94	95	96	97	98	99	100

16. A test has 86 questions. Glenda needs to answer 23 more questions to finish the test. How many test questions has Glenda answered already?

_____ questions

17. **Higher Order Thinking** Chris wants to subtract 76 – 42. Write the steps he can take to subtract 42 from 76 on the hundred chart.

_____

_____

_____

18. © **Assessment** Lu has 75 buttons. 49 of the buttons are green. The rest of the buttons are red. How many of the buttons are red?

Ⓐ 16   Ⓑ 20   Ⓒ 26   Ⓓ 36

© Pearson Education, Inc. 2

Name _____

Another Look! Here is another way to subtract on a hundred chart.

Find 36 − 24.

I. Start at 36.

2. Move up 2 rows to subtract _2_ tens.

3. Move left 4 columns to subtract _4_ ones.

So 36 − 24 = 12.

1	2	3	4	5	6	7	8	9	10
11	12	13	14	15	16	17	18	19	20
21	22	23	24	25	26	27	28	29	30
31	32	33	34	35	36	37	38	39	40
41	42	43	44	45	46	47	48	49	50
51	52	53	54	55	56	57	58	59	60
61	62	63	64	65	66	67	68	69	70
71	72	73	74	75	76	77	78	79	80
81	82	83	84	85	86	87	88	89	90
91	92	93	94	95	96	97	98	99	100

HOME ACTIVITY Ask your child to subtract 58 − 23 on a hundred chart and explain how he or she subtracted.

Subtract using the hundred chart.

I. 87 − 7 = _____

2. 79 − 48 = _____

3. 65 − 41 = _____

4. 99 − 52 = _____

5. 35 − 13 = _____

6. _____ = 84 − 33

Algebra Write the digits that make each equation true.

7. $\boxed{}3 - 2\boxed{} = 71$

8. $5\boxed{} - \boxed{}1 = 14$

9. $78 - \boxed{}5 = 4\boxed{}$

10. © **MP.7 Look for Patterns** A treasure is hidden under one of the rocks. Follow the clues to find the treasure. Color each rock you land on.

A. Start at 55.   B. Subtract 20.

C. Add 5.   D. Add 20.

E. Add 10.   F. Subtract 5.

G. Subtract 20.   H. Add 5.

I. Subtract 20.   J. Subtract 5.

1	2	3	4	5	6	7	8	9	10
11	12	13	14	15	16	17	18	19	20
21	22	23	24	25	26	27	28	29	30
31	32	33	34	35	36	37	38	39	40
41	42	43	44	45	46	47	48	49	50
51	52	53	54	55	56	57	58	59	60
61	62	63	64	65	66	67	68	69	70
71	72	73	74	75	76	77	78	79	80
81	82	83	84	85	86	87	88	89	90
91	92	93	94	95	96	97	98	99	100

The treasure is hidden under the last rock that you colored. What is the number of that rock? _____
Describe the pattern you see in the numbers you colored.

_____

11. © **Assessment** A pan holds 36 biscuits. Kiana put 12 biscuits on the pan. How many more biscuits will fit on the pan?

Ⓐ 24   Ⓑ 23   Ⓒ 22   Ⓓ 21

12. © **Assessment** A garden has room for 22 flowers. Dan needs to plant 11 more flowers to fill the garden. How many flowers did Dan already plant?

Ⓐ 10   Ⓑ 11   Ⓒ 12   Ⓓ 13

© Pearson Education, Inc. 2

Solve & Share

Jesse had 50 balloons at the fair.
A strong wind blew away 30 balloons.
How many balloons does Jesse have left?
Use the number line below to show your work.

I can ...
use an open number line to subtract tens.

© **Content Standards** 2.NBT.B.5, 2.NBT.B.9
Mathematical Practices MP.2, MP.3, MP.5, MP.8

POPCORN

_____ ◯ _____ = _____

Find 56 − 20.

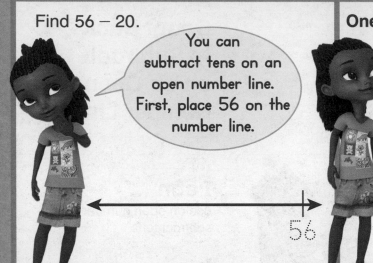

You can subtract tens on an open number line. First, place 56 on the number line.

56

One Way

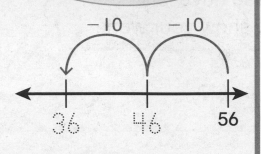

20 is 2 tens. So, count back by 10 two times. Show each 10 on the number line as you count.

−10   −10

36   46   56

Another Way

Moving back 2 tens from 56 is the same as 56 − 20.

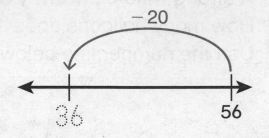

− 20

36   56

You land on 36. So, 56 − 20 = __36__.

Do You Understand?

Show Me! How can an open number line help you subtract numbers?

☆ **Guided Practice** ☆ Use an open number line to find each difference.

1. 70 − 20 = _____

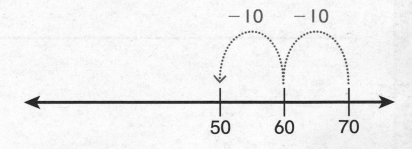

−10   −10

50   60   70

2. 67 − 30 = _____

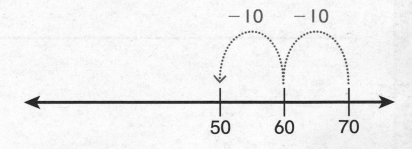

© Pearson Education, Inc. 2   **Topic 5** | Lesson 2

Name _____

Independent Practice ✩   Use an open number line to find each difference.

3. 60 − 40 = _____

4. 85 − 20 = _____

5. 99 − 40 = _____

6. 42 − 30 = _____

7. 34 − 10 = _____

The number you are subtracting from should be put on the right side of the line.

8. Higher Order Thinking Jada drew this number line to find 79 − 40. She circled her answer. Did Jada get the correct answer? Explain.

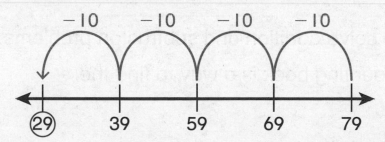

9. © MP.2 Reasoning Evan has 62 baseball cards. He gives 30 cards to Bridget. How many cards does Evan have left?

_____ baseball cards

10. Math and Science 45 icicles hang from a roof. 20 icicles melt and fall. How many icicles are left?

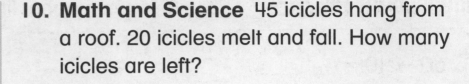

_____ icicles

11. **A-Z** **Vocabulary** Complete each sentence using one of the terms below.

| sum | open number line | difference |

You can use an _____

_____

to solve addition and subtracton problems.

Counting back is a way to find the

_____.

The _____ is the answer to an addition problem.

12. © Assessment Which does the number line show? Choose all that apply.

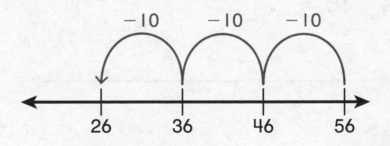

☐ Count back by 10 two times from 56.

☐ Count back by 10 three times from 56.

☐ $56 - 30 = 26$

☐ $26 + 56 = 82$

© Pearson Education, Inc. 2

Help Tools Games

Another Look! Find 45 − 20 using an open number line.

You can use an open number line to make subtracting tens easier.

Place 45 on the number line. Then count back by 10 twice to subtract 20.

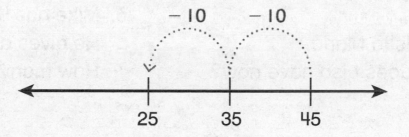

$$-10 \qquad -10$$

25   35   45

So, ___45___ − ___20___ = ___25___.

HOME ACTIVITY Draw an open number line on a sheet of paper. Then have your child find 33 − 20 using the number line.

Use an open number line to find each difference.

1. 30 − 20 = _____

2. 95 − 30 = _____

© MP.5 Use Tools Use an open number line to solve each problem.

3. $21 - 20 = $ _____

4. $15 - 10 = $ _____

5. Lisa has 25 beads.
She gives 10 beads to Maria.
How many beads does Lisa have now?

_____ beads

6. Mike has 43 balloons.
He gives away 20 balloons.
How many balloons does Mike have left?

_____ balloons

7. **Higher Order Thinking** Jackson drew this number line to solve a subtraction problem. Write the equation he solved.

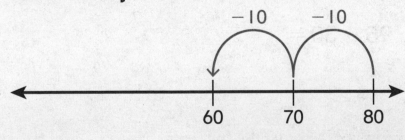

_____ − _____ = _____

8. **© Assessment** Which does the number line show? Choose all that apply.

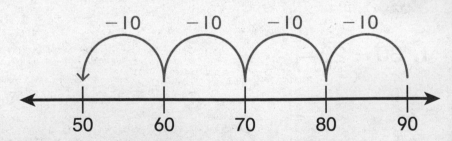

☐ Count back 4 tens from 90.

☐ Count back 40 from 90.

☐ $90 - 30 = 60$

☐ $90 - 40 = 50$

© Pearson Education, Inc. 2

Topic 5 | Lesson 2

Solve

Solve & Share

Jeremy had 56 bug stickers.
He gave 24 stickers to Eric.
How many bug stickers does Jeremy have left?
Use the open number line below to show your work.

I can ...
use an open number line to subtract tens and ones.

Content Standards 2.NBT.B.5, 2.NBT.B.9
Mathematical Practices MP.1, MP.4, MP.5

⟵———————————————⟶

_____ − _____ = _____

Find 68 − 23.

Let's use an open number line and count back. First, place 68 on the line.

68

One Way
23 is 2 tens and 3 ones.
So, count back 2 tens from 68.
58, 48
Then, count back 3 ones from 48.
47, 46, 45

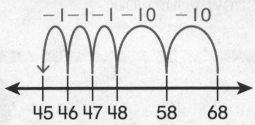

−1−1−1 −10 −10

45 46 47 48   58   68

Another Way
You can subtract 68 − 20 = 48,
then 48 − 3 = 45.

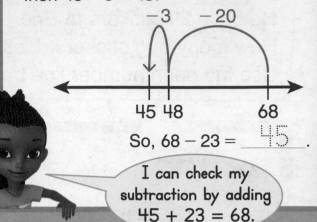

−3   − 20

45 48   68

So, 68 − 23 = __45__.

I can check my subtraction by adding 45 + 23 = 68.

Do You Understand?

Show Me! How can the open number line help you keep track as you count back?

⭐ **Guided Practice** ⭐   Use an open number line to find each difference.

1. 28 − 24 = _____

−4   −10   −10

4   8   18   28

2. 50 − 35 = _____

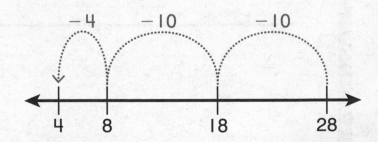

© Pearson Education, Inc. 2

Name _____

Independent Practice ☆   Use an open number line to find each difference.

3. 45 − 13 = _____

4. 63 − 22 = _____

5. 78 − 46 = _____

6. 92 − 37 = _____

7. 80 − 44 = ?

Break apart the number you are subtracting into tens and ones.

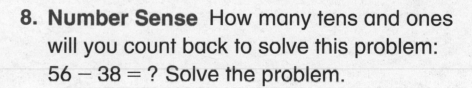

_____ − _____ = _____

8. Number Sense How many tens and ones will you count back to solve this problem: 56 − 38 = ? Solve the problem.

_____ tens _____ ones

_____ − _____ = _____

9. **© MP.5 Use Tools** There are 47 raffle tickets to sell for the fair. Ms. Brown's class sells 23 raffle tickets. How many raffle tickets are left to sell?

_____ raffle tickets

10. **© MP.5 Use Tools** Ethan counts 78 carrots. He sells 35 carrots at the farmers market. How many carrots does Ethan have left?

_____ carrots

11. **Higher Order Thinking** Show two different ways to find 63 − 25 using the open number lines.

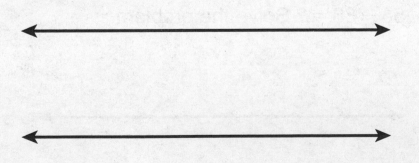

63 − 25 = _____

12. **© Assessment** Jen solved a subtraction problem using the open number line shown. Write the equation that her work below shows.

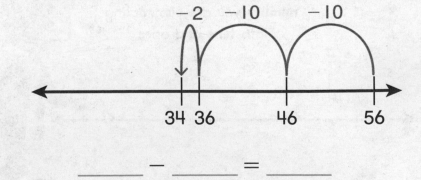

_____ − _____ = _____

© Pearson Education, Inc. 2

Name _____

Help   Tools   Games

Another Look! Find 83 − 35.

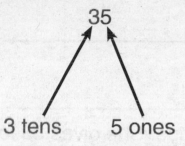

35

3 tens   5 ones

How many tens and ones do you need to subtract?

First place 83 on an open number line. Then count back 3 tens and 5 ones to subtract 35.

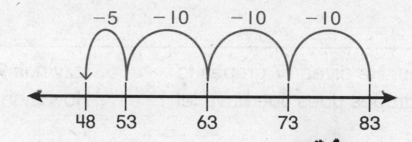

−5   −10   −10   −10

48   53   63   73   83

HOME ACTIVITY Tell your child a subtraction story for 36 − 15. Have your child draw an open number line and use it to solve the problem.

So, 83 − 35 = 48.

Use an open number line to find each difference.

1. 95 − 23 = _____

2. 30 − 15 = _____

© MP.5 Use Tools Use an open number line to solve each problem.

3. 87 − 23 = _____

4. 54 − 19 = _____

5. Joe has 43 grapes. He gives 17 grapes to Dee. How many grapes does Joe have left?

_____ grapes

6. Izzy has 99 bottle caps. She gives 33 to Max. How many bottle caps does Izzy have left?

_____ bottle caps

7. Higher Order Thinking Write a story problem for 36 − 14. Draw and use an open number line to solve the problem.

8. © Assessment Manuel solved a subtraction problem using the open number line shown. Write the equation his open number line shows.

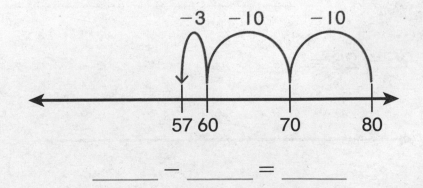

_____ − _____ = _____

© Pearson Education, Inc. 2

Name _____

Solve & Share

There are 50 children at the park. 28 are boys and the rest are girls. How many girls are at the park?

Use the open number line to solve. Show your work.

I can ...
add up to subtract using an open number line.

© **Content Standards** 2.NBT.B.5, 2.NBT.B.9
Mathematical Practices MP.1, MP.2, MP.5, MP.6

←————————————————————→

_____ ◯ _____ = _____

Find 57 − 28.

You can add up from 28 to subtract. Place 28 on the number line first.

28

You can add 2 to get to 30.

Then add 10, and 10 again, to get to 50.

Then add 7 to land on 57.

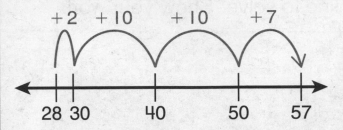

+2 +10   +10   +7

28 30   40   50   57

Add the tens and ones.

$2 + 10 + 10 + 7 = 29$

So, $57 − 28 = 29$.

I can check by adding!
$28 + 29 = 57$

Do You Understand?

Show Me! How can you add up to find $42 − 17$?

☆ **Guided Practice** ☆ Add up to find each difference. Use an open number line.

1. $45 − 27 = $ _____

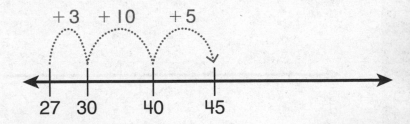

+3 +10 +5

27 30   40   45

2. $66 − 39 = $ _____

© Pearson Education, Inc. 2

Topic 5 | Lesson 4

Tools   Assessment

Independent Practice

Add up to find each difference.
Use an open number line.

3. 41 − 19 = _____

4. 63 − 34 = _____

5. 83 − 58 = _____

6. 74 − 46 = _____

7. 72 − 34 = _____

8. **Math and Science** Rob had 34 snowballs. Some melted and now he has 18 snowballs. How many snowballs melted?

_____ − _____ = _____

Don't forget to find the sum of the tens and the ones you added up. That is the difference.

Add up to solve each problem. Use an open number line. Write the equations.

9. © **MP.6 Be Precise** Dino has 41 crayons. He gives 23 crayons to Bridget, and 7 crayons to Dan. How many crayons does Dino have left? Solve using two steps.

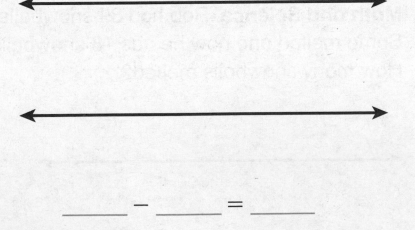

The answer to the first step is needed for the second step. Is your work precise?

Step 1: _____ ◯ _____ = _____

Step 2: _____ ◯ _____ = _____

10. **Higher Order Thinking** Show two different ways to add up to find 72 − 35.

_____ − _____ = _____

11. © **Assessment** Add up to solve 46 − 25. Show your work on the open number line and then write an equation.

_____ − _____ = _____

Help Tools Games

Another Look!

You can add up on an open number line to subtract 73 − 45.

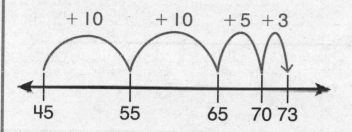

$+10$ $+10$ $+5$ $+3$

45 55 65 70 73

You can start at 45. Add 10, and 10 again, to get to 65. Then add 5 to get to 70. Then add 3 to get to 73.

Add tens and ones to find the difference:

$\underline{10} + \underline{10} + \underline{5} + \underline{3} = \underline{28}$

So, 73 − 45 = 28.

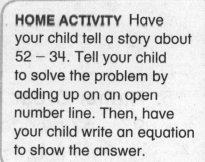

HOME ACTIVITY Have your child tell a story about 52 − 34. Tell your child to solve the problem by adding up on an open number line. Then, have your child write an equation to show the answer.

Add up to find each difference. Use an open number line.

1. 93 − 65 = _____

2. 84 − 67 = _____

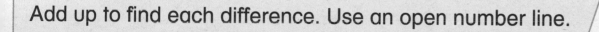

Add up to solve each problem. Use an open number line. Write the equations.

3. © **MP.5 Use Tools** Misha has 36 bows. She gives 19 bows to Alice. How many bows does Misha have left?

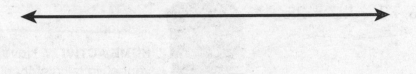

_____ − _____ = _____

4. © **MP.5 Use Tools** Remi has 80 golf balls. He hits 53 of them. How many golf balls does Remi have left?

_____ − _____ = _____

5. Higher Order Thinking Richard found 93 − 67 by adding up on the open number line. Is he correct? Explain. Then write an addition equation to show how you could check his work.

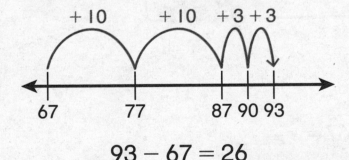

$$93 - 67 = 26$$

_____

_____

_____ ◯ _____ = _____

6. © **Assessment** Use the open number lines. Show two different ways to add up to find 91 − 56.

One way

Another way

$$91 - 56 = \_\_\_\_\_$$

© Pearson Education, Inc. 2

Name _____

Solve & Share

Don wants to find 42 − 7 by breaking apart the 7 into two numbers. Use and draw place-value blocks to show how Don could find the difference.

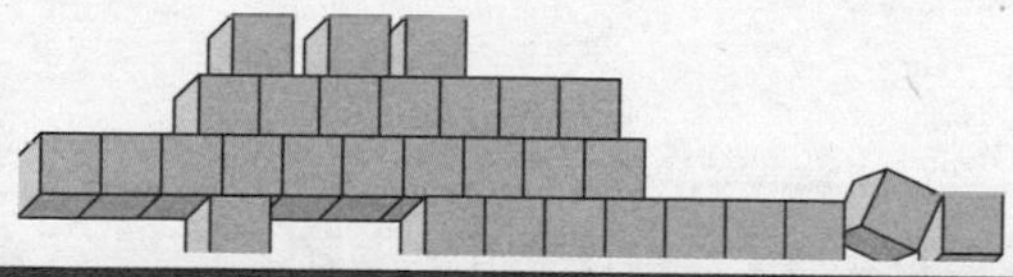

I can ...
break apart 1-digit numbers to help me subtract mentally.

© **Content Standards** 2.NBT.B.5, 2.NBT.B.9
Mathematical Practices MP.3, MP.6, MP.7

33 − 6 = ?

You can break apart the number you are subtracting to find the difference.

Here are 3 ways to break apart 6. Which is best for subtracting 6 from 33?

6
△
1 + 5

6
△
2 + 4

6
△
3 + 3

33 − 6 = _____ ?

3   3

Start at 33. Subtract 3 to get to 30. Then subtract 3 more.

11	12	13	14	15	16	17	18	19	20
21	22	23	24	25	26	27	28	29	30
31	32	33	34	35	36	37	38	39	40

33 − 6 = _27_

Do You Understand?

Show Me! Look at the problem above. Why wasn't the 6 broken apart into 1 + 5 to find 33 − 6?

 **Guided Practice** Subtract. Break apart the number you are subtracting. Show your work.

1. 43 − 9 = _____

☐   ☐

2. _____ = 24 − 6

☐   ☐

11	12	13	14	15	16	17	18	19	20
21	22	23	24	25	26	27	28	29	30
31	32	33	34	35	36	37	38	39	40
41	42	43	44	45	46	47	48	49	50

© Pearson Education, Inc. 2

Name _____

Independent Practice Subtract. Break apart the number you are subtracting. Show your work. Use a hundred chart if needed.

3. $35 - 8 =$ _____

4. $41 - 5 =$ _____

5. _____ $= 82 - 7$

6. $53 - 7 =$ _____

7. $97 - 8 =$ _____

8. $64 - 9 =$ _____

9. $86 - 8 =$ _____

10. _____ $= 32 - 9$

11. $93 - 6 =$ _____

12. **Algebra** One number makes both equations true. Find the missing number.

$48 + \boxed{} = 56$ $56 - \boxed{} = 48$

Think about how addition and subtraction are related.

The missing number is _____.

13. © **MP.3 Explain** Karen has 7 pencils. Karen's teacher has 45 pencils. How many fewer pencils does Karen have than her teacher? Explain how you solved the problem.

_____

_____

_____

Is your explanation clear?

_____ fewer pencils

14. **Higher Order Thinking** Write a story problem about 63 − 8. Then solve.

_____

_____

_____

_____

$63 - 8 =$ _____

15. © **Assessment** Duane has 24 seashells. He gives 9 shells to his cousin Rob. How many seashells does Duane have now?

$24 - 9 = ?$

Ⓐ 16   Ⓒ 14

Ⓑ 15   Ⓓ 13

Name _____

Another Look! Find 55 − 8.

You can break apart 8 to find 55 − 8.

One way is 8 = 5 + 3.

There is a 5 in the ones place in 55. It's easy to subtract 55 − 5.

$$55 − 5 = 50$$

Next, subtract 50 − 3. You can count back 3 from 50.

$$50 − 3 = 47$$

So, 55 − 8 = ___47___.

HOME ACTIVITY Ask your child to show you how to break apart the 5 in 43 − 5 to find the difference.

Subtract. Break apart the number you are subtracting. Show your work.

1. 65 − 9 = _____

2. 24 − 7 = _____

3. _____ = 84 − 8

© **MP.3 Explain** Subtract. Break apart the number you are subtracting. Show your work to explain your thinking.

4. 41 − 5 = _____

5. _____ = 94 − 8

6. 25 − 9 = _____

7. **Higher Order Thinking** The table shows how many spools of thread Smith's Fabric Store sold on Monday.

Before the sale, there were 34 red spools and 53 black spools. How many red spools were left at the end of Monday? How many black spools were left?

_____ red spools _____ black spools

Spools of Thread Sold	
Thread Color	**Number of Spools**
Red	8
Blue	7
Black	6

8. © **Assessment** Ron has 21 comic books. He sells 6 of them to a friend. How many comic books does Ron have now?

Ⓐ 17 Ⓒ 15

Ⓑ 16 Ⓓ 14

9. © **Assessment** Yelena has 5 animal stickers. Vera has 41 animal stickers. How many fewer animal stickers does Yelena have than Vera?

Ⓐ 26 Ⓒ 35

Ⓑ 34 Ⓓ 36

© Pearson Education, Inc. 2

Solve & Share

Gina wants to find 53 − 28 by breaking apart 28 into two numbers. Use place-value blocks and the hundred chart to show how Gina could find the difference.

Solve

Lesson 5-6

Continue to Break Apart Numbers to Subtract

I can ...
break apart 2-digit numbers to help me subtract.

© **Content Standards** 2.NBT.B.5, 2.NBT.B.9
Mathematical Practices MP.1, MP.3, MP.6, MP.7

21	22	23	24	25	26	27	28	29	30
31	32	33	34	35	36	37	38	39	40
41	42	43	44	45	46	47	48	49	50
51	52	53	54	55	56	57	58	59	60
61	62	63	64	65	66	67	68	69	70

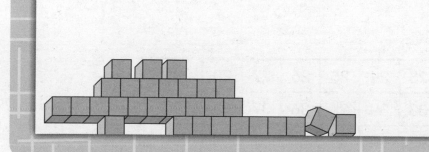

81 − 27 = ?

You can use place value to break apart the number you are subtracting.

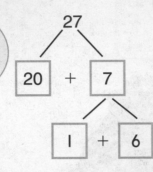

Break apart 27 into tens and ones. Then break apart the ones.

27
20 + 7
1 + 6

81 − 27 = _____?

20   7

1   6

51	52	53	54	55	56	57	58	59	60
61	62	63	64	65	66	67	68	69	70
71	72	73	74	75	76	77	78	79	80
81	82	83	84	85	86	87	88	89	90

Start at 81. Subtract 20 to get to 61. Then subtract 1 to get to 60. Then subtract 6 more.

So, 81 − 27 = 54.

Do You Understand?

Show Me! How do you decide how to break apart the ones?

☆ Guided Practice ☆

Subtract. Break apart the number you are subtracting. Show your work.

1. 54 − 26 = _____

2. 43 − 18 = _____

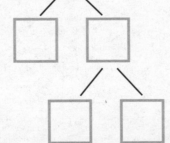

21	22	23	24	25	26	27	28	29	30
31	32	33	34	35	36	37	38	39	40
41	42	43	44	45	46	47	48	49	50
51	52	53	54	55	56	57	58	59	60

Topic 5 | Lesson 6

Name _____

Independent Practice

Subtract. Break apart the number you are subtracting. Show your work. Use a hundred chart if needed.

3. _____ = 32 − 13

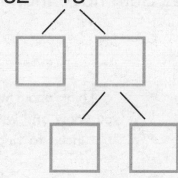

4. 74 − 28 = _____

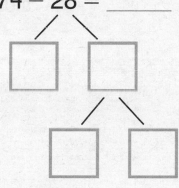

5. _____ = 61 − 47

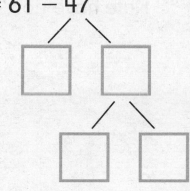

6. 84 − 46 = _____

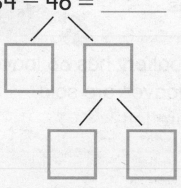

7. 46 − 17 = _____

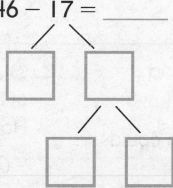

8. _____ = 95 − 38

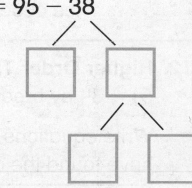

9. **Higher Order Thinking** Tina found 53 − 27 by breaking apart 27 into 23 and 4. Does Tina's way work?

Show another way you could break apart 27 to find 53 − 27. Then find the difference.

10. Math and Science Kate had 32 ice cubes. She put 14 of them in the sun and they melted. How many ice cubes does Kate have now?

_____ ice cubes

11. ⓒ MP.1 Make Sense Mark has 27 stamps. Sam has 82 stamps. Lena has 42 stamps. How many more stamps does Sam have than Mark?

Think about what you know and what you need to find.

_____ more stamps

12. Higher Order Thinking Allison found 51 − 34 by breaking apart 34 into 31 + 3.

Write equations to show how Allison could have found the difference.

13. ⓒ Assessment A bakery has 66 loaves of bread. 27 of the loaves are sold. How many loaves are left?

Ⓐ 39

Ⓑ 38

Ⓒ 37

Ⓓ 36

© Pearson Education, Inc. 2 **Topic 5** | Lesson 6

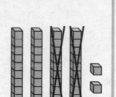

Help   Tools   Games

Another Look! Find 43 − 27.

To find 43 − 27, you can break apart 27.

One way is 20 + 7.

It's easy to find 43 − 20.

$$43 - 20 = 23$$

Next, subtract 23 − 7.
You can break apart
7 into 3 + 4.

$$23 - 3 = 20$$ and

$$20 - 4 = 16$$

So, 43 − 27 = 16.

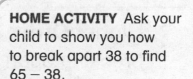

HOME ACTIVITY Ask your child to show you how to break apart 38 to find 65 − 38.

Subtract. Break apart the number you are subtracting.
Show your work to explain your thinking.

1. 76 − 29 = _____

2. _____ = 82 − 39

3. 92 − 16 = _____

© MP.3 Explain Subtract. Break apart the number you are subtracting. Show your work. Be ready to explain why your way works.

4. $75 - 27 =$ _____

5. _____ $= 61 - 34$

6. $87 - 28 =$ _____

---

7. Higher Order Thinking Brian found $42 - 19$ by breaking apart 19 into $12 + 7$. Write equations to show how Brian could have found the difference.

How can place value help you solve the problem?

---

8. © Assessment Rosita has 55 grapes. She gives a friend 26 of her grapes. How many grapes does Rosita have now?

Ⓐ 17

Ⓑ 29

Ⓒ 28

Ⓓ 37

9. © Assessment Can you use the equations to find $86 - 27$? Choose Yes or No.

$86 - 20 = 66$ ○ Yes ○ No
$66 - 7 = 59$

$26 - 10 = 16$ ○ Yes ○ No
$16 - 6 = 10$

$86 - 20 = 66$ ○ Yes ○ No
$66 - 6 = 60$
$60 - 1 = 59$

© Pearson Education, Inc. 2

Name _____

Solve

Solve & Share

Yuri found 86 − 29 using mental math.
He changed 29 so it would be easier to find the difference.

Show how Yuri could have found the difference.
Explain how he could have used mental math.

Lesson 5-7
Subtract Using Compensation

I can ...
make numbers that are easier to subtract, then use mental math to find the difference.

© **Content Standards** 2.NBT.B.5, 2.NBT.B.9
Mathematical Practices MP.1, MP.4, MP.7, MP.8

43 − 18 = ?

You can use compensation to make numbers that are easier to subtract.

It is easier to subtract 20, than 18.

One Way Add 2 to both numbers. Then subtract using mental math.

$$43 \quad - \quad 18 \quad = \quad ?$$
$$\downarrow +2 \qquad \downarrow +2$$
$$45 \quad - \quad 20 \quad = \quad 25$$

So, 43 − 18 = 25.

Another Way Add 2 to 18. Then subtract using mental math. Then add 2 to find the answer.

$$43 \quad - \quad 18 = ?$$
$$\downarrow +2$$
$$43 \quad - \quad 20 = 23$$
$$\downarrow +2$$

So, 43 − 18 = 25.

I subtracted 2 more than 18, so I need to add 2 to 23 to find the answer.

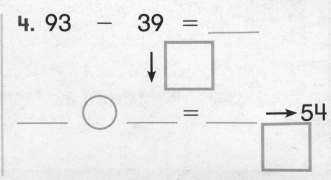

Do You Understand?

Show Me! Marc says to find 61 − 13, it's easier to subtract 10 instead of 13. He says if you subtract 3 from 13 to get 10, you must subtract 3 more from your answer. Do you agree? Explain.

Guided Practice

Use compensation to make numbers that are easier to subtract. Then solve. Show your work.

1. $52 \quad - \quad 8 \quad = \underline{\quad}$

$\downarrow \boxed{+2} \qquad \downarrow \boxed{+2}$

$54 \quad - \quad 10 \quad = \quad 44$

2. $76 \quad - \quad 27 \quad = \underline{\quad}$

$\downarrow \Box \qquad \downarrow \Box$

$\underline{\quad} \quad - \quad \underline{\quad} \quad = \underline{\quad}$

3. $52 - 15 = \underline{\quad}$

$\downarrow \boxed{+5}$

$52 \quad - \quad 20 \quad = \quad 32 \dashrightarrow 37$

$\boxed{+5}$

4. $93 \quad - \quad 39 \quad = \underline{\quad}$

$\downarrow \Box$

$\underline{\quad} \bigcirc \underline{\quad} = \underline{\quad} \longrightarrow 54$

$\Box$

© Pearson Education, Inc. 2

Independent Practice

Use compensation to make numbers that are easier to subtract. Then solve. Show your work.

5. 73 − 9 = _____

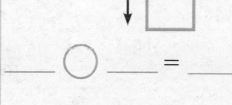

___ ◯ ___ = ___ → 64

6. 35 − 16 = _____

↓ ▢

___ ◯ ___ = ___ → 19

7. 43 − 28 = _____

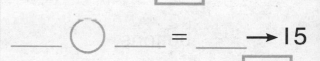

___ ◯ ___ = ___ → 15

8. 51 − 27 = _____

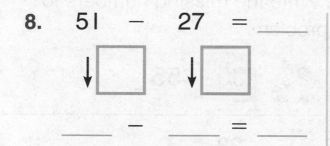

___ − ___ = ___

9. 74 − 35 = _____

↓ ▢   ↓ ▢

___ − ___ = ___

10. 99 − 21 = _____

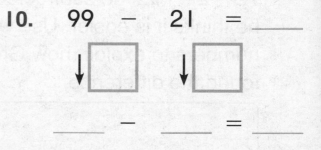

___ − ___ = ___

11. **Higher Order Thinking** Yoshi says that to find 91 − 32, she can subtract 2 from both numbers. Then subtract using mental math. She says the answer is 59. Do you agree?

12. © **MP.1 Make Sense** There were some buttons in a jar. Mrs. Kim puts 19 more buttons in the same jar. Now there are 45 buttons in the jar. How many buttons were in the jar to begin with?

_____ buttons

13. Romi has 42 cards. Lisa has 75 cards. How many more cards does Lisa have than Romi?

_____ more cards

Think about what you are trying to find.

14. **Higher Order Thinking** Greg found 72 − 24. First he subtracted 20 because he thinks it is easier. Use words and numbers to explain how Greg could have found the difference.

15. © **Assessment** Use the numbers on the cards. Write the missing numbers to solve the problem.

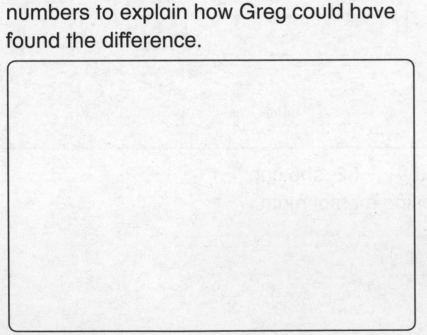

| 2 | 25 | 30 | 55 |

$$53 \quad - \quad 28 \quad = \quad \rule{1cm}{0.4pt}$$

$$+\ 2 \qquad + \ \square$$

$$\rule{1cm}{0.4pt} \quad - \quad \rule{1cm}{0.4pt} \quad = \quad \rule{1cm}{0.4pt}$$

© Pearson Education, Inc. 2

Name _____

Another Look! You can use compensation to find 64 − 27.

27 is close to __30__.

27 + __3__ = __30__

It's easy to find 64 − 30.

64 − 27 = ?
        ↓+ 3
64 − 30 = 34 → 37
            + 3

So, 64 − 27 = __37__.

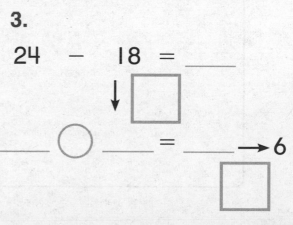

Since I subtracted 30, I subtracted 3 more than 27.

So, I need to add 3 to 34 to find the answer.

HOME ACTIVITY Ask your child to show you how to use compensation to find 82 − 49.

Use compensation to make numbers that are easier to subtract. Then solve. Show your thinking.

1.
   65 − 48 = ____
        ↓ □
   ___ ○ ___ = ___ → 17
        □

2.
   96 − 37 = ____
        ↓ □
   ___ ○ ___ = ___ → 59
        □

3.
   24 − 18 = ____
        ↓ □
   ___ ○ ___ = ___ → 6
        □

Solve each problem. Show your work.

4. © MP.I Make Sense A store had 45 hats for sale. On Friday, 26 of the hats were still for sale. How many hats sold? Think about what you are trying to find.

_____ hats

5. A-Z Vocabulary Complete each sentence using one of the terms below.

regroup   **subtract**

To find 56 + 38, you can _____ 14 ones as 1 ten and 4 ones.

You can use compensation to help

you add and _____ mentally.

6. Higher Order Thinking Use compensation to find 93 − 78. Use words, pictures, or numbers to explain how you found the difference.

7. © Assessment Use the numbers on the cards. Write the missing numbers to solve the problem.

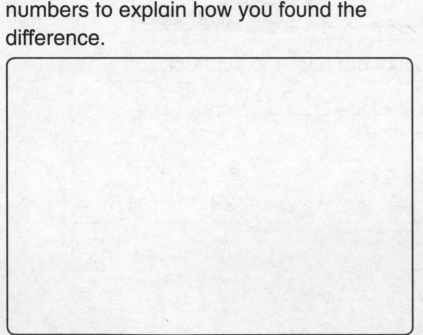

© Pearson Education, Inc. 2

Name _____

Solve & Share

Some frogs were sitting on a pond.
16 more frogs joined them.
Now there are 49 frogs on the pond.
How many frogs were on the pond at first?
Show how you know.

I can ...
solve one- and two-step problems using addition or subtraction.

© **Content Standard** 2.OA.A.1
Mathematical Practices MP.1, MP.2, MP.4, MP.5

_____ frogs

Brian had some baseball cards. Eric gave Brian 6 more cards. Now Brian has 15 cards. How many baseball cards did Brian have at first?

You can use a model to keep track of the numbers.

You know the whole and one part.

15

? | 6

You can use addition or subtraction to solve the problem.

__9__ + 6 = 15

or

15 − 6 = __9__

So, Brian had __9__ cards at first.

Check that your answer makes sense.

Brian had 9 cards. Then Eric gave him 6 more cards. Now he has 15 cards.

9 + 6 = 15

My answer makes sense!

Do You Understand?

Show Me! Cory scored some points. Then he scored 8 more points. He scored 14 points in all. How many points did Cory score at first? How can you solve the problem?

☆ **Guided Practice** ☆ Complete both equations to solve the problem. Use the model to help you.

1. Some people got on the bus at the first stop.
   9 more people got on the bus at the second stop.
   There are 21 people on the bus now.
   How many people got on the bus at the first stop?

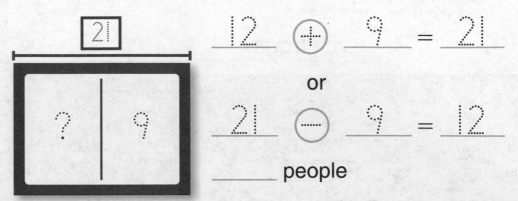

21

? | 9

__12__ ⊕ __9__ = __21__

or

__21__ ⊖ __9__ = __12__

_____ people

© Pearson Education, Inc. 2

Topic 5 | Lesson 8

Name _____

Independent Practice ☆ Solve each problem. Show your work.

2. Mr. Wing's class collected some cans to recycle on Tuesday. They collected 18 more cans on Wednesday. The class collected 44 cans in all. How many cans did the class collect on Tuesday?

You can use addition or subtraction to solve this problem.

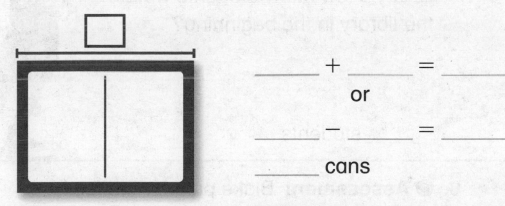

_____ + _____ = _____

or

_____ − _____ = _____

_____ cans

3. Sue took out 5 books from the library on Monday. She took out 6 books from the library on Tuesday. Then she returned 3 books on Wednesday. How many books does Sue have on Thursday?

_____ books

4. **Higher Order Thinking** There are 24 peas on Kim's plate. Kim eats 15 peas. Then Kim's mother puts 8 more peas on her plate. How many peas are on Kim's plate now?

Step 1

_____ − _____ = _____

Step 2

_____ + _____ = _____

_____ peas

Write two equations to solve each problem. Show your work.

Think about what you know and what you are trying to find.

5. © **MP.1 Make Sense** Elaine put 13 photos in the album. Ken put some more photos in the album. There are 32 photos in the album in all. How many photos did Ken add?

_____ photos

6. © **MP.1 Make Sense** Kris sees some students in the library. Then 10 more students enter the library. Now Kris sees 20 students in the library. How many students were in the library in the beginning?

_____ students

7. **Higher Order Thinking** There are 15 vocabulary words in Week 1. There are 8 more vocabulary words in Week 2 than in Week 1.

How many words are there in both weeks?

Step 1: _____ + _____ = _____

Step 2: _____ + _____ = _____

_____ words

8. © **Assessment** Blake puts 8 marbles in the bag. Cole puts 9 marbles in the bag. Then Blake takes out 7 marbles from the bag. How many marbles are in the bag now?

Solve. Show your work in the table.

Step 1
Step 2
Answer: _____ marbles

© Pearson Education, Inc. 2

Help   Tools   Games

Another Look! You can solve a two-step problem by writing two equations.

Rena counts 6 birds in the tree. 3 birds fly away. Then 8 more birds land in the tree. How many birds does Rena count in the tree now?

Step I
Subtract to find how many birds are in the tree after 3 birds fly away.

Step 2
Add the number of birds that landed in the tree.

$$\underline{6} - \underline{3} = \underline{3}$$

$$\underline{3} + \underline{8} = \underline{11}$$

$$\underline{11} \text{ birds}$$

HOME ACTIVITY Make up a two-step story problem for your child to solve.

Complete both equations to solve each problem.

I. Lucy collects 9 rocks. She gives 4 rocks to Sam. Then Lucy collects 7 more rocks. How many rocks does Lucy have now?

_____ rocks

Step I:

_____ – _____ = _____

Step 2:

_____ + _____ = _____

2. 4 boys ride their bicycles to the park. 6 more boys ride their bicycles to the park. Then 2 boys go home. How many boys are at the park now?

_____ boys

Step I:

_____ + _____ = _____

Step 2:

_____ – _____ = _____

Solve each problem. Show your work.

3. © **MP.4 Model** Michael put some of the dishes away. Scott put 17 dishes away. They put away 32 dishes in all. Use the bar diagram to model the story. Then write 2 equations the model shows. How many dishes did Michael put away?

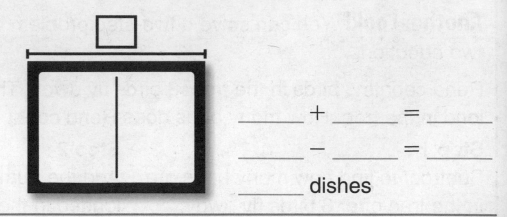

_____ + _____ = _____

_____ − _____ = _____

_____ dishes

---

4. **Higher Order Thinking** Kina picked 14 green apples. Her dad picked 8 red apples. Then they each ate 2 apples. How many apples do they have now? Explain how you solved the problem.

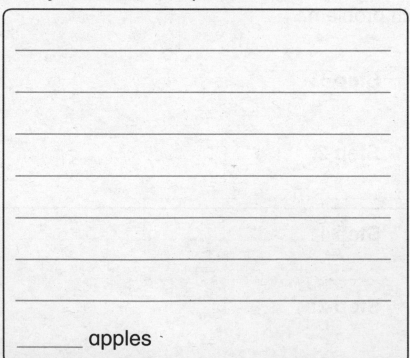

_____ apples

5. © **Assessment** 3 black cats were in the alley. 5 cats joined them. Then 6 cats walked away. How many cats are still in the alley?

Solve. Show your work in the table.

| **Step 1** |
| **Step 2** |
| Answer: _____ cats |

Name _____

Solve & Share

Bill collects and sells seashells. He has 45 shells, finds 29 shells, and sells 20 shells. How many seashells does Bill have now?

Tara says you have to subtract 45 − 29 and then add 20 to solve the problem. Do you agree with Tara's thinking? Circle your answer. Use pictures, words, or equations to explain.

I can ...
critique the thinking of others by using what I know about addition and subtraction.

© **Mathematical Practices** MP.3 Also MP.1, MP.4, MP.7 **Content Standards** 2.OA.A.1, 2.NBT.B.5

Agree   **Do Not Agree**

Thinking Habits
What questions can I ask to understand other people's thinking?

Are there mistakes in other people's thinking?

42 people are swimming. Some people leave. Now 15 people are swimming.

Kelly added up to subtract and she says 17 people left.

How can I decide if I agree with Kelly?

I can check for mistakes or ask Kelly questions.

I can draw a number line and add up to check for mistakes.

$+5$ $+10$ $+2$

15 20   30 32

$5 + 10 + 2 = 17$,
but $15 + 17$ is only 32.

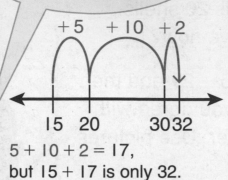

Kelly's strategy of adding up is good, but her answer is not correct.

$+5$ $+10$ $+10$ $+2$

15 20   30   40 42

$15 + 27 = 42$
So, 27 people left.

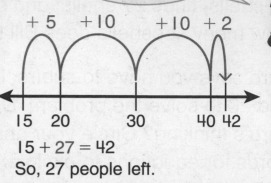

Do You Understand?

Show Me! What question would you ask Kelly to help her check her reasoning?

☆ **Guided Practice** ☆   Circle the answer. Use pictures, words, or equations to explain your reasoning.

1. 51 people were on a train. 33 people left the train. How many people are on the train now?

Agree	Do Not Agree

Ryan says 18 people. He broke apart 33 into 30 and 3. Then he subtracted each number. Does Ryan's reasoning make sense?

© Pearson Education, Inc. 2

Tools   Assessment

Independent Practice

Circle the answer. Use pictures, words, or equations to explain your reasoning.

---

2. Jill put 53 buttons in a box. Marci put 17 buttons in another box.

Jarod says Marci has 33 fewer buttons than Jill. He thinks 53 − 20 is easier to subtract than 53 − 17. He subtracts 53 − 20 and gets 33.

Do you agree or not agree with Jarod's thinking?

Agree   **Do Not Agree**

---

3. Rob has 68 more puzzle pieces than Gina. Rob has 90 puzzle pieces.

Carol says Gina has 22 puzzle pieces. Carol says she found 90 − 68 using an open number line. She added up 2 and 20 more from 68 and got 90.

Does Carol's reasoning make sense?

Agree   **Do Not Agree**

Math Practices and Problem Solving

Reading Books

Ricky read the first 3 chapters of a book. Chapter 1 has 11 pages. Chapter 2 has 7 pages. Chapter 3 has 9 pages.

Sally read 46 pages of her book. How many more pages did Sally read than Ricky?

4. **MP.1 Make Sense** What steps do you need to take to solve the problem?

_____

_____

_____

5. **MP.7 Look for a Pattern** Is there a shortcut to find how many pages Ricky read? Explain.

_____

_____

_____

_____

6. **MP.3 Explain** Sally drew this open number line. Sally says she read 21 more pages than Ricky. Do you agree? Explain.

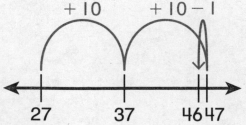

_____

_____

_____

_____

Another Look!

Shane has 62 stamps. Jake has 36 stamps.

Nita says Jake has 26 fewer stamps than Shane, because she can break apart 36 and subtract 62 − 30 = 32 and 32 − 6 = 26. Is Nita correct?

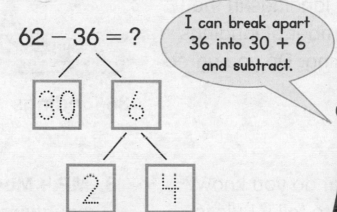

$62 - 36 = ?$

I can break apart 36 into 30 + 6 and subtract.

$62 - 30 = 32$
$32 - 2 = 30$ and $30 - 4 = 26$
So, $62 - 36 = 26$.
Yes, Nita is correct.

HOME ACTIVITY Take turns writing your own subtraction problems involving two-digit numbers. Make some mistakes in some of your solutions. Then challenge each other to find the mistakes.

Circle the answer. Use pictures, words, or equations to explain.

1. There were 64 runners in a race last year. This year there were 25 fewer runners.

Latoya says 39 runners were in the race this year. She says 64 − 30 is easy to subtract. So she added 25 + 5 = 30. Then she found 64 − 30 = 34, and added 5 to 34 to get 39.

Agree   **Do Not Agree**

Landing Planes

Luis says the number of landings in the afternoon equals the number of landings in the morning and evening. Do you agree with Luis?

Morning
36 landings

Afternoon
74 landings

Evening
38 landings

2. **MP.1 Make Sense** What do you know? What do you need to do to tell if Luis is correct?

_____

_____

_____

3. **MP.4 Model** Use pictures, words, or equations to explain if Luis's thinking is correct.

_____

_____

_____

4. **MP.3 Explain** Luis got his answer by finding $74 - 38 = 36$.

Do you agree with Luis's thinking? Use pictures, words, or equations to explain.

© Pearson Education, Inc. 2

Find a Match

Find a partner. Point to a clue. Read the clue.

Look below the clues to find a match. Write the clue letter in the box next to the match.

Find a match for every clue.

I can ...
add and subtract within 20.

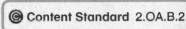

© Content Standard 2.OA.B.2

Clues

A Every difference is 10.

B Every sum is 11.

C Every sum and difference is 6.

D Exactly three sums are the same.

E Exactly three differences are the same.

F Every sum is the same as $9 + 4$.

G Every difference is odd.

H Exactly three sums are even.

☐ $12 - 5$ $17 - 8$ $14 - 7$ $16 - 9$	☐ $10 - 0$ $20 - 10$ $14 - 4$ $19 - 9$	☐ $6 + 6$ $2 + 8$ $7 + 4$ $5 + 7$	☐ $14 - 8$ $3 + 3$ $15 - 9$ $0 + 6$
☐ $8 + 6$ $7 + 8$ $9 + 6$ $10 + 5$	☐ $15 - 8$ $18 - 9$ $12 - 7$ $13 - 6$	☐ $5 + 6$ $4 + 7$ $9 + 2$ $3 + 8$	☐ $7 + 6$ $3 + 10$ $8 + 5$ $4 + 9$

Understand Vocabulary

Choose a term from the Word List to complete each sentence.

1. You can count back or add up to subtract on an

   _____.

2. To find 42 − 7, you can _____ 7 into 2 + 5.

3. The answer to a subtraction problem is called the _____.

4. There are 6 _____ in the number 36.

---

5. In 43, there are _____ tens.

6. In 76, there are _____ tens and _____ ones.

7. Break apart 8 to find 65 − 8.

   _____

Use Vocabulary in Writing

8. Use words to tell how to find 54 − 19. Use terms from the Word List.

   _____

   _____

   _____

   _____

Name _____

Set A

You can use a hundred chart to help you subtract. Find 65 − 31.

Start at 31. Move right 4 ones to 35.
Then move down 3 tens to 65.
3 tens and 4 ones is 34.

So, 65 − 31 = __34__.

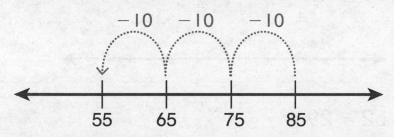

Use a hundred chart to solve the problems.

1. 67 − 42 = _____

2. 70 − 33 = _____

3. 58 − 42 = _____

4. 63 − 38 = _____

Set B

You can use an open number line to find 85 − 30.

Place 85 on the number line.

−10 −10 −10

55   65   75   85

30 is 3 tens. Count back by 10 three times from 85.

So, 85 − 30 = __55__.

Use an open number line to find each difference.

5. 60 − 20 = _____

6. 78 − 40 = _____

You can use an open number line to find 57 − 24.

Place 57 on the number line. There are 2 tens in 24. So, count back by 10 two times. There are 4 ones in 24. Then count back 4 from 37.

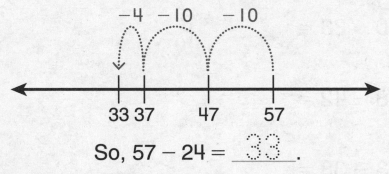

So, 57 − 24 = _33_.

Find 62 − 37.

Place 37 on the line. Add 3 to get to 40. Then add two 10s to get to 60. Then add 2 to get to 62. Add the tens and ones: $3 + 10 + 10 + 2 = 25$.

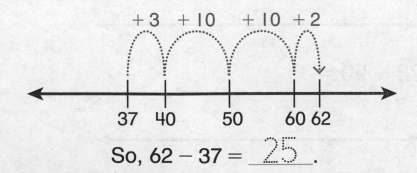

So, 62 − 37 = _25_.

Use an open number line to find each difference.

7. 38 − 13 = _____

8. 93 − 36 = _____

Add up on an open number line to find each difference.

9. 75 − 47 = _____

10. 52 − 29 = _____

© Pearson Education, Inc. 2

Name _____

Set E

Break apart 17 to find 54 − 17.

21	22	23	24	25	26	27	28	29	30
31	32	33	34	35	36	37	38	39	40
41	42	43	44	45	46	47	48	49	50
51	52	53	54	55	56	57	58	59	60

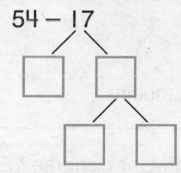

$$54 - 17$$

Start at 54. Subtract 10. Then subtract 4 to get to 40. Then subtract 3 more.

So, 54 − 17 = __37__.

Set F

74 − 27 = ?

Use compensation to solve.

$$74 - 27$$
$$\big\downarrow +3$$
$$74 - 30 = 44 \dashrightarrow 47$$
$$+3$$

So, 74 − 27 = __47__.

Reteaching Continued

Subtract. Break apart the number you are subtracting. Show your work.

11. 52 − 23 = _____

12. 45 − 19 = _____

Use compensation to make numbers that are easier to subtract. Then solve.

13. 42 − 18 = _____

14. 84 − 37 = _____

Mason reads 34 pages in two days. He reads 8 of the pages on the second day. How many pages does Mason read the first day?

26 + 8 = 34 and
34 − 8 = 26

_26_ pages

Add or subtract to solve the problem. Show your work.

15. Gene bakes 60 muffins in one day. He bakes 24 of the muffins before lunch. How many muffins does he bake after lunch?

_____ ◯ _____ = _____

_____ muffins

Thinking Habits

Critique Reasoning

What questions can I ask to understand other people's thinking?

Are there mistakes in other people's thinking?

Do you agree or disagree? Explain.

16. Ken has 29 more stamps than Jamie. Ken has 52 stamps. Lisa says Jamie has 23 stamps.

Lisa added up 1 from 29, then 20 more from 30, and 2 more to get to 52. Does Lisa's reasoning make sense?

© Pearson Education, Inc. 2

1. A store has 68 candles. Then they sell 29 of the candles.
How many candles are left?

Ⓐ 29   Ⓑ 38   Ⓒ 39   Ⓓ 97

---

2. Which does the number line show? Choose all that apply.

☐   Count back by 10 two times from 48.

☐   Count back by 10 three times from 48.

☐   48 − 30 = 18

☐   18 + 48 = 66

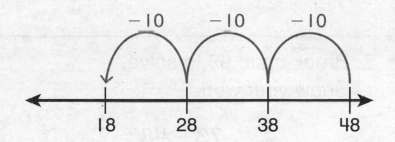

---

3. Tony has 66 rocks.
He gives 23 rocks to Chris.

How many rocks does Tony have now?

_____ ◯ _____ = _____

_____ rocks

21	22	23	24	25	26	27	28	29	30
31	32	33	34	35	36	37	38	39	40
41	42	43	44	45	46	47	48	49	50
51	52	53	54	55	56	57	58	59	60
61	62	63	64	65	66	67	68	69	70

---

4. Raven solved a subtraction problem
using the number line. Write the equation
that the number line shows.

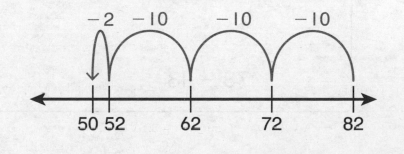

_____ − _____ = _____

5. Ella has 7 carrots.
Ann has 34 carrots.
How many fewer carrots does
Ella have than Ann?

(A) 7   (C) 34

(B) 27   (D) 41

6. Keena has 64 balloons.
28 of the balloons are red.
14 balloons are green.
The rest of the balloons are purple.
How many of the balloons are purple?

(A) 22   (C) 42

(B) 36   (D) 50

7. Break apart 48 to solve.
Show your work.

$$73 - 48 = ?$$

$$73 - 48 = \underline{\hspace{1.5cm}}$$

8. Joe has 43 stickers.
Then he gives away 9 stickers.
How many stickers does Joe have left?

Can you use the two equations to solve?
Choose Yes or No.

43 + 7 = 50   ◯ Yes   ◯ No
50 + 2 = 52

43 + 10 = 53   ◯ Yes   ◯ No
53 − 1 = 52

43 − 3 = 40   ◯ Yes   ◯ No
40 − 6 = 34

43 − 10 = 33   ◯ Yes   ◯ No
33 + 1 = 34

Name _____

9. Which does the number line show? Choose all that apply.

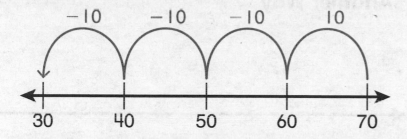

☐ Count back 4 tens from 70.

☐ Count back 4 from 70.

☐ $70 - 30 = 40$

☐ $70 - 40 = 30$

10. Use the open number line to find the difference.

$$80 - 42 = ?$$

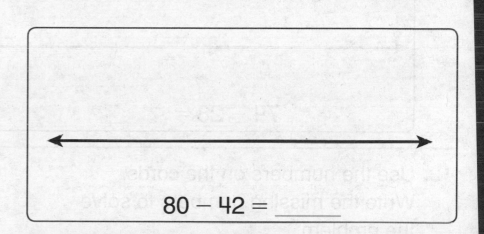

$80 - 42 =$ _____

11. Part A 33 ants are on a leaf. 15 ants leave. How many ants are left?
Jay adds 2 to 33 to make an easier problem, 35–15. He says 20 ants are left. Circle whether you agree or do not agree.

Agree   **Do Not Agree**

Part B Explain why you agree or do not agree with Jay's strategy.

_____

_____

_____

_____

_____

12. Use the open number lines. Show two different ways to find 74 − 28.
Show your work.

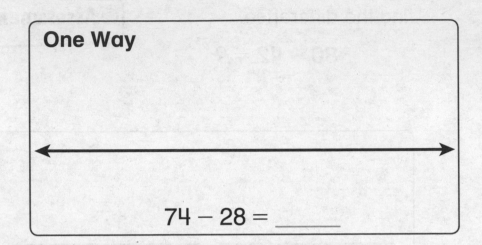

One Way

74 − 28 = _____

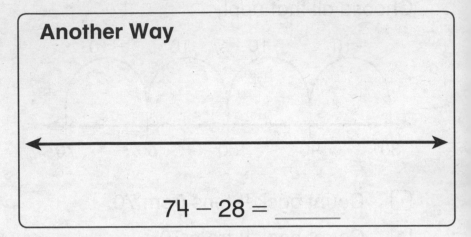

Another Way

74 − 28 = _____

13. Use the numbers on the cards.
Write the missing numbers to solve
the problem.

| 3 | 35 | 40 | 75 |

72 − 37 = _____

+3   + [ ]

_____ − _____ = _____

14. 5 black cows are at the ranch.
9 brown cows join them.
Then 6 cows leave the ranch.
How many cows are still at the ranch?

Solve. Show your work in the table.

Step I
Step 2
Answer
_____ cows

Name _____

Beautiful Boats

Chen's family goes to the lake for a vacation.
They count the boats that they see.

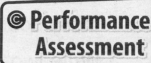

12 sailboats   28 rowboats   36 motorboats

2. Maria's family saw 57 rowboats on their vacation. How many more rowboats did they see than Chen's family?

Use compensation to solve.
Explain how you found your answer.

1. How many more motorboats does Chen see than sailboats?

Use the open number line to solve.

_____ more motorboats

_____ more rowboats

3. Chen's sisters play with toy boats at the lake. They have 21 yellow boats. They have 9 fewer red boats than yellow boats. How many boats do they have in all?

Write two equations to solve the problem.

_____ − _____ = _____

_____ + _____ = _____

_____ boats

4. Julie's family saw 94 boats on their vacation. How many more boats did they see than Chen's family?

Part A What do you need to do to solve the problem?

Part B How many boats did Chen see? Show your work. Then explain how you found your answer.

_____ boats

Part C Julie said that her family saw 18 more boats than Chen's family. She broke apart 76 into 70 + 4 + 2. Then she subtracted each number from 94. Does Julie's reasoning make sense? Explain.

© Pearson Education, Inc. 2

TOPIC 6 Fluently Subtract Within 100

Essential Question: What are strategies for subtracting numbers to 100?

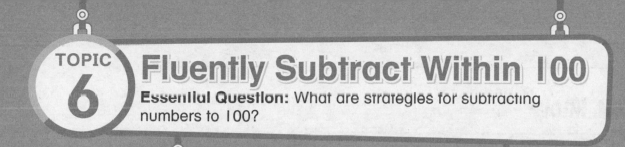

More of Earth is covered with water than with land!

And some of the land is covered with snow and ice!

Wow! Let's do this project and learn more.

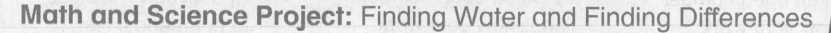

Math and Science Project: Finding Water and Finding Differences

Find Out Use globes, maps, books, and other sources to find out where water, snow, and ice can be found on Earth. Make a list of different names of bodies of water and names of bodies of snow and ice.

Journal: Make a Book Show what you learn in a book. In your book, also:

• Tell about how globes are models that show where water is found on Earth.

• Tell about how to use a subtraction model to find differences.

Topic 6

three hundred twenty-one **321**

Name _____

★ Review What You Know ★

A-Z Vocabulary

1. **Break apart** 56 into tens and ones. Draw place value blocks to show the parts.

   56 = _____ + _____

2. Complete the drawing to show how to **regroup** 1 ten as ones.

   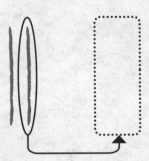

3. Complete the **bar diagram** to model
   64 − 31 = ?

   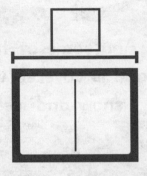

Open Number Lines

4. Find 40 − 25 by counting back on an open number line. Show your work.

   40 − 25 = _____

5. Find 45 − 22 by adding up on an open number line. Show your work.

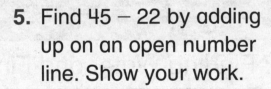

   45 − 22 = _____

Math Story

6. Lea has 30 cookies. She gives 17 cookies to her friends. How many cookies does Lea have now?

   _____ cookies

© Pearson Education, Inc. 2

Solve & Share

How can you use tens and ones to find 23 − 6? Use place-value blocks to help you. Show your work.

I can ...
exchange 1 ten for 10 ones.

© **Content Standards** 2.NBT.B.5, 2.NBT.B.9
Mathematical Practices MP.1, MP.3, MP.5, MP.8

_____ − _____ = _____

Find 34 − 6. Show 34. There are not enough ones to subtract 6.

Tens	Ones

You need to regroup.

Regroup 1 ten as 10 ones.

Tens	Ones

Subtract 6.

Tens	Ones

Cross out 6 ones to subtract. Now there are 2 tens and 8 ones left that show the difference.

34 − 6 = 28

Do You Understand?

Show Me! Do you need to regroup when you subtract 5 from 44? Explain why or why not.

☆ **Guided Practice** ☆ Subtract. Use your workmat and place-value blocks. Regroup if you need to.

	Show.	Subtract.	Do you need to regroup?	Find the difference.
1.	35	8	Yes No	35 − 8 = 27
2.	46	3	Yes No	46 − 3 = ___
3.	62	4	Yes No	62 − 4 = ___
4.	50	7	Yes No	50 − 7 = ___

Topic 6 | Lesson 1

Tools   Assessment

Independent Practice

Subtract. Use your workmat and place-value blocks. Regroup if you need to.

	Show.	Subtract.	Do you need to regroup?		Find the difference.
5.	81	2	Yes	No	81 − 2 = _____
6.	29	1	Yes	No	29 − 1 = _____
7.	60	4	Yes	No	60 − 4 = _____
8.	24	9	Yes	No	24 − 9 = _____
9.	75	3	Yes	No	75 − 3 = _____
10.	43	5	Yes	No	43 − 5 = _____

11. **Higher Order Thinking** Which one-digit numbers can you subtract from 74 without first regrouping? Explain how you know.

Think about what each digit stands for in 74.

_____

_____

Solve each problem below.

12. © **MP.1 Make Sense** There are 21 snails in a garden. 6 snails leave. How many snails are still in the garden?

_____ snails

13. © **MP.1 Make Sense** Kate has 45 marbles. She gives 3 marbles to her brother. How many marbles does Kate have now?

_____ marbles

14. Higher Order Thinking Sammie has 9 fewer rings than Emilio. Sammie has 7 more rings than Sara. Emilio has 34 rings. Complete the sentences below. Draw a picture to explain your work.

Sammie has _____ rings.

Sara has _____ rings.

15. © **Assessment** Malcolm has 38 seeds. Juan has 4 fewer seeds than Malcolm. Juan gives 8 seeds to his friend. How many seeds does Juan have now?

Ⓐ 22
Ⓑ 26
Ⓒ 36
Ⓓ 46

Think about what you know and what you are trying to find. Can drawing place-value blocks help?

© Pearson Education, Inc. 2

Name _____

Help   Tools   Games

Another Look! Use place-value blocks to find 42 − 7.

Show 42.

Tens	Ones

Regroup.

Tens	Ones

Subtract 7 ones.

Tens	Ones

HOME ACTIVITY Ask your child to show you how to subtract 26 − 7 using small objects such as buttons, marbles, or paper clips. Have your child explain and show you how to regroup.

$12 - 7 = \underline{5}$ ones

$42 - 7 = \underline{35}$

Subtract. Use the pictures to help.

1. Subtract 5 from 31.

Show 31.

Tens	Ones

Regroup.

Tens	Ones

Subtract _____ ones.

Tens	Ones

$11 - 5 = \underline{}$ ones

$31 - 5 = \underline{}$

2. A-Z **Vocabulary** Circle the missing word.

addend   equation

$42 - 7 = 35$ is an _____ .

3. **Algebra** What number is missing?

_____ $- 5 = 20$

4. **Algebra** What number is missing?

$37 -$ _____ $= 28$

© **MP.1 Make Sense** Solve. Think about what you know and need to find.

5. Maria buys 36 beads.
She uses 9 of the beads.
How many beads does Maria have left?

_____ beads

6. Luke buys 7 new pencils.
Now he has 21 pencils.
How many pencils did Luke have at first?

_____ pencils

7. **Higher Order Thinking** A flag pole is 30 feet tall. A bug crawls 14 feet up the pole. Then it crawls another 4 feet up the pole. How much farther must the bug crawl to get to the top?

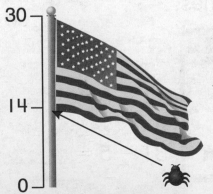

_____ feet

8. © **Assessment** An old building has 48 big windows.
The building has 12 small windows.
There are 9 broken windows.
How many windows are **NOT** broken?

Ⓐ 51

Ⓑ 48

Ⓒ 41

Ⓓ 37

© Pearson Education, Inc. 2

Solve & Share

There are 22 students drawing pictures.
4 students finish drawing. How many students are still drawing?

Use place-value blocks to help you solve.
Show the tens and ones you have.

I can ...
use place value and models to subtract 2-digit and 1-digit numbers.

© **Content Standards** 2.NBT.B.5, 2.NBT.B.9
Mathematical Practices MP.3, MP.4, MP.5

Tens	Ones

_____ tens   _____ ones

$$22 - 4 = \underline{\hspace{1cm}}$$

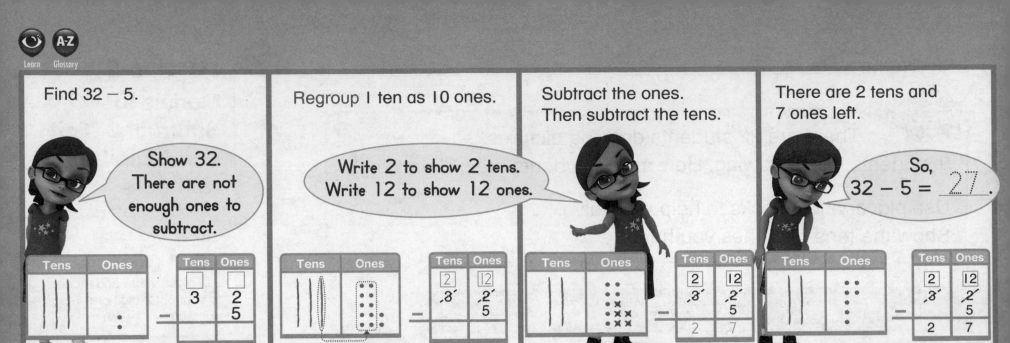

Find 32 − 5.

Show 32. There are not enough ones to subtract.

Tens	Ones
|||	::

−
Tens	Ones
3	2 5

Regroup 1 ten as 10 ones.

Write 2 to show 2 tens. Write 12 to show 12 ones.

Tens	Ones
|||	:::::

−
Tens	Ones
2 8́	12 2́ 5

Subtract the ones. Then subtract the tens.

Tens	Ones
||	:::::

−
Tens	Ones
2 8́	12 2́ 5
	2	7

There are 2 tens and 7 ones left.

So, 32 − 5 = 27.

Tens	Ones
||	:::::

−
Tens	Ones
2 8́	12 2́ 5
2	7

Do You Understand?

Show Me! Why do you need to regroup when you subtract 32 − 5?

☆ **Guided Practice** ☆ Subtract. Draw place-value blocks to show your work. Regroup if needed.

1.

Tens	Ones
3	14
4́	4́
−	9
3	5

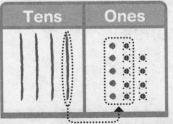

Tens	Ones

2.

Tens	Ones
2	3
−	5

Tens	Ones

3.

Tens	Ones
3	5
−	8

Tens	Ones

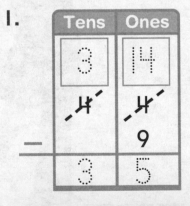

330 three hundred thirty

© Pearson Education, Inc. 2

Topic 6 | Lesson 2

Independent Practice

Subtract. Draw place-value blocks to show your work. Regroup if needed.

4.

Tens	Ones
☐	☐
6	3
−	2

Tens	Ones

5.

Tens	Ones
☐	☐
9	1
−	7

Tens	Ones

6.

Tens	Ones
☐	☐
6	6
−	9

Tens	Ones

7.

Tens	Ones
☐	☐
5	2
−	6

Tens	Ones

Write the missing numbers in the boxes. Draw a picture to show and explain your work.

8. Algebra What numbers will complete the subtraction equations?

$$\boxed{} - 8 = 17 \qquad 34 - \boxed{} = 29$$

Math Practices and Problem Solving

☺ **MP.4 Model** Solve the problems below. Draw place-value blocks to model.

9. There are 23 students playing tag. 9 students go home. How many students are still playing tag?

Tens	Ones

_____ students

10. There are 67 books on the shelf. Dion takes 5 of them. How many books are left on the shelf?

Tens	Ones

_____ books

11. Higher Order Thinking What mistake did Alia make when she subtracted 72 – 4? Show how to fix her mistake.

Alia's Work

$$\begin{array}{r} 72 \\ -\ 4 \\ \hline 72 \end{array}$$

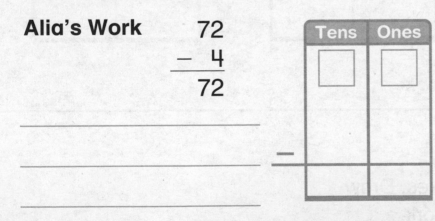

Tens	Ones

_____

_____

_____

_____

12. ☺ Assessment You draw place value blocks to model each subtraction. Would you regroup to show the difference? Choose Yes or No.

29 – 3 = ? ◯ Yes ◯ No

30 – 0 = ? ◯ Yes ◯ No

77 – 8 = ? ◯ Yes ◯ No

55 – 5 = ? ◯ Yes ◯ No

Name _____

Help · Tools · Games

Another Look! Regroup when there are not enough ones. Find 52 − 8.

Step 1

Show 52. There are not enough ones to subtract 8.

Tens	Ones
|||||	:

Tens	Ones
□	□
5	2
−	8

Step 2

Regroup 1 ten as 10 ones.

Tens	Ones
||||(|)	::::::

Tens	Ones
4	12
5̶	2̶
−	8

Step 3

Subtract the ones. Then subtract the tens.

Tens	Ones
||||	•••• ✗✗

Tens	Ones
4	12
5̶	2̶
−	8
4	4

So, 52 − 8 = __44__.

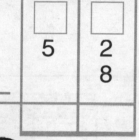
Subtract. Draw place-value blocks to show your work. Regroup if needed.

1.

Tens	Ones
□	□
2	6
−	7

Tens	Ones

2.

Tens	Ones
□	□
4	3
−	9

Tens	Ones

3. There are 40 students in the gym. 9 students are jumping rope. How many students are **NOT** jumping rope?

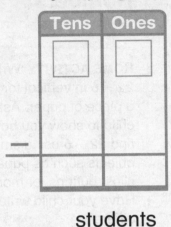

Tens	Ones

_____ students

4. Kate writes on 7 pages in her notebook. There are 34 pages in her notebook. How many pages are blank?

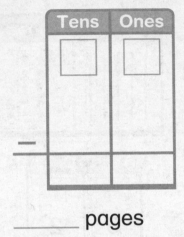

Tens	Ones

_____ pages

5. **Higher Order Thinking** Write a subtraction story about $45 - 8$. Then solve.

_____

_____

_____

Tens	Ones

6. © **Assessment** You draw place value blocks to model each subtraction. Choose all of the problems that need regrouping to show the difference.

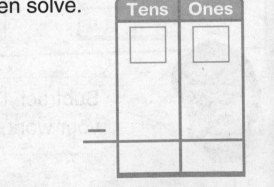

☐ $62 - 4 = ?$ ☐ $75 - 7 = ?$

☐ $58 - 7 = ?$ ☐ $35 - 5 = ?$

Name _____

Solve & Share

Ari has 31 stickers.
He puts 8 of his stickers in a scrapbook.
How many stickers are left?

Solve. Explain why your strategy works.

I can ...
use place value and
regrouping to subtract.

© **Content Standards** 2.NBT.B.5,
2.NBT.B.9
Mathematical Practices MP.4,
MP.5, MP.6, MP.8

Tens	Ones
−	

Find 42 – 9.

Show 42.

Tens	Ones
‖‖	:

Tens	Ones
4	2
−	9

Look at the ones.
There are not enough
ones to subtract.

Regroup!

Tens	Ones
‖‖	⦙

Tens	Ones
3 4	12 2
−	9

Subtract the ones.
Then subtract the tens.

Tens	Ones
‖‖	✗✗✗

Tens	Ones
3 4	12 2
−	9
3	3

There are 3 tens
and 3 ones left.

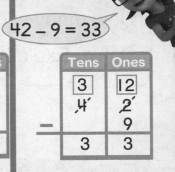

42 – 9 = 33

Tens	Ones
3 4	12 2
−	9
3	3

Do You Understand?

Show Me! Look at the regrouping in the problem above. Why is 12 written above the 2 in the ones column?

Guided Practice Subtract. Use drawings if needed.

1.

Tens	Ones
2 3	16 6
−	8
2	8

2.

Tens	Ones
2	9
−	4

3.

Tens	Ones
4	1
−	4

4.

Tens	Ones
6	3
−	5

5.

Tens	Ones
5	0
−	1

6.

Tens	Ones
4	8
−	7

Topic 6 | Lesson 3

Independent Practice ✩ Subtract. Use drawings if needed.

7.
Tens	Ones
☐	☐
3	2
−	6

8.
Tens	Ones
☐	☐
2	0
−	3

9.
Tens	Ones
☐	☐
6	7
−	6

10.
Tens	Ones
☐	☐
5	2
−	4

11.
Tens	Ones
☐	☐
3	5
−	0

12.
Tens	Ones
☐	☐
7	5
−	3

13.
Tens	Ones
☐	☐
5	6
−	7

14.
Tens	Ones
☐	☐
8	5
−	1

15.
Tens	Ones
☐	☐
9	8
−	9

16.
Tens	Ones
☐	☐
7	7
−	9

Use words or a picture to solve.

17. **Number Sense** What is the missing number? Explain how to solve.

$$45 - 9 = 46 - \boxed{}$$

Solve the problems below.

18. © **MP.8. Generalize** There are 25 bikes at a bike store. The store owner sells 7 bikes. How many bikes are left?

Tens	Ones

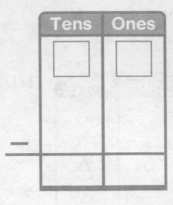

You can repeat steps to subtract. First subtract the ones. Regroup if needed. Then subtract the tens. 7 has zero tens.

_____ bikes

19. **Higher Order Thinking** A bike store sold 10 fewer locks on Wednesday than on Tuesday. How many more locks did the store sell on Wednesday than on Monday?

Bike Locks Sold	
Monday	9
Tuesday	33
Wednesday	

Tens	Ones

_____ locks

20. © **Assessment** Use the numbers on the cards to find the missing numbers in the problem. Write the missing numbers.

15	9	3

Think: How will I regroup to subtract?

Tens	Ones
3	
4	5
−	6

© Pearson Education, Inc. 2

Homework & Practice 6-3
Subtract 2-Digit and 1-Digit Numbers

Another Look! Find 42 − 6. You can subtract the ones first.

Think: Are there enough ones to subtract?

Regroup if you need to. Then subtract the tens. Draw pictures if needed.

1-digit numbers have 0 tens.

There are **NOT** enough ones to subtract.

Tens	Ones
~~3~~ ~~4~~	12 ~~2~~
−	6
3	6

Regroup? (Yes)   No

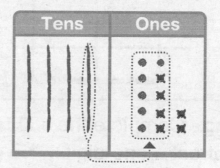

So, 42 − 6 = 36.

HOME ACTIVITY Write 34 − 9 in vertical form on a sheet of paper. Have your child use pencil and paper to solve.

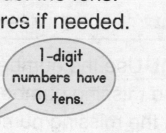

Subtract. Use drawings if needed.

1.

Tens	Ones
☐	☐
2	5
−	4

2.

Tens	Ones
☐	☐
4	1
−	8

3.

Tens	Ones
☐	☐
6	5
−	7

4.

Tens	Ones
☐	☐
7	8
−	9

5.

Tens	Ones
☐	☐
8	3
−	6

© **MP.8. Generalize** Solve the problems. Show your work and regroup if needed.

6. 53 grapes are on a plate. Andrea eats 5 of them. How many grapes are on the plate now?

Tens	Ones
☐	☐
−	

_____ grapes

7. Chato reads 7 pages. His book has 67. How many pages does Chato have left to read?

Tens	Ones
☐	☐
−	

_____ pages

8. Higher Order Thinking Complete the subtraction frame. Subtract a one-digit number from a 2-digit number.

Tens	Ones
☐	☐
−	
7	6

You know the difference! Work backwards to check your work. There is more than one correct answer.

9. © **Assessment** Use the numbers on the cards to find the missing numbers in the problem. Write the missing numbers.

1	8	11

Tens	Ones
2	1
−	3
1	☐

Solve & Share

You have 42 pipe cleaners.
You use 19 of the pipe cleaners.
How many pipe cleaners do you have now?

Use place-value blocks to help you solve.
Draw your place-value blocks.
Tell if you need to regroup.

I can ...
use place value and models to
subtract 2-digit numbers.

© **Content Standards** 2.NBT.B.5,
2.NBT.B.9
Mathematical Practices MP.3,
MP.4, MP.5, MP. 7

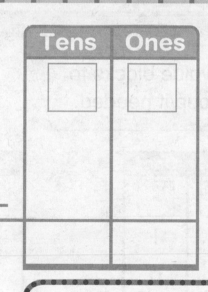

Tens	Ones
−	

Regroup?

Yes   No

_____ pipe cleaners

Find 31 − 14.

Show 31. There are not enough ones to subtract.

Tens	Ones

Tens	Ones
3	1
1	4

Regroup 1 ten as 10 ones.

Write 2 to show 2 tens. Write 11 to show 11 ones.

Tens	Ones
2	11
3	1
1	4

Subtract the ones.

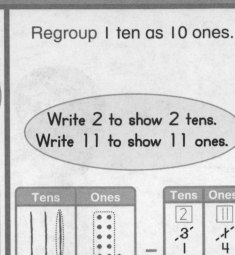

Tens	Ones
2	11
3	1
1	4
	7

Subtract the tens.

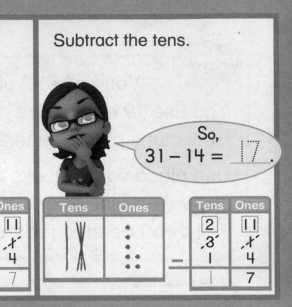

So, 31 − 14 = 17 .

Tens	Ones
2	11
3	1
1	4
1	7

Do You Understand?

Show Me! Explain why you need to regroup to find 65 − 17.

Subtract. Draw place-value blocks to show your work. Regroup if needed.

1.

Tens	Ones
4	12
5	2
1	3
3	9

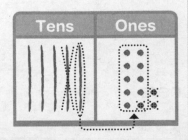

Tens	Ones

2.

Tens	Ones
4	1
2	6

Tens	Ones

3.

Tens	Ones
6	4
4	7

Tens	Ones

© Pearson Education, Inc. 2   **Topic 6 | Lesson 4**

Name _____

Independent Practice

Subtract. Draw place-value blocks to show your work. Regroup if needed.

4.

Tens	Ones
□	□
5	6
− 3	1

Tens	Ones

5.

Tens	Ones
□	□
6	6
− 5	8

Tens	Ones

6.

Tens	Ones
□	□
8	5
− 4	6

Tens	Ones

7.

Tens	Ones
□	□
4	3
− 1	5

Tens	Ones

8. Algebra Write numbers to complete the equations. Draw pictures to help if needed.

$37 - 18 = \boxed{}$

$46 - \boxed{} = 18$

$\boxed{} - 17 = 16$

9. Number Sense

Do these models show the same value? Explain.

_____

_____

_____

_____

Solve each problem.

10. © MP.4 Model Anita has $63. She spends $24 and saves the rest. How much does Anita save?

$ _____

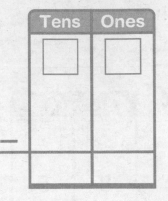

Tens	Ones

What kind of picture can you draw to model the subtraction?

11. Higher Order Thinking Write a subtraction story about 36 − 17. Explain how to solve the problem.

_____

_____

_____

_____

_____

_____

12. © Assessment Sara has 70 beads. There are 11 beads that are **NOT** round. The rest are round. How many round beads does Sara have?

- Ⓐ 59
- Ⓑ 49
- Ⓒ 47
- Ⓓ 11

Name _____

Another Look! Find 43 − 16.

Step 1	**Step 2**	**Step 3**
Show 43. There are not enough ones to subtract 6.	Regroup 1 ten as 10 ones.	Subtract the ones. Then subtract the tens.

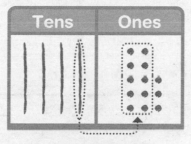

HOME ACTIVITY Ask your child to use paper clips or other small objects to find 25 − 16. Have your child explain how he or she regrouped.

Tens	Ones
☐	☐
4	3
− 1	6

Tens	Ones
3	13
4̸	3̸
− 1	6

Tens	Ones
3	13
4̸	3̸
− 1	6
2	7

So, 43 − 16 = **27**.

Subtract. Draw place-value blocks to show your work. Regroup if needed.

1.

Tens	Ones
☐	☐
5	0
− 1	3

Tens	Ones

2.

Tens	Ones
☐	☐
7	6
− 2	8

Tens	Ones

3. Jamal has 54 marbles. Lucas has 70 marbles. How many more marbles does Lucas have than Jamal?

Tens	Ones
☐	☐

_____ more marbles

4. Latoya has 95 pennies. She gives 62 pennies to her cousin. How many pennies does Latoya have now?

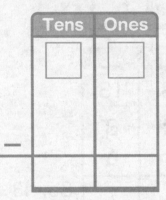

_____ pennies

5. **Higher Order Thinking** Fill in the missing numbers to make the subtraction problem true.

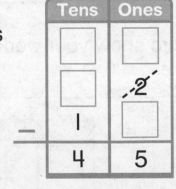

6. © **Assessment** To find 36 − 17, how can you regroup 36?

Ⓐ 2 tens and 6 ones

Ⓑ 2 tens and 16 ones

Ⓒ 3 tens and 16 ones

Ⓓ 4 tens and 16 ones

Name _____

Solve & Share

How is subtracting 23 from 71 like subtracting 3 from 71?
How is it different from subtracting 3 from 71? Explain.
Find both differences. Use blocks if you need to.

I can ...
use place value to subtract 2-digit numbers.

© **Content Standards** 2.NBT.B.5, 2.NBT.B.9
Mathematical Practices MP.2, MP.3, MP.4, MP.5, MP.6

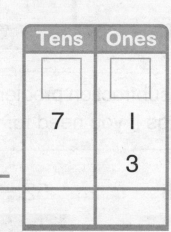

Tens	Ones
7	1
−	3

Tens	Ones
7	1
− 2	3

Find 43 − 18.
Show and write the subtraction.

Tens	Ones
| | | |	• • •

Tens	Ones
☐	☐
4	3
− 1	8

You can use a frame to write the subtraction.

There are not enough ones to subtract. Regroup 1 ten as 10 ones.

Tens	Ones
| | | | ⟨|⟩	• • • • • • • • • • • • •

Tens	Ones
3	13
4	3
− 1	8

Write 4 tens and 3 ones as 3 tens and 13 ones.

Subtract: 13 ones − 8 ones = 5 ones
3 tens − 1 ten = 2 tens

Tens	Ones
| | ✕	• ✕ • ✕ • ✕ ✕ • ✕ ✕ • ✕ ✕

Tens	Ones
3	13
4	3
− 1	8
2	5

So, 43 − 18 = 25.

Do You Understand?

Show Me! Why can you regroup 1 ten as 10 ones when there are not enough ones to subtract?

☆ **Guided Practice** ☆ Write each subtraction problem. Find the difference. Use drawings if you need to.

1. 34 − 15

Tens	Ones
2	14
3	4
− 1	5
1	9

Sometimes you need to regroup. Sometimes you don't.

2. 52 − 31

Tens	Ones
☐	☐
−	

3. 67 − 48

Tens	Ones
☐	☐
−	

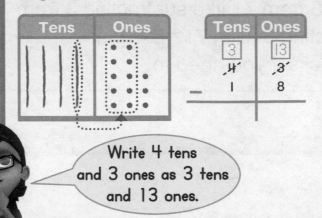

Tools   Assessment

Independent Practice ☆   Write each subtraction problem. Find the difference.

4.   52 − 36

Tens	Ones
☐	☐

−

5.   94 − 54

Tens	Ones
☐	☐

−

6.   41 − 25

Tens	Ones
☐	☐

−

7.   33 − 28

Tens	Ones
☐	☐

−

8.   65 − 42

Tens	Ones
☐	☐

−

9.   70 − 48

Tens	Ones
☐	☐

−

10.   96 − 37

Tens	Ones
☐	☐

−

11.   87 − 45

Tens	Ones
☐	☐

−

Solve. Draw a model to help.

12. Higher Order Thinking Tia's basketball team
scored 61 points. They won by 23 points.
How many points did the other team score?

_____ points

13. © **MP.4 Model** Don has 72 marbles. Josie has 56 marbles. How many more marbles does Don have than Josie?

Tens	Ones

_____ more marbles

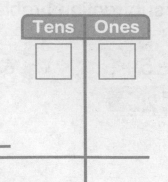

Can you use a drawing or objects to show the problem?

---

14. **Higher Order Thinking** Write a subtraction story using two two-digit numbers. Then solve the problem in your story.

Tens	Ones

15. © **Assessment** Eric can fit 90 cards in a scrapbook. He already has 46 cards in the scrapbook.

How many more cards will fit?

Ⓐ 44

Ⓑ 45

Ⓒ 46

Ⓓ 54

Name _____

Another Look! Remember the steps for subtracting.

Step 1
Think: Are there enough ones to subtract?

Step 2
Regroup if you need to.

Step 3
Subtract the ones.
Subtract the tens.

Write the problems in the frames. Find each difference.

38 − 13

Tens	Ones
3	8
− 1	3
2	5

54 − 17

Tens	Ones
4	14
5̶	4̶
− 1	7
3	7

Be sure to cross out if you regroup.

You can use drawings to help.

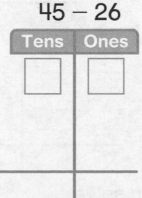

HOME ACTIVITY Have your child use paper and pencil to solve 65 − 37. Have your child explain the steps he or she takes to subtract.

Write each problem in a frame. Find the difference.

1. 37 − 14

Tens	Ones
−	

2. 64 − 18

Tens	Ones
−	

3. 45 − 26

Tens	Ones
−	

4. 73 − 25

Tens	Ones
−	

© MP.6 Be Precise Decide which one item each child will buy. Subtract to find how much money is left.

Stickers 14¢

Craft sticks 36¢

Paint set 42¢

Crayons 58¢

---

5. Bonnie has 47¢.
She buys the

_____.

Bonnie has _____ ¢ left.

Tens	Ones
☐	☐

− _____

---

6. Ricky has 59¢.
He buys the

_____.

Ricky has _____ ¢ left.

Tens	Ones
☐	☐

− _____

---

7. Lani has 63 grapes. She gives 36 grapes to Carla. How many grapes does Lani have left?

_____ grapes

Tens	Ones
☐	☐

− _____

---

8. Write a number to make this a subtraction problem with regrouping. Then find the difference.

Tens	Ones
☐	☐

−   2   3

---

9. Higher Order Thinking Use each number below.

| 1 | 2 | 4 | 5 |

Write the subtraction problem that has the greatest difference. Then solve.

Tens	Ones
☐	☐
☐	☐

− _____

---

10. © Assessment Norma has 48 buttons. Grace has 14 buttons. Connie has 29 buttons. How many fewer buttons does Connie have than Norma?

34   29   19   15
Ⓐ   Ⓑ   Ⓒ   Ⓓ

Lesson 6-6

Use Addition to Check Subtraction

Solve & Share

Find 52 − 24.
Use the bar diagram and subtraction frame to help you show and solve the problem.
How can you use addition to check your answer?

I can ...
add to check my subtraction.

© **Content Standards** 2.NBT.B.5, 2.NBT.B.9
Mathematical Practices MP.1, MP.2, MP.3, MP.4

Remember that addition and subtraction are related. So, you can add to check subtraction.

Find 24 − 9.

The sum of the parts equals the whole.

$$\begin{array}{r} {}^{1\,14}\\ 2\!\!\!/4 \\ -\ 9 \\ \hline 15 \end{array} \quad \begin{array}{r} {}^{1}\\ 15 \\ +\ 9 \\ \hline 24 \end{array}$$

```
   24
 ┌──────┐
 │ 9 │15 │
 └──────┘
```

Find 52 − 17.

Add to check your subtraction.

The two parts equal the whole!

$$\begin{array}{r} {}^{4\,12}\\ 5\!\!\!/2 \\ -\ 17 \\ \hline 35 \end{array} \quad \begin{array}{r} {}^{1}\\ 35 \\ +\ 17 \\ \hline 52 \end{array}$$

```
   52
 ┌──────┐
 │17 │35 │
 └──────┘
```

Do You Understand?

Show Me! Why can you use addition to check 63 − 19 = 44?

☆ Guided Practice ☆

Subtract. Check your answer by adding. Write the missing part.

1.

$$\begin{array}{r} {}^{2\,12}\\ 32 \\ -\ 13 \\ \hline 19 \end{array} \quad \begin{array}{r} {}^{1}\\ 19 \\ +\ 13 \\ \hline 32 \end{array}$$

```
   32
 ┌──────┐
 │13 │19 │
 └──────┘
```

2.

$$\begin{array}{r} 78 \\ -\ 49 \\ \hline \end{array} \quad \begin{array}{r} 29 \\ +\ 49 \\ \hline \end{array}$$

```
   78
 ┌──────┐
 │49 │   │
 └──────┘
```

You can show the parts in any order.

Name _____

 Independent Practice — Subtract. Check your answer by adding. Write the missing part.

3.
$$\begin{array}{r} 52 \\ -\ 27 \\ \hline \end{array}$$

52

27 |

4.
$$\begin{array}{r} 80 \\ -\ 14 \\ \hline \end{array}$$

80

14

5.
$$\begin{array}{r} 54 \\ -\ 19 \\ \hline \end{array}$$

54

19 |

6.
$$\begin{array}{r} 75 \\ -\ 62 \\ \hline \end{array}$$

75

62

7.
$$\begin{array}{r} 83 \\ -\ 29 \\ \hline \end{array}$$

83

29 |

8.
$$\begin{array}{r} 48 \\ -\ 21 \\ \hline \end{array}$$

48

21 |

9. Higher Order Thinking Maria uses $35 + 24$ to check her answer to a subtraction problem. Write two subtraction problems Maria could have solved.

10. Math and Science 62 students are doing science experiments. 48 students have cups of water. The rest have ice cubes. How many students have ice cubes?

_____ − _____   _____ + _____

_____ students

11. © MP.1 Make Sense
37 students make clay pots. 16 students use brown clay. The rest use green clay. How many students use green clay?

_____ students

12. Higher Order Thinking Write a subtraction story about 65 − 41. Solve the story. Check your answer by adding.

_____

_____

_____

13. © Assessment Bill has 17 more craft sticks than Roger. Bill has 45 craft sticks. How many craft sticks does Roger have? Which shows the solution and how to check it?

Ⓐ 15 sticks; $30 + 15 = 45$

Ⓑ 28 sticks; $28 + 17 = 45$

Ⓒ 45 sticks; $28 + 17 = 45$

Ⓓ 62 sticks; $45 + 17 = 62$

Name _____

Another Look!

You can think of subtraction as starting with the whole. Then you take away one part. The other part is left.

```
  37   Whole
- 12   Part
  25   Part
```

```
  25   Part
+ 12   Part
  37   Whole
```

To check your work, add to put the parts back together. Your answer should be the whole.

If no regrouping is needed, then add or subtract the tens and the ones.

Tens	Ones

Tens	Ones
and	and

HOME ACTIVITY Ask your child to find 65 − 32. Then have him or her use addition to show you how to check the subtraction.

Subtract. Check your answer by adding.

1.
```
  86
-  9
```
+ _____

2.
```
  54
- 19
```
+ _____

3.
```
  63
- 37
```
+ _____

4. Mei Ling has 71 marbles.
   Then she loses 25 marbles.
   How many marbles does Mei Ling have left?

   _____ marbles

   Subtract   **Check**

   $-$ _____ $+$ _____

> Think about how addition and subtraction are related.

5. Denise has 51 beads.
   Then she uses 32 beads to make a bracelet.
   How many of her beads does Denise have left to use?

   _____ beads

   Subtract   **Check**

   $-$ _____ $+$ _____

6. **Number Sense** Write the number that makes each equation true.

   $63 - 20 = 20 +$ _____

   $58 - 40 = 18 +$ _____

   $75 - 30 = 15 +$ _____

   $89 - 46 = 30 +$ _____

> In an equation, each side of the equals sign shows the same value.

7. © **Assessment** Lana subtracts to find $52 - 39$. Which addition equation could Lana use to check her answer?

   Ⓐ $13 + 26 = 39$

   Ⓑ $39 + 52 = 91$

   Ⓒ $13 + 39 = 52$

   Ⓓ $52 + 13 = 65$

© Pearson Education, Inc. 2

Name _____

Solve & Share

Find 82 − 56. Use any strategy you have learned or your own strategy. Show your work. Explain why your strategy works.

I can ...
subtract 2-digit numbers and decide when to regroup and when not to regroup.

© **Content Standards** 2.NBT.B.5, 2.NBT.B.9
Mathematical Practices MP.1, MP.2, MP.6, MP.7

Find 72 − 24.

One way is to break apart numbers.

72 − 24 = ?   72 − 20 = 52

20   4   52 −   2 = 50

2   2   50 −   2 = 48

So, 72 − 24 = 48.

Another way is to line up the numbers by place value.

6 12
7̶ 2̶
− 2 4
4 8

I get the same difference either way!

So, 72 − 24 = 48.

You can check your subtraction with addition.

My work checks. My subtraction is correct.

1
2 4
+ 4 8
7 2

Do You Understand?

Show Me! Could you solve 72 − 24 in another way? Explain.

☆ **Guided Practice** ☆   Use any strategy to subtract. Show your work. Check your work with addition.

1. 67 − 39 = _____

67 − 40 = 27

27 + 1 = 28

Check:

1
2 8
+ 3 9
6 7

2. 78 − 42 = _____

Independent Practice Use any strategy to subtract. Show your work. Check your work with addition.

3. 73 − 34 = _____

4. 78 − 25 = _____

5. 83 − 46 = _____

6. 36 − 27 = _____

7. 98 − 51 = _____

8. 45 − 34 = _____

9. 86 − 29 = _____

10. 71 − 38 = _____

11. 85 − 23 = _____

Algebra Find the missing number.

Look for a pattern. Use mental math.

12. 34 − 8 = 35 − ☐

13. 27 − 9 = 28 − ☐

14. The hardware store has 32 hammers in stock. The store sells 16 hammers on Saturday. How many hammers are left?

_____ hammers

15. A barber does 15 haircuts on Monday. He does 28 haircuts on Friday. How many more haircuts does he do on Friday than on Monday?

_____ more haircuts

16. 🄰🄯 **Vocabulary** Complete each sentence. Use two of the words below.

addend   equation   difference   sum

$93 - 53 = 40$ is an _____.

40 is called the _____ of 93 and 53.

17. Higher Order Thinking
Fill in the missing digits.

$$\begin{array}{r} \square\;\square \\ -\;2\quad 3 \\ \hline 2\quad 9 \end{array}$$

18. © **Assessment** Circle the problem that you will use regrouping to solve. Then find both differences. Show your work.

$56 - 38$ $74 - 52$

$$\begin{array}{r} 56 \\ -\;38 \\ \hline \end{array} \qquad \begin{array}{r} 74 \\ -\;52 \\ \hline \end{array}$$

Name _____

Another Look! Find 82 − 37.

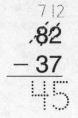

```
   7 12
   8̶2̶
 − 37
   45
```

Check

You can use addition to check your subtraction.

```
   37
 + 45
   82
```

Or you can break apart the numbers to check your work.

82 − 37 = ?

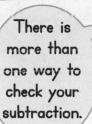

30   7

2   5

82 − 30 = 52
52 − 2 = 50
50 − 5 = 45

So, 82 − 37 = 45.

I can subtract in different ways. I will line up the numbers by place value!

There is more than one way to check your subtraction.

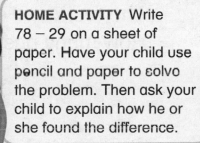

HOME ACTIVITY Write 78 − 29 on a sheet of paper. Have your child use pencil and paper to solve the problem. Then ask your child to explain how he or she found the difference.

Use any strategy to subtract. Show your work. Check your work.

1. 56 − 37 = _____

2. 46 − 18 = _____

3. 75 − 22 = _____

4. 45 basketballs are in a closet.
38 basketballs are full of air.
The rest need air.
How many basketballs need air?

_____ basketballs

5. Sue buys a box of 60 craft sticks.
She uses 37 craft sticks for her project.
How many craft sticks are left?

_____ craft sticks

6. **Higher Order Thinking** 36 berries are in a
bowl. James eats 21 of the berries. Then he
puts 14 more berries in the bowl. How many
fewer berries are in the bowl now?

Is there a shortcut you can use?

_____ fewer berries

7. © **Assessment** Circle the problem that
you will use regrouping to solve. Then
find both differences. Show your work.

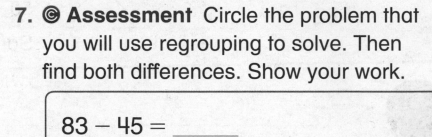

$83 - 45 =$ _____

$65 - 33 =$ _____

© Pearson Education, Inc. 2

Name _____

Solve & Share

Trevor made 20 apple muffins for the bake sale. Ryan made 15 banana muffins. They sold 23 muffins in all. How many muffins are left?

Solve any way you choose. Then write two equations to show your work.

I can ...
use models and equations to solve word problems.

© **Content Standard** 2.OA.A.1
Mathematical Practices MP.1, MP.2, MP.4, MP.7

_____ ◯ _____ = _____

_____ ◯ _____ = _____

_____ muffins

Some students are in the gym. 13 students leave. Now there are 15 students in the gym.

How many students were in the gym at the start?

What is happening in the story?

You can write an equation. First, think about what you need to find.

How many students were in the gym at the start?

You can use a ? for the unknown.

$$? - 13 = 15$$

You can also use a bar diagram to show the parts and the whole.

?

| 13 | 15 |

You can add to solve the problem.

$$\begin{array}{r} 1\ 3 \\ +\ 1\ 5 \\ \hline 2\ 8 \end{array}$$

So, 28 students were in the gym at the start.

Do You Understand?

Show Me! How does the bar diagram show what happens in the story problem?

☆ **Guided Practice**   Solve each problem. Show your work.

1. Some key chains are in a bag. Aki takes out 17 key chains. 14 key chains are left in the bag. How many key chains were in the bag at the start?

   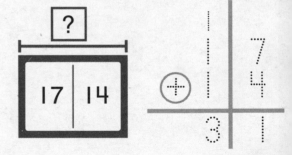

?

   | 17 | 14 |

   $$\begin{array}{r} 1\ 7 \\ +\ 1\ 4 \\ \hline 3\ 1 \end{array}$$

   _____ key chains

2. Some leaves are in a pile. 26 leaves blow away. 22 leaves are left. How many leaves were in the pile at the start?

   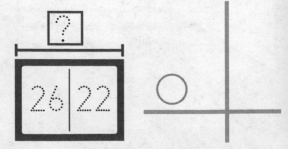

?

   | 26 | 22 |

   _____ leaves

© Pearson Education, Inc. 2   **Topic 6 | Lesson 8**

Name _____

Independent Practice   Use a bar diagram to solve each problem.
Show your work.

3. Some balls are in the closet. Mr. Thomas takes out 15 balls for class. Now there are 56 balls in the closet. How many balls were in the closet in the beginning?

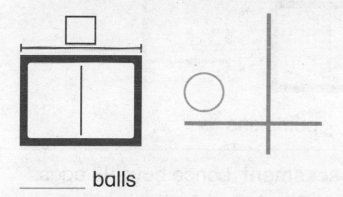

_____ balls

4. Corey buys a box of 96 paper clips from the store. He uses 34 paper clips. How many paper clips does Corey have left?

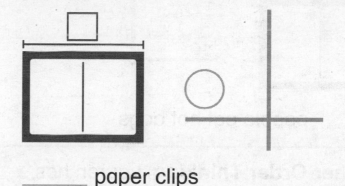

_____ paper clips

5. A.J. counts 44 acorns in his yard. He picks up 27 acorns. Then 16 more acorns fall from the tree. How many acorns are in the yard now? Show your work.

Think about what to find first. Then use that answer to solve the problem.

Step 1

____ ◯ ____ = ____

Step 2

____ ◯ ____ = ____

_____ acorns

Topic 6 | Lesson 8

6. 27 people are at a picnic. 14 people eat hamburgers. The rest eat hot dogs. How many people eat hot dogs?

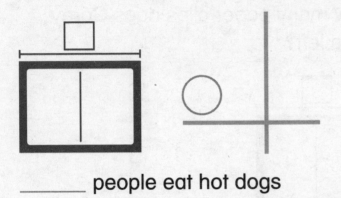

_____ people eat hot dogs

7. Some pumpkins are in a patch. 41 pumpkins are picked. Now there are 33 pumpkins in the patch. How many pumpkins were in the patch at the start?

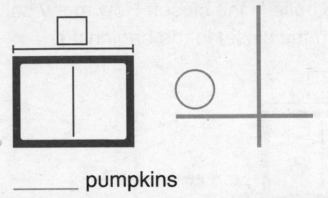

_____ pumpkins

8. Higher Order Thinking Lauren has a stamp collection. She gives Kristen 12 stamps and Ethan 15 stamps. Lauren has 22 stamps left. How many stamps did she have at the start?

Step 1

_____ ◯ _____ = _____

Step 2

_____ ◯ _____ = _____

_____ stamps

9. © **Assessment** Lance buys 48 eggs. He uses 24 of them for baking. Then he buys 12 more eggs. How many eggs does Lance have now?

Which set of equations can you use to solve this problem?

Ⓐ 48 + 24 = 72
72 − 12 = 60

Ⓒ 48 + 24 = 72
72 + 12 = 84

Ⓑ 48 − 24 = 24
24 + 12 = 36

Ⓓ 48 − 24 = 24
24 − 12 = 12

Name _____

Another Look! 52 cars are parked in the lot. 18 cars leave. Then 10 more cars leave. How many cars are in the lot now?

Use the answer from Step 1 to solve Step 2.

Step 1: Subtract to find how many cars are still in the lot after 18 cars leave.

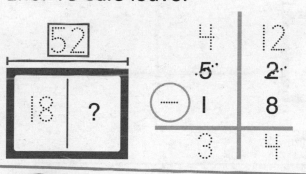

52

18 | ?

$$\begin{array}{r} 4\,\,12 \\ \cancel{5}\,\,2 \\ -\,1\,\,8 \\ \hline 3\,\,4 \end{array}$$

Step 2: Then subtract to find how many cars are still in the lot after 10 more cars leave.

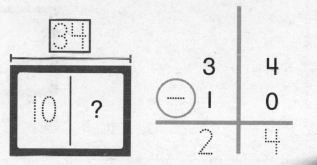

34

10 | ?

$$\begin{array}{r} 3\,\,4 \\ -\,1\,\,0 \\ \hline 2\,\,4 \end{array}$$

Use the answer from Step 1 to solve Step 2.

HOME ACTIVITY Have your child solve this problem: Some birds are sitting on the roof. Then thunder scares away 12 birds. Now there are 32 birds sitting on the roof. How many birds were sitting on the roof at the start?

1. 73 people are on the train. At a train stop 24 people get off and 19 people get on. How many people are on the train now?

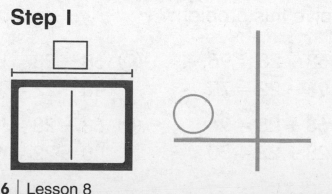

Step 1

Step 2

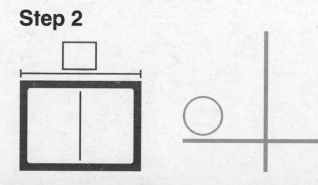

_____ people

2. Rosa's book has 88 pages in all. She reads some pages on Monday. She has 59 pages left to read. How many pages did she read on Monday?

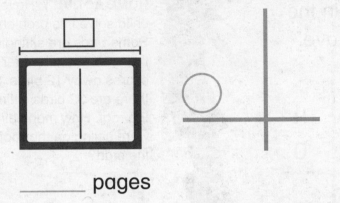

_____ pages

3. Jackie runs 19 laps on Monday. She runs 12 laps on Tuesday. How many laps did she run on both days?

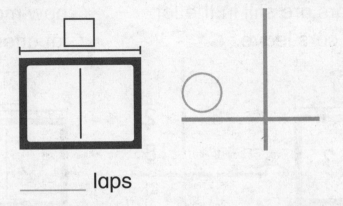

_____ laps

4. Higher Order Thinking Zak has a bag of cherries. He gives away 18 cherries to Tim and 18 cherries to Janet. Now he has 25 cherries. How many cherries did Zak have at the start?

Step I

_____ ◯ _____ = _____

Step 2

_____ ◯ _____ = _____

_____ cherries

5. © **Assessment** There are 68 runners in a marathon. 28 runners finish the race. Then 22 more runners finish the race. How many runners have **NOT** finished the race?

Which pair of equations can you use to solve this problem?

Ⓐ 68 + 28 = 96;
96 − 22 = 74

Ⓑ 68 + 28 = 96;
28 + 22 = 50

Ⓒ 68 − 28 = 40;
40 − 22 = 18

Ⓓ 68 − 28 = 40;
40 + 22 = 66

Name _____

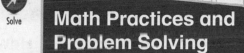
Solve & Share

Farmer Davis has 52 chickens.
He sells 15 chickens at the market.
How many chickens does Farmer Davis have now?

Use the bar diagram and equation to help you solve.
Be ready to explain how the numbers in the problem are related.

I can ...
reason about word problems, and use bar diagrams and equations to solve them.

© **Mathematical Practices** MP.2
Also MP.1, MP.4, MP.5, MP.6
Content Standards 2.OA.A.1, 2.NBT.B.9

Thinking Habits

How are the numbers in the problem related?

How can I show a word problem using pictures or numbers?

_____ ◯ _____ ◯ _____ chickens

45 beads are in a jar. Jenny uses some beads to make a necklace.
Now 17 beads are in the jar.

How many beads does Jenny use to make the necklace?

How can I use reasoning to solve the problem?

45 beads − beads in = 17 beads
           necklace   left

I can think about how the numbers are related. 45 - ? = 17 A bar diagram can show this.

I know the whole. So, I can subtract the part I know to find the missing part.

45
? | 17

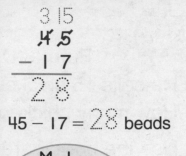

$$\begin{array}{r} 3\;15 \\ \cancel{4}\;\cancel{5} \\ -\;1\;7 \\ \hline 2\;8 \end{array}$$

45 − 17 = 28 beads

My bar diagram and equation show how the numbers relate.

Do You Understand?

Show Me! Why can you subtract 45 − 17 to solve 45 − ? = 17?

Guided Practice

Reason about the numbers in each problem. Complete the bar diagram and write an equation to solve. Show your work.

1. Wendy has 38 cents to spend on a snack. She buys an apple that costs 22 cents. How many cents does Wendy have left?

38 ⊖ 22 ⊜ _____ cents

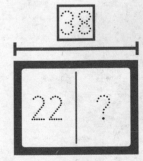

38
22 | ?

2. Joe has 46 crayons. Tamila has 18 more crayons than Joe. How many crayons does Tamila have?

_____ ◯ _____ ◯ _____ crayons

© Pearson Education, Inc. 2

Tools Assessment

Independent Practice

Reason about how the numbers in each problem relate. Complete the bar diagram and write an equation to solve. Show your work.

3. **Math and Science** Andy's class wants to test samples of river water. They want to test 47 water samples. So far, they tested 34 samples. How many more samples do they need to test?

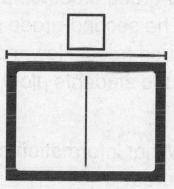

_____ ◯ _____ ◯ _____ more samples

4. 93 dimes are in a box. Grant uses some to buy a game. Now, 66 dimes are in the box. How many dimes did Grant use to buy the game?

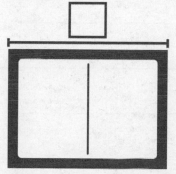

_____ ◯ _____ ◯ _____ dimes

5. Maria paints 62 squares for a mural. Oscar paints 38 squares. How many more squares does Maria paint than Oscar?

_____ ◯ _____ ◯ _____ more squares

Math Practices and Problem Solving

Planting Trees

The second and third-grade students planted these trees in Wing Park. The second-grade students planted 26 of the spruce trees. How many spruce trees did the third-grade students plant?

38 Oak   **44 Spruce**

6. **MP.1 Make Sense** What information can you get from the pictures?

_____

_____

_____

_____

7. **MP.4 Model** Complete the bar diagram. Decide how the numbers in the problem relate. Then write an equation that shows how to solve the problem.

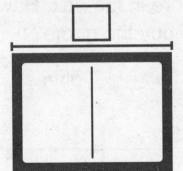

8. **MP.2 Reasoning** How many spruce trees did the third-grade students plant? Explain how you solved the problem.

_____ spruce trees

© Pearson Education, Inc. 2

Name _____

Another Look! Robin collects 36 acorns.
Trisha collects 19 more acorns than Robin.
How many acorns does Trisha collect?

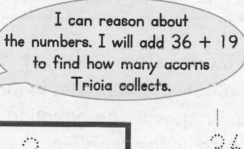

I can reason about the numbers. I will add 36 + 19 to find how many acorns Tricia collects.

This bar diagram shows comparison. The diagram and the equation show how the numbers and the unknown in the problem relate.

HOME ACTIVITY Ask your child to find 76 − 42 by drawing a bar diagram and writing an equation. Then ask your child to explain what the numbers and symbols mean.

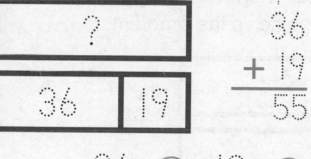

$$\begin{array}{r} 36 \\ + 19 \\ \hline 55 \end{array}$$

36 $\oplus$ 19 $\ominus$ 55 acorns

Reason about how the numbers in the problem relate. Complete the bar diagram and write an equation to solve. Show your work.

I. The Tigers scored 53 points in a basketball game.
The Lions scored 12 fewer points than the Tigers.
How many points did the Lions score?

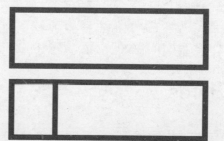

_____ ◯ _____ ◯ _____ points

Topic 6 | Lesson 9

Vacation Pictures

Adam, Tessa, and Nicki take pictures on their vacation. How many fewer pictures did Adam take than Nicki?

Use the information in the table to solve.

Number of Pictures Taken

Adam	Tessa	Nicki
19	92	78

2. **MP.1 Make Sense** Will you use each number in the table to solve the problem? Explain.

_____

_____

_____

3. **MP.4 Model** Complete the bar diagram. Decide how the numbers in the problem relate. Then write an equation that shows how to solve the problem.

4. **MP.2 Reasoning** How many fewer pictures did Adam take than Nicki? Explain how you solved the problem.

_____ fewer pictures

Name _____

Point & Tally

Find a partner. Get paper and a pencil. Each partner chooses a different color: light blue or dark blue.

Partner 1 and Partner 2 each point to a black number at the same time. Both partners add those numbers.

If the answer is on your color, you get a tally mark. Work until one partner gets seven tally marks.

I can ...
add within 100.

© Content Standard 2.NBT.B.5

Partner 1							Partner 2
49	34	76	74	61	63	89	**40**
60	58	80	93	78	95	100	**25**
36	85	74	69	50	98	65	**14**
55	45	87	60	84	89	49	**38**
20							**29**

Tally Marks for Partner 1	Tally Marks for Partner 2

 A-Z Glossary

Word List
- bar diagram
- difference
- equation
- ones
- regroup
- tens

Understand Vocabulary

Write *always*, *sometimes*, or *never*.

1. A bar diagram shows subtraction. _____

2. An 8 in the ones place of a number equals 80. _____

3. A 5 in the tens place of a number equals 50. _____

Draw a line from each term to its example.

4. equation

5. regroup

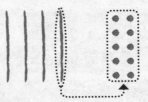

The answer to 75 − 23

6. difference

$72 + 25 = 97$

Use Vocabulary in Writing

7. Explain how you can make a model to show and help you solve the problem. Use terms from the Word List.

Molly has 64 marbles.
Leslie has 29 marbles.
How many fewer marbles does Leslie have?

_____

_____

_____

© Pearson Education, Inc. 2

Name _____

Set A

You can regroup 1 ten as 10 ones when you subtract. Find 46 − 8.

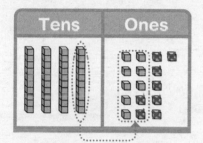

Tens | Ones

46 − 8 = _38_

Did you need to regroup?

(Yes)   No

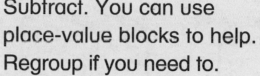
Reteaching

Subtract. You can use place-value blocks to help. Regroup if you need to.

1. 61 − 3 = _____

Did you need to regroup?

Yes   No

2. 57 − 5 = _____

Did you need to regroup?

Yes   No

Set B

You can draw place-value blocks to help you regroup. Find 72 − 6.

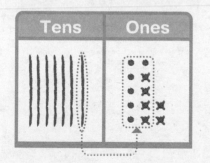

Tens | Ones

Tens	Ones
6	12
7̶	2̶
−	6
6	6

72 − 6 = _66_

Subtract. Draw place-value blocks. Regroup if you need to.

3.

Tens	Ones
□	□
2	7
−	9

Tens	Ones

Find 53 − 6. Regroup if you need to.

Tens	Ones

Tens	Ones
4	13
5	3
−	6
4	7

Subtract. Use drawings if needed.

4.

Tens	Ones
☐	☐
3	8
−	9

5.

Tens	Ones
☐	☐
6	1
−	4

You can draw place-value blocks to help you regroup when subtracting two-digit numbers.

Find 43 − 15.

You can regroup 1 ten as 10 ones.

Tens	Ones
3	13
4	3
− 1	5
2	8

43 − 15 = 28

Subtract. Draw place-value blocks. Regroup if you need to.

6.

Tens	Ones
☐	☐
7	2
3	6
−	

Tens	Ones

© Pearson Education, Inc. 2

Name _____

Set E

You can write subtraction problems in a frame. Find 52 − 33. Draw pictures if needed.

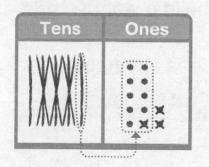

Tens	Ones
4	12
5	2
− 3	3
1	9

Write each subtraction problem in the frame. Find the difference.

7. 84 − 47

Tens	Ones
☐	☐
−	

8. 62 − 36

Tens	Ones
☐	☐
−	

Set F

You can check subtraction by adding. The sum of the parts equals the whole.

```
  4 8          32
− 1 6        + 1 6
  3 2          4 8
```

48
16	32

Subtract. Check your answer by adding.

9. 6 7
   − 4 8

10. 4 9
    − 2 7

11. 9 5
    − 4 3

12. 7 0
    − 3 6

Topic 6 | Reteaching

Thinking Habits

Reasoning

What do the numbers and symbols in the problem mean?

How are the numbers in the problem related?

How can I show a word problem using pictures or numbers?

Complete the bar diagram and write an equation to show the problem. Then solve. Show your work.

13. 94 bricks are needed to build a wall.
Lindy has 65 bricks.
How many more bricks does she need?

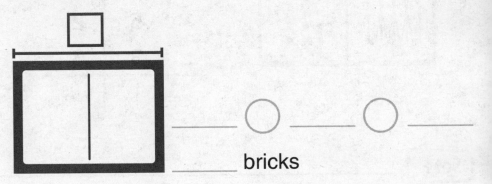

_____ bricks

14. Explain why making a bar diagram can help you solve the problem above.

_____

_____

_____

_____

Name _____

1. Would you regroup to find each difference?
Choose Yes or No.

$45 - 8 = ?$ ○ Yes   ○ No

$51 - 9 = ?$ ○ Yes   ○ No

$77 - 6 = ?$ ○ Yes   ○ No

$83 - 4 = ?$ ○ Yes   ○ No

2. Sam has 74 books.
He puts 28 books on a shelf.
How many books are **NOT**
on the shelf? Show your work.

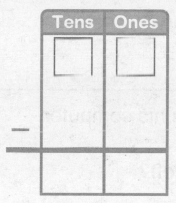

_____ books are **NOT** on the shelf.

3. Ryan has 46 marbles.
John has 4 fewer marbles than Ryan.
John gives 9 marbles to his friend.
How many marbles does John have now?

Ⓐ 23

Ⓑ 33

Ⓒ 35

Ⓓ 42

4. A ship has 68 round windows.
The ship also has 16 square windows.
7 of the windows are broken.
How many windows are **NOT** broken?

Ⓐ 45

Ⓑ 61

Ⓒ 77

Ⓓ 91

5. Choose all of the problems that you will solve by regrouping.

☐ $45 - 0 = ?$

☐ $68 - 49 = ?$

☐ $84 - 37 = ?$

☐ $99 - 33 = ?$

6. Ben wants to find $54 - 18$. How can he regroup 54?

Ⓐ 4 tens and 4 ones

Ⓑ 4 tens and 14 ones

Ⓒ 5 tens and 4 ones

Ⓓ 6 tens and 14 ones

7. Jason has 86 photos in his computer. He deletes 61 photos. How many photos are left?

Use the frame to help you.

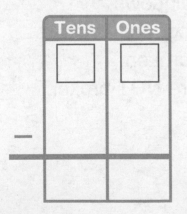

Ⓐ 5   Ⓑ 15   Ⓒ 25   Ⓓ 35

8. Claire has 53 beads. Grace has 26 beads. Bella has 39 beads. How many fewer beads does Bella have than Claire?

Show your work.

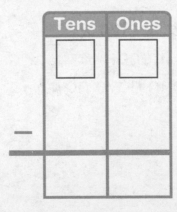

_____ fewer beads

9. Circle the problem that you will use regrouping to solve.
Then explain how you know.

$$54 - 23 \qquad 82 - 44$$

10. A book has 72 pages.
Dan reads 38 pages on Monday.
He reads 26 pages on Tuesday.
How many pages does Dan have left to read?

Which pair of equations can you use to solve the problem?

Ⓐ $38 + 26 = 64$
$72 - 64 = 8$

Ⓒ $72 + 26 = 98$
$98 - 38 = 60$

Ⓑ $72 - 38 = 34$
$34 + 26 = 60$

Ⓓ $72 - 26 = 46$
$46 + 38 = 84$

11. Part A
Subtract. Write the missing part in the bar diagram.

$$\begin{array}{r} 24 \\ -\ 16 \\ \hline \end{array}$$

Part B
Which addition equation can you use to check your answer?

Ⓐ $24 - 8 = 16$

Ⓑ $8 + 8 = 16$

Ⓒ $16 + 8 = 24$

Ⓓ $16 + 24 = 40$

12. Peter collects 54 stamps. He gives 29 stamps to Ruth. How many stamps does Peter have now? Show the problem in the bar diagram with a ? for the unknown number. Then write an equation to solve the problem.

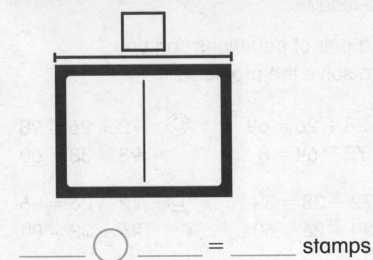

_____ ◯ _____ = _____ stamps

13. Match each number from the cards to a missing number in the problem. Write the missing numbers.

| 4 | 5 | 13 |

Tens	Ones
4 5	3
−	8

14. Find 72 − 38.
Use any strategy to solve. Then explain why your strategy works.

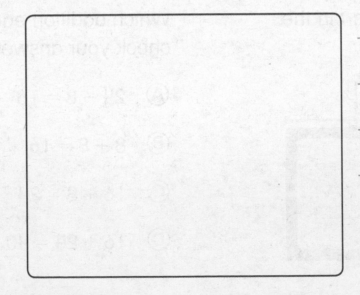

_____

_____

_____

_____

© Pearson Education, Inc. 2

Name _____

Stamp Collection

Mary collects stamps.
The table shows the number of different kinds of stamps that she has.

Number of Stamps	
Flags	8
Butterflies	34
Birds	27
Flowers	61

1. How many more stamps with butterflies does Mary have than stamps with flags? Show your work and draw pictures.

Tens	Ones
☐	☐
—	

_____ more stamps with butterflies

2. How many fewer stamps with birds does Mary have than stamps with flowers? Use subtraction to solve. Then use addition to check your work.

_____ fewer stamps with birds

3. Can you add in a different order to check your work in Item 2? Explain.

4. Luke also collects stamps.
He has 57 stamps.
His friend gives him 25 more stamps.

Then Luke gives away some stamps.
Now Luke has 44 stamps.
How many stamps did Luke give away?

Part A
How many stamps does Luke have
after his friend gives him more stamps?

_____ ◯ _____ = _____

_____ stamps

Part B
How many stamps did Luke give away?

_____ ◯ _____ = _____

_____ stamps

5. Mary puts 54 of her stamps in a book.
The book holds 96 stamps.
How many more stamps can Mary put in
the book?

Part A
Complete the bar diagram to model the problem.

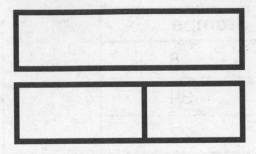

Explain how the bar diagram helps you
understand the problem.

_____

_____

_____

_____

Part B
Write an equation to solve the problem.

_____ ◯ _____ = _____

_____ more stamps

Topic 6 | Performance Assessment

More Solving Problems Involving Addition and Subtraction

Essential Question: How can you solve word problems that use adding or subtracting?

Digital Resources

Solve Learn Glossary

Tools Assessment Help Games

This row of trees can help slow down the wind!

This is only one of the ways to help protect land from wind or water.

Wow! Let's do this project and learn more.

Math and Science Project: Solving Problems

Find Out Find and share books that tell about ways to protect land from damage that wind or water can cause. Compare the different ways to protect the land.

Journal: Make a Book Show what you learn in a book. In your book, also:

• Show ways to solve problems caused by wind or water.

• Show ways to solve problems using addition or subtraction.

Name _____

A-Z Vocabulary

1. Write the subtraction problem below as an **equation**.

$$75$$
$$-\ 30$$
$$\overline{45}$$

2. Complete the **bar diagram** to model $77 + 22 = ?$

3. Circle the two addends below that are **compatible numbers**.

$$18 + 6 + 4 = ?$$

Adding to Check Subtraction

4. Use addition to check if the subtraction equation is correct.

$$51 - 22 = 29$$

Is it correct? _____

Subtracting to Check Addition

5. Use subtraction to check if the addition is correct.

$$37 + 26 = 53$$

Is it correct? _____

Number Story

6. Jim and Maria are counting birds. Jim counts 17 birds. Maria counts 33 birds. How many more birds does Maria count than Jim?

_____ more birds

Solve & Share

Jenn has some red cubes and 11 blue cubes. She has 24 red and blue cubes in all.

She says the problem can be shown with the equation below.

$$? + 11 = 24$$

Draw what the ? represents.
Explain your answer.

I can ...
model problems using equations with unknowns in any position.

© **Content Standard** 2.OA.A.1
Mathematical Practices MP.2, MP.4, MP.5, MP.8

Robert has 27 toy robots. He buys some more. Now he has 58 robots. How many robots did Robert buy?

58 is the whole. 27 is one part.

You can show the problem with an equation.

$$27 + ? = 58$$

The ? shows the addend you don't know.

58

| 27 | ? |

You can solve the problem by adding on from 27 until you get to 58.

$27 + 10 = 37$
$37 + 10 = 47$
$47 + 10 = 57$
$57 + 1 = 58$
$10 + 10 + 10 + 1 = 31$
So, $27 + 31 = 58$.

Robert bought 31 robots.

You can subtract to solve the problem.

$$\begin{array}{r} 58 \\ - 27 \\ \hline 31 \end{array}$$

You can check by adding.
$31 + 27 = 58$

Robert bought 31 robots.

Do You Understand?

Show Me! Could you show Robert's robot problem with the equation below? Explain.

$$58 = 27 + ?$$

Guided Practice Write an equation with a ? for the unknown to model the problem. Then solve. Show your work.

1. Mary has some game tickets. She gives 14 tickets away and now has 17 tickets left. How many tickets did she have at first?

Equation:  _____ tickets

2. Tamara has $25. She earns $34 more by working. How much money does she have now?

Equation: _____ $ _____

© Pearson Education, Inc. 2

Tools Assessment

Independent Practice

Write an equation with a ? for the unknown to model the problem. Then solve. Show your work.

3. Erin has 32 books on her bookshelf. She gives some to friends and now has 19 books left. How many books did she give away?

Equation: _____

_____ books

4. A store sells 38 men's bikes and 47 women's bikes. How many bikes did the store sell in all?

Equation: _____

_____ bikes

5. Math and Science A field has 25 trees in it. 14 trees are new and the rest are old. How many trees are old? Write two different equations that represent the problem. Then solve.

Equation: _____

Equation: _____

_____ old trees

6. Number Sense Harry buys 22 fish. He has a round fish bowl and a rectangular fish tank. How could he place the fish in the bowl and tank?

Equation: _____

_____ fish in the bowl _____ fish in the tank

Write an equation with a ? for the unknown to model the problem. Then solve. Show your work.

7. **© MP.4 Model** Rodney collects 17 leaves and Sheila collects 23 leaves. How many more leaves does Sheila collect than Rodney?

Equation: _____

_____ more leaves

8. **© MP.4 Model** Jun swims 18 laps and Mara swims 25 laps. How many fewer laps did Jun swim than Mara?

Equation: _____

_____ fewer laps

9. **Higher Order Thinking** Jim has 44 roses. 14 are white and the rest are red. How many are red? Write two different equations to model the problem. Then solve.

Equation: _____

Equation: _____

_____ red roses

10. **© Assessment** Some wolves howl in the woods. 12 wolves join them. Now 30 wolves howl. How many wolves howled at first?

Write an equation to model the problem. Use a ? for the unknown. Then solve.

© Pearson Education, Inc. 2

Name _____

Another Look! Jamal has some green apples and 17 red apples. He has 29 apples in all. How many green apples does he have?

You can show word problems with drawings.

You can write an equation with a ? or another symbol for the part you don't know.

12 + 17 = 29, so Jamal has 12 green apples.

29

| ? | 17 |

? + 17 = 29

Add mentally.

17 + 10 = 27

27 + 2 = 29

HOME ACTIVITY Ask your child to write an equation for each of 2 different problems you make up. Then have him or her show you how to solve the problems.

Write an equation with a ? for the unknown to model the problem. Then solve. Show your work.

1. Jill bikes 15 miles in the morning and 17 miles in the afternoon. How many miles does she bike in all?

   Equation: _____

   _____ miles

2. Maria makes 21 thank you cards. She mails 13 of the cards. How many cards does she have left?

   Equation: _____

   _____ cards

Write an equation with a ? for the unknown to model the problem. Then solve. Show your work.

3. **© MP.4 Model** Latisha eats 12 grapes with lunch and then eats some more with dinner. She eats 26 grapes in all. How many grapes does she eat with dinner?

Equation: _____

_____ grapes

4. **© MP.4 Model** Jack read 24 pages of a book and John read 19 pages of a book. How many more pages did Jack read than John?

Equation: _____

_____ more pages

5. **Higher Order Thinking** A train has 43 cars. 15 cars are red and the rest are blue. How many blue cars does the train have? Write two different equations that represent the problem. Then solve.

Equation: _____

Equation: _____

_____ blue cars

6. **© Assessment** 63 boys enter a marathon. 48 boys finish the race and some boys do not. How many boys do **NOT** finish the race?

Write an equation to model the problem. Use a ? for the unknown. Then solve.

© Pearson Education, Inc. 2

Solve & Share

Aiden has 27 fewer crayons this week than last week. Last week he had 56 crayons. How many crayons does Aiden have this week? Show your work.

I can ...
use drawings and equations to make sense of the words in problems.

Content Standard 2.OA.A.1
Mathematical Practices MP.1, MP.2, MP.3, MP.4

_____ crayons

Sally has 28 fewer blocks than Nigel.
Sally has 26 blocks.
How many blocks does Nigel have?

Let's think about who has fewer blocks and who has more blocks.

A bar diagram can help you think about the problem.

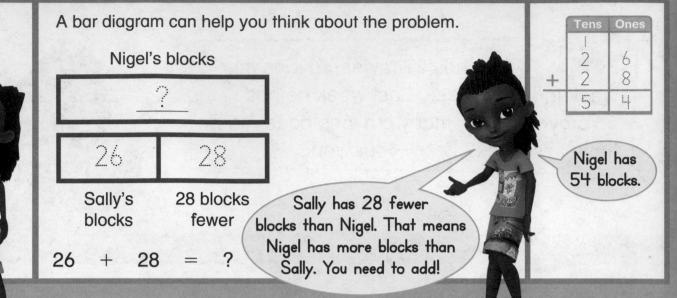

Nigel's blocks

?

26   28

Sally's   28 blocks
blocks   fewer

26   +   28   =   ?

Sally has 28 fewer blocks than Nigel. That means Nigel has more blocks than Sally. You need to add!

Nigel has 54 blocks.

Tens	Ones
1	
2	6
+ 2	8
5	4

Do You Understand?

Show Me! How are these statements alike and different? Cal has 12 fewer blocks than Mia. Mia has 12 more blocks than Cal.

Guided Practice   Solve the problem any way you choose. Use drawings and equations to help.

1. Lakota has 11 fewer magnets than Jeffrey. Lakota has 25 magnets. How many magnets does Jeffrey have?

?

25   11

25
+ 11
____

_____ magnets

Tools Assessment

Independent Practice

Solve each problem any way you choose. Use drawings and equations to help. Show your work.

2. There are 28 more students than adults at the school fair. There are 96 students at the school fair. How many adults are at the school fair?

_____ adults

3. Ellie the elephant has some peanuts. She eats 49 peanuts. Now Ellie the elephant has 31 peanuts. How many peanuts did she have before?

_____ peanuts

4. The blue team scores 16 fewer points than the green team. The blue team scores 41 points. How many points did the green team score?

_____ points

5. Higher Order Thinking Sean studies 16 fewer vocabulary words than Chris. Chris studies 10 fewer vocabulary words than Tia. Tia studies 34 words. How many words does Sean study? Explain your answer.

_____

_____

_____

Solve the problem any way you choose. Use drawings and equations to help. Show your work.

6. © MP.2 Reasoning Kevin practices kicks for soccer. He kicks 13 times at recess. He kicks 14 times after school. Then he kicks 16 times before bed. How many practice kicks did Kevin take in all?

I can think about what the numbers in the problem mean.

_____ kicks

---

7. **Higher Order Thinking** There are 48 red tacks and blue tacks in a bag. There are fewer red tacks than blue tacks. There are at least 26 blue tacks but no more than 30 blue tacks. How many of each color could be in the bag?

Complete the chart to solve the problem.

Red Tacks	Blue Tacks	Total
22	26	48
21		48
	28	48
19		48
	30	48

8. © **Assessment** Jim has 14 fewer baseball cards than Sara. Sara has 27 cards. How many baseball cards does Jim have?

Draw a line to show where each number and the unknown could be in the equation. Then solve.

| 27 | ? | 14 |

_____ – _____ = _____

_____ cards

© Pearson Education, Inc. 2

Name _____

Another Look! A bar diagram can help you solve word problems.

Bridget has 15 fewer crackers than Jessica. Bridget has 20 crackers. How many crackers does Jessica have?

Jessica's crackers

| 20 | 15 |

Bridget's crackers   15 crackers fewer

Jessica has __35__ crackers.

$$\begin{array}{r} 20 \\ + 15 \\ \hline 35 \end{array}$$

Bridget has 15 fewer, which means Jessica has 15 more. Add to find the number of crackers Jessica has.

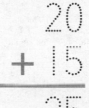

HOME ACTIVITY Tell your child Max has 10 fewer shells than Becca. Max has 20 shells. How many shells does Becca have? Then have your child write the equation. $20 + 10 = 30$.

 Solve each problem any way you choose. Use drawings and equations to help. Show your work.

1. Ann puts 37 photos in one book and 24 photos in another book. How many photos does she use in all?

_____ photos

2. Jorge's puzzle has 20 fewer pieces than Rosi's puzzle. Jorge's puzzle has 80 pieces. How many pieces does Rosi's puzzle have?

_____ pieces

Solve each problem any way you choose. Use drawings and equations to help. Show your work.

3. © **MP.2 Reasoning** Lucy makes 37 get well cards and some thank you cards. She makes 60 cards in all. How many thank you cards does Lucy make?

Think about what the numbers in the problem mean.

_____ thank you cards

4. **Higher Order Thinking** Jeff finds some bugs. He finds 10 fewer grasshoppers than crickets. He finds 5 fewer crickets than ladybugs. If Jeff finds 5 grasshoppers, how many ladybugs does Jeff find? How many crickets does he find? Write two equations to solve the problem.

_____ crickets   _____ ladybugs

5. © **Assessment** Sandy has 17 fewer hockey cards than Al. Al has 55 hockey cards. How many hockey cards does Sandy have?

Draw a line to show where each number and unknown could be in the equation. Then solve.

| 17 | ? | 55 |

_____ + _____ = _____

_____ cards

Solve & Share

Erin has 17 more books than Isabella. Erin has 44 books. How many books does Isabella have?

Solve any way you choose. Show your work.

Continue Practice with Addition and Subtraction Problems

I can ...
use drawings and equations to make sense of the words in problems.

© **Content Standard** 2.OA.A.1
Mathematical Practices MP.1, MP.2, MP.4, MP.8

_____ books

Julie has 18 more pictures than Landon.
Julie has 37 pictures. How many pictures does Landon have?

Julie's pictures

37

?	18

Landon's   18 pictures
pictures   more

The diagram helps you show what you know.

Landon has 18 fewer pictures than Julie. You can subtract to find the answer.

$37 - 18 = ?$

```
  2 17
  3̶ 7̶
-  1 8
—————
  1 9
```

Add to check your answer.

```
    1
   1 9
 + 1 8
—————
   3 7
```

So, Landon has 19 pictures.

You can solve word problems using models, drawings, or mental math.

Do You Understand?

Show Me! Compare the two statements:
Sam has 18 more markers than Zoey.
Zoey has 18 fewer markers than Sam.

Guided Practice Solve the problem any way you choose. Use drawings and equations to help.

1. The second grade has 19 more students than the first grade. The second grade has 68 students. How many students does the first grade have?

68

?	19

```
  5 18
  6̶ 8̶
-  1 9
—————
```

_____ students

© Pearson Education, Inc. 2   **Topic 7 | Lesson 3**

Independent Practice

Solve each problem any way you choose. Use drawings and equations to help. Show your work.

2. There are 11 more adults than children at a craft fair. There are 54 adults at the craft fair. How many children are at the craft fair?

_____ children

3. Caleb is 17 years old. His sister is 12 years younger. How old is Caleb's sister?

_____ years old

4. Dylan and his friends had some blueberries. They ate 39 blueberries. They have 21 blueberries left. How many blueberries did Dylan and his friends have at first?

_____ blueberries

5. Math and Science Addison made a dam with 18 more rocks than James. Addison's dam had 42 rocks. How many rocks did James's dam have? Explain your answer.

_____

_____

_____

_____

Solve each problem any way you choose. Use drawings and equations to help. Show your work.

6. **© MP.2 Reasoning** Connor has 39 sheets of green paper and some sheets of yellow paper. He has 78 sheets of paper in all. How many yellow sheets of paper does Connor have?

I can think about how the numbers in the problem are related.

_____ yellow sheets

7. **Higher Order Thinking** There are 58 red pens and blue pens in a bag. There are more red pens than blue pens. There are at least 36 red pens but no more than 40 red pens. How many of each color could be in the bag?

Complete the chart to solve the problem.

Red Pens	Blue Pens	Total
36	22	58
37		58
	20	58
39		58
	18	58

8. **© Assessment** Andrew has 63 more beanbags than Evan. Andrew has 92 beanbags. How many beanbags does Evan have?

Explain how you will solve the problem. Then solve.

_____ bean bags

© Pearson Education, Inc. 2

Name _____

Another Look!

Derek has some sheets of blue paper. He has 34 sheets of red paper. He has a total of 67 sheets of paper. How many sheets of blue paper does Derek have?

You know one of the parts and the whole.

$? + 34 = 67$

Subtract $67 - 34$ to find the missing part.

$67 - 30 = 37$ $37 - 4 = 33$

So, Derek has 33 sheets of blue paper.

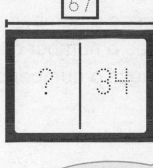

67

? | 34

Don't forget to check that your answer makes sense!

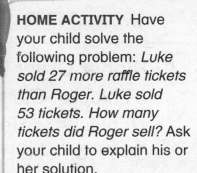

HOME ACTIVITY Have your child solve the following problem: *Luke sold 27 more raffle tickets than Roger. Luke sold 53 tickets. How many tickets did Roger sell?* Ask your child to explain his or her solution.

Solve each problem any way you choose. Use drawings and equations to help. Show your work.

1. Joshua used 23 more craft sticks on his project than Candice. Joshua used 41 craft sticks. How many craft sticks did Candice use?

_____ craft sticks

2. Gavin painted 14 pictures last week. He painted some more pictures this week. He painted 25 pictures in all. How many pictures did Gavin paint this week?

_____ pictures

3. © **MP.2 Reasoning** Daniel tosses a number cube 19 fewer times than Jayden. Daniel tosses a number cube 38 times. How many times does Jayden toss a number cube?

I can represent a word problem with the correct numbers and symbols.

_____ times

4. **Higher Order Thinking** Wyatt has 34 blocks. Stella has 36 blocks. They give 14 blocks to Henry. Now how many blocks do Wyatt and Stella have together?

Complete the steps to solve the problem.

Step 1

_____ ◯ _____ = _____

Step 2

_____ ◯ _____ = _____

_____ blocks

5. © **Assessment** Oliver runs 23 fewer laps than Nate. Nate runs 61 laps. How many laps does Oliver run?

Explain how you will solve the problem. Then solve.

_____ laps

© Pearson Education, Inc. 2

Solve & Share

3 bees land on some flowers.
10 more bees join them. Then 4 bees fly away.
How many bees are left?

Solve the problem any way you choose.
Write equations to show how you solved each part of the problem.

I can ...
model and solve two-step problems using equations.

© **Content Standard** 2.OA.A.1
Mathematical Practices MP.1,
MP.2, MP.4, MP.6

_____ ◯ _____ = _____   _____ ◯ _____ = _____

Bop picked 18 flowers and then 5 more.

He gave 10 flowers to Buzz. How many flowers does Bop have now?

Look for the hidden question that you need to answer first, before you can solve the problem.

> I need to find how many flowers Bop picked in all, before I can solve the problem.

$18 + 5 = ?$

$\underline{18} + \underline{5} = \underline{23}$

Bop picked 23 flowers. Then he gave 10 flowers to Buzz.

$23 - 10 = ?$

$\underline{23} - \underline{10} = \underline{13}$

Now Bop has 13 flowers.

> I added 2 ones to make the next ten and then added the 3 leftover ones to find $18 + 5 = 23$. Then I subtracted 10 from 23 to get 13.

Do You Understand?

Show Me! Tom bought 15 pencils and then 7 more. He gave 10 pencils to Nyla. If you want to find how many pencils Tom has left, why do you need to solve the first part of the problem before the second part?

✩ Guided ✩ Practice

Solve any way you choose. Show your work. Write equations to solve both parts of the problem.

1. Carmen found 14 shells on Monday and 15 more shells on Tuesday. She found 6 more shells on Wednesday. How many shells did she have then?

$\underline{14} \, (+) \, \underline{15} = \underline{29}$

$\underline{29} \, (+) \, \underline{6} = \underline{}$

$$\begin{array}{r} \overset{1}{14} \\ + 15 \\ \hline 29 \end{array} \qquad \begin{array}{r} 29 \\ + 6 \\ \hline \end{array}$$

_____ shells

Tools Assessment

Independent Practice

Solve any way you choose. Show your work.
Write equations to solve both parts of the problem.

2. There are 6 red birds and
17 brown birds in a tree.
If 8 more brown birds come,
how birds will there be in all?

____ ◯ ____ = ____

____ ◯ ____ = ____

_____ birds

3. Erika saw 16 frogs on a lily
pad and 8 frogs in the mud.
If 7 of the frogs hop away,
how many frogs will be left?

____ ◯ ____ = ____

____ ◯ ____ = ____

_____ frogs

Think: How can
I break apart the problem
into steps? What is the
hidden problem that I need
to solve first?

4. **Higher Order Thinking** Kevin
has 15 photos in his scrapbook.
He adds 21 photos. Then
Kevin takes out some photos.
Now he has 28 photos in the
scrapbook. How many photos
did Kevin take out?

____ ◯ ____ = ____

____ ◯ ____ = ____

_____ photos

5. ⓒ MP.4 Model There are 35 test questions. Kareem answers 10 of the questions. Then he answers 12 more questions. How many more questions does Kareem still need to answer?

_____ more questions

---

6. Ⓐ⁻ᶻ Vocabulary Circle the equations that have a **sum**. Underline the equations that have a **difference**.

$33 - 18 = 15$ $79 + 16 = 95$

$46 + 34 = 80$ $52 - 52 = 0$

7. Algebra Find the missing numbers.

$35 + \blacksquare = 100$ $\blacksquare = $ _____

$100 - \triangle = 18$ $\triangle = $ _____

---

8. Higher Order Thinking There are 25 friends at a party. Another 20 friends arrive. Then some friends leave the party. Only 7 friends stay. How many friends leave the party?

Write two equations to solve the problem.

_____

_____ friends leave the party.

9. ⓒ Assessment Bill caught 22 fish and threw 6 fish back. He caught 8 more fish. How many fish does Bill have now?

Which equations can be used to solve the problem?

Ⓐ $22 + 6 = 28$ and $28 - 8 = 20$

Ⓑ $22 - 6 = 16$ and $8 - 6 = 2$

Ⓒ $22 - 6 = 16$ and $16 + 8 = 24$

Ⓓ $22 + 6 = 28$ and $28 + 8 = 36$

Help   Tools   Games

Another Look! You can solve problems in different ways.

Jenna had 13 red markers and 15 blue markers. Then she lost 12 markers. How many markers does Jenna have left?

Step 1
Add to find out how many markers Jenna had in all.

Step 2
Subtract the number of markers Jenna lost.

```
  13            28
+ 15          - 12
  28            16
```

13 (+) 15 = 28   28 (−) 12 = 16   16 markers

> I broke apart the problem into two parts. I wrote the numbers like this. Then I used place value to solve each part.

HOME ACTIVITY Make up story problems that take two questions, or steps, to solve. Ask your child to solve both parts of each problem.

Solve any way you choose. Show your work. Write equations to solve both parts of the problem.

1. There were 15 red apples and 6 green apples in a bowl. Eric ate 2 of the apples. How many apples are in the bowl now?

Step 1 _____ ◯ _____ = _____

Step 2 _____ ◯ _____ = _____

_____ apples

2. © MP.6 Be Precise Three students use the table to record how many jumping jacks they did each day. Complete the table and the sentences.

Hank did _____ jumping jacks on Friday.

Emma did _____ jumping jacks on Thursday.

Tana did _____ jumping jacks on Wednesday.

Jumping Jacks				
	Wednesday	Thursday	Friday	**Total**
Emma	30	_____	15	88
Hank	33	32	_____	85
Tana	_____	35	25	100

3. **Higher Order Thinking** Kendra drew 26 stars. She erased 12 stars. Then Kendra drew some more stars. Now there are 29 stars. How many more stars did Kendra draw? Write an equation for each part. Then solve.

4. © **Assessment** Ken needs to buy 100 nails. He buys 25 nails at one store and 36 nails at another store. How many more nails does Ken need to buy?

Ⓐ 75

Ⓑ 64

Ⓒ 61

Ⓓ 39

It helps to break apart the problem into steps.

Solve & Share

You have 26 library books. You return some books. Then you take out 15 more books. Now you have 27 books. How many books did you return?

Solve any way you choose. Show your work.

Mia sees 15 yellow birds and 16 red birds. Some birds fly away and now Mia sees 14 birds. How many birds flew away?

I need to solve the first step of the problem in order to solve the second step.

Mia sees __31__ birds in all.

There are 14 birds left after __17__ fly away.

The bar diagrams helped me see the parts and the whole in each step of the problem.

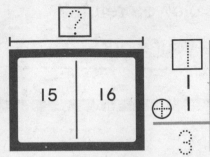

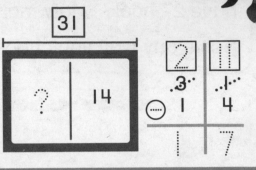

Do You Understand?

Show Me! Why do you need two steps to solve the problem above?

⭐ **Guided Practice**   Complete the equations to solve.

1. There are some boys painting and 9 girls painting. In all, 17 children are painting. Then some more boys come to paint. Now there are 15 boys painting. How many more boys come to paint?

Step 1	Step 2

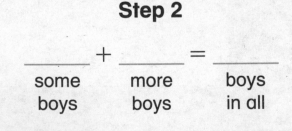

$$\underline{8} + \underline{9} = \underline{17}$$
some boys   girls   children in all

$$\underline{} + \underline{} = \underline{}$$
some boys   more boys   boys in all

_____ more boys come to paint.

© Pearson Education, Inc. 2

Topic 7 | Lesson 5

Independent Practice Solve each problem any way you choose. Show your work.

2. Jake has 16 toy cars. Lidia has 5 fewer toy cars than Jake. How many toy cars do they have in all?

They have _____ cars in all.

3. Sandy has 12 balloons. Tom has 11 more balloons than Sandy. Some of Tom's balloons popped and now he has 14 balloons. How many balloons popped?

_____ balloons popped.

4. 25 wolves howl together in the woods. 14 wolves join them. Then 22 wolves run away. How many wolves are left?

_____ wolves are left.

5. **Higher Order Thinking** Explain how you solved Item 4.

_____

_____

_____

_____

6. © MP.1 Make Sense Tim bakes 24 more muffins than Gina. Gina bakes 13 muffins. Lea bakes 16 fewer muffins than Tim.

How many muffins does Lea bake?

I can check that my work and answer make sense.

_____ muffins

---

7. Higher Order Thinking Write a two-step math story using the numbers 36, 65, and 16. Then solve the problem. Write equations to show each step.

_____

_____

_____

_____

8. © Assessment There are 44 marbles in a jar. Some are red and 23 are blue. Julie adds 13 red marbles to the jar. Now how many red marbles are in the jar?

Which equations show a way to solve the problem?

Ⓐ $44 - 23 = 21$
   $21 + 13 = 34$

Ⓒ $23 + 21 = 44$
   $44 - 13 = 31$

Ⓑ $44 - 23 = 21$
   $21 - 13 = 8$

Ⓓ $23 + 44 = 67$
   $67 + 13 = 80$

Help   Tools   Games

Another Look! Use the answer from Step 1 to solve Step 2.

Tomas has 14 toy cars. Jonah has 6 more toy cars than Tomas. How many toy cars do they have in all?

HOME ACTIVITY Ask your child to solve two-step problems. Use small objects found at home as props.

Step 1: Add to find out how many toy cars Jonah has in all.

$$14 + 6 = 20$$

Step 2: Add to find the number of toy cars they have in all.

$$20 + 14 = 34$$

They have 34 toy cars in all.

Use the answer from Step 1 to solve Step 2.

1. Dani picked some red flowers and 9 pink flowers for a total of 21 flowers. Then Dani gave Will 5 red flowers. How many red flowers does Dani have left?

Step 1: Subtract to find how many red flowers Dani picked.

_____ − _____ = _____

Step 2: Subtract to find how many red flowers Dani has left.

_____ − _____ = _____

_____ red flowers

Mr. and Mrs. Morley picked their crops. Use the data in the chart to solve each problem.

Fruit and Vegetables Picked				
Apples	Peaches	Pumpkins	Corn	Squash
?	23	47	25	17

2. © MP.1 Make Sense Mr. Morley takes the apples and peaches to his fruit stand. He takes 58 pieces of fruit in all. He sells 13 apples. How many apples are at the fruit stand now?

_____ apples

3. Higher Order Thinking Write and solve a two-step problem about the data in the chart above.

_____

_____

_____

_____

_____

4. A-Z Vocabulary Complete the bar diagram. Use two possible addends with a sum of 25. Then complete the equation.

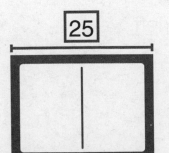

_____ + _____ = 25

5. © Assessment There are 21 students at the school picnic. Then 42 more students join them. Later, 30 students leave.

How many students are still at the picnic?

21   33   63   93
Ⓐ   Ⓑ   Ⓒ   Ⓓ

© Pearson Education, Inc. 2

Solve & Share

Write a number story for this equation.

$$20 = ? + ?$$

Then complete the equation to match your story.

Solve

I can ...
use reasoning to write and solve number stories.

Ⓒ Mathematical Practices
MP.2 Also MP.1, MP.3, MP.4, MP.7
Content Standard 2.OA.A.1

Thinking Habits
How are the numbers in the problem related?

How can I use a word problem to show what the equation means?

$$20 = \_\_\_\_ + \_\_\_\_$$

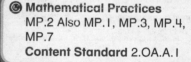

Write a number story for 68 − 33. Then write an equation to match your story.

How can I show what numbers and symbols mean?

I think about what 68, 33 and the − sign mean in the problem. I can use that to write a story.

Subtraction stories can be about separating or about comparing. This story is about separating.

Harry finds 68 acorns. He gives 33 acorns to Joyce. How many acorns does Harry have left?

68 − 33 = ?

Subtract to answer the question in the problem.

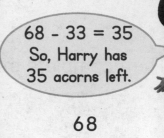

68 - 33 = 35
So, Harry has 35 acorns left.

$$68$$
$$-33$$
$$35$$

Do You Understand?

Show Me! Write a number story about comparing for 68 − 33 = ?.

☆ Guided Practice ☆

Complete the number story. Then complete the equation to match the story. Draw a picture to help, if needed.

1. 47 − 18 = _____

Blake collects __47__ cans.

He recycles __18__ cans.

How many cans does Blake have now?

_____ cans

Independent Practice

Write a number story to show the problem.
Complete the equation to match your story.

2. 22 - 17 = _____

_____

_____

_____

_____

_____

3. 84 − 62 = _____

_____

_____

_____

_____

_____

4. 28 + 12 = _____

_____

_____

_____

_____

5. 39 + 47 = _____

_____

_____

_____

_____

Math Practices and Problem Solving

Toy Car Collection

The picture at the right shows a toy car collection. Use the picture to write and solve number story problems.

6. **MP.2 Reasoning** Write an addition story about the toy car collection.

_____

_____

_____

_____

7. **MP.2 Reasoning** Write a subtraction comparison story about the collection.

_____

_____

_____

_____

8. **MP.4 Model** Write an equation for each number story that you wrote in Item 6 and Item 7. Then solve any way you choose. Show your work.

Another Look! You can write a number story about each problem.
Then complete the equation to match the story.

$22 - 15 = ?$

There are ___22___ red buttons.

There are ___15___ blue buttons.
How many more red buttons
are there than blue buttons?

$22 - 15 = \underline{7}$

So, there are ___7___ more red buttons.

$36 - 17 = ?$

___36___ grapes are on the table.

___17___ are red and the rest are green.
How many grapes are green?

$36 - 17 = \underline{19}$

So, ___19___ grapes are green.

HOME ACTIVITY Write problems such as $41 - 28 = ?$ and $55 + 37 = ?$. Ask your child to write or say a number story about the problem. Have your child complete the equation to match the story.

Write a number story to show the problem.
Complete the equation to match your story.

1. $31 - 8 = $ _____

_____

_____

_____

_____

2. $23 + 37 = $ _____

_____

_____

_____

_____

Bakery Muffins

The picture at the right shows information about muffins at Herb's Bakery. Use the picture to write and solve number story problems.

Herb's Bakery

33 Berry   18 Bran   29 Apple

3. **MP.2 Reasoning** Write an addition story about the muffins at the bakery.

_____

_____

_____

_____

4. **MP.2 Reasoning** Write a subtraction story about the muffins at the bakery.

_____

_____

_____

5. **MP.4 Model** Write an equation for each number story that you wrote in Item 3 and Item 4. Then solve any way you choose. Show your work.

Find a Match

Find a partner. Point to a clue. Read the clue.

Look below the clues to find a match. Write the clue letter in the box next to the match.

Find a match for every clue.

Clues

A Is equal to $5 + 4$

B Is equal to $8 + 7$

C Is equal to $20 - 10$

D Is equal to $12 - 7$

E Is equal to $9 + 3$

F Is equal to $13 - 9$

G Is equal to $11 - 8$

H Is equal to $7 + 6$

I Is equal to $2 + 4$

J Is equal to $5 + 6$

K Is equal to $14 - 7$

L Is equal to $10 + 6$

☐ $10 - 7$	☐ $19 - 9$	☐ $8 + 8$	☐ $12 - 8$
☐ $18 - 9$	☐ $13 - 8$	☐ $13 - 7$	☐ $8 + 3$
☐ $4 + 9$	☐ $15 - 8$	☐ $9 + 6$	☐ $6 + 6$

Vocabulary Review

A-Z
Glossary

Understand Vocabulary

Write T for *true* or F for *false*.

1. _____ An equation is a model you can use to help solve a problem.

2. _____ 43 is the difference in the equation $43 - 16 = 27$.

3. _____ Addition and subtraction can be shown using a bar diagram.

4. _____ An equation is a model you can use to represent a problem.

5. _____ A sum is the answer to a subtraction problem.

Draw a line from each term to its example.

6. regroup

7. sum   The answer to $18 + 45$

8. open number line   15 ones = 1 ten and 5 ones

Use Vocabulary in Writing

9. Explain how you can count on to find $58 + 23$. Use at least one term from the Word List.

Name _____

Set A

You can model problems.

A store has some rings. Then 34 rings are sold. Now the store has 47 rings. How many rings did the store have at first?

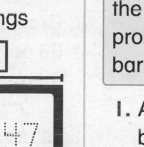

$? - 34 = 47$

$$\begin{array}{r} 1 \\ 47 \\ + 34 \\ \hline 81 \text{ rings} \end{array}$$

Write an equation with a ? for the unknown to represent the problem. Then solve using the bar diagram.

1. A store has 52 juice boxes. Then some juice boxes are sold. Now the store has 35 juice boxes. How many juice boxes were sold?

Equation: _____

_____ juice boxes

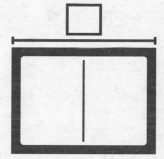

Set B

Trent has 29 more toy cars than Bill. Trent has 72 toy cars. How many toy cars does Bill have?

$$\begin{array}{r} 6\;12 \\ 7\!\!\!/2 \\ - 29 \\ \hline 43 \end{array}$$

This means Bill has 29 fewer toy cars than Trent. Subtract to solve. Bill has 43 toy cars.

Solve the problem any way you choose. Show your work.

2. A game has 19 more red cards than blue cards. The game has 43 red cards. How many blue cards does the game have?

_____ blue cards

Lacie buys 28 peaches. She gives 12 to Ted. Then she buys 15 more. How many peaches does Lacie have now?

$28 - 12 =$ 16 $16 + 15 =$ 31

31 peaches

Use the answer from the first step to solve the second step. Use the bar diagrams to help.

3. Craig scores 27 points. Next he scores 33 points. Then he loses 14 points. How many points does Craig have now?

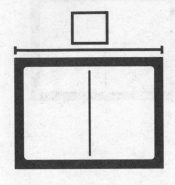
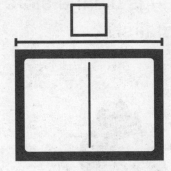

$27 + 33 =$ _____   _____ $-$ _____ $=$ _____

_____ points

Thinking Habits

Reasoning

How are the numbers in the problem related?

How can I use a word problem to show what the equation means?

Write a number story for the problem. Complete the equation to match your story.

$28 + 35 =$ _____

_____

_____

_____

_____

© Pearson Education, Inc. 2

1. Jodi has 28 apples. She buys some more.
Now Jodi has 43 apples.
How many apples did she buy?

Use the bar diagram to help you
write an equation. Then use
the open number line to solve.

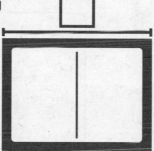

_____ ◯ _____ = _____

_____ apples

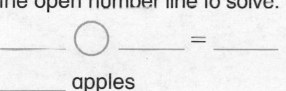

2. Alayna draws 18 more stars than Pearl. Alayna draws 37 stars. How many stars does Pearl draw?

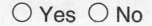 **Assessment**

Can you use the equation to solve the problem? Choose Yes or No.

$37 - 18 = ?$ ◯ Yes ◯ No

$18 + 37 = ?$ ◯ Yes ◯ No

$18 + ? = 37$ ◯ Yes ◯ No

$? + 18 = 37$ ◯ Yes ◯ No

3. Emily has 17 fewer ribbons than Piper.
Piper has 48 ribbons.
How many ribbons does Emily have?

Solve any way you choose.
Show your work.

_____ ribbons

4. Write a number story for $72 - 36 = ?$.
Then solve the story problem.

$72 - 36 =$ _____

5. Joy needs 99 coats for children in need.
She gets 54 coats from her school.
She gets 22 coats from friends.
How many more coats does Joy need?

Write equations to solve.
Then write the answer.

_____ ◯ _____ = _____

_____ ◯ _____ = _____

Joy needs _____ more coats.

6. Shane has 27 more cards than Tom.
Shane has 62 cards.
How many cards does Tom have?

Explain how you will solve the problem.
Then solve.

Tom has _____ cards.

7. Grace found 36 shells.
She threw 8 shells back into the sea.
Then she found 9 more shells.
How many shells does Grace have now?

Which pair of equations shows a way to
solve the problem?

Ⓐ $36 - 8 = 28$
$28 - 9 = 19$

Ⓒ $36 + 9 = 45$
$45 + 8 = 53$

Ⓑ $36 - 8 = 28$
$28 + 9 = 37$

Ⓓ $36 + 8 = 44$
$44 + 9 = 53$

Name _____

School Fair

Meadow School is having a school fair. The table shows the number of tickets Ms. Davis's class has sold.

 **Performance Assessment**

Number of Tickets Sold	
Monday	42
Tuesday	17
Wednesday	21

1. How many fewer tickets did Ms. Davis's class sell on Wednesday than on Monday?
Complete the bar diagram to model the problem. Then solve.

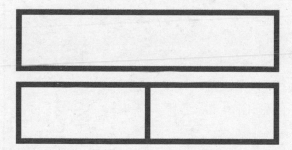

_____ fewer tickets

2. Ms. Davis says the class can have a party if they sell 95 tickets.

Part A

Write an equation to show how many tickets the class has sold.

Then solve the equation. Show your work.

_____ tickets sold

Part B

How many more tickets does the class have to sell to have a party? Explain.

_____ tickets

3. The table shows the number of tickets Mr. Rios's class has sold.

How many more tickets did his class sell on Monday and Tuesday than on Wednesday?

Number of Tickets Sold	
Monday	24
Tuesday	18
Wednesday	28

Write two equations to solve both parts of the problem.

_____ ◯ _____ = _____

_____ ◯ _____ = _____

_____ more tickets

Here are some models you can use or make.

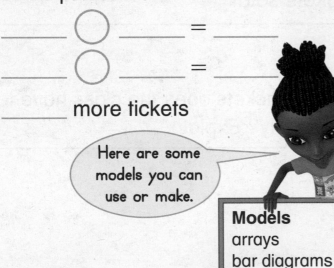

Models
arrays
bar diagrams
drawings
equations
open number lines
place-value blocks

4. Part A
Write a number story about selling tickets for the school fair. Use numbers that you can add or subtract.

_____

_____

_____

_____

Part B
Write an equation to match your story. Then solve any way you choose. Show your work.

© Pearson Education, Inc. 2

Topic 7 | Performance Assessment

Work with Time and Money

Essential Question: How can you solve problems about counting money or telling time to the nearest 5 minutes?

Digital Resources

Solve Learn Glossary

Tools Assessment Help Games

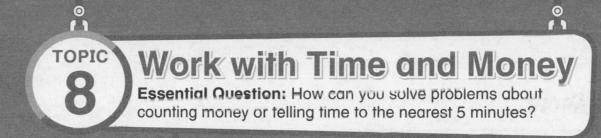

Different materials are used to make money!

How would you describe different types of money?

Wow! Let's do this project and learn more.

Math and Science Project: Money Matters

Find Out Collect examples of different types of coins and dollar bills. Describe how different coins and bills look and feel. Sort the money by size, color, and whether or not you can bend it.

Journal: Make a Book Show what you find out in a book. In your book, also:

• Tell how different types of coins are alike. Tell how they are different.

• Show as many different ways as you can to make 25¢.

Name _____

Review What You Know

A-Z Vocabulary

1. Draw the hands to show **8 o'clock**.

2. Circle the number of minutes in one **hour**.

30 minutes

50 minutes

60 minutes

3. Write the time below to the **half hour**.

_____ o'clock

Doubles Facts

4. Write each sum.

$$
\begin{array}{ccc}
7 & 9 & 10 \\
+7 & +9 & +10 \\
\end{array}
$$

Doubles facts are fun.

Array

5. Use mental math. How many squares are in the array?

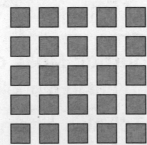

_____ squares

Math Story

6. Some pennies are in a cup. Jan takes out 22 of the pennies. Now, 14 pennies are left in the cup. How many pennies were in the cup at the start?

_____ pennies

A-Z Glossary

dime

nickel

penny

quarter

half-dollar

cents (¢)

I cent
or I¢

10 cents
or 10¢

My Word Cards

Use what you know to complete the sentences.
Extend learning by writing your own sentence using each word.

✂

A _____

is 1 cent or 1¢.

A _____

is 5 cents or 5¢.

A _____

is 10 cents or 10¢.

The value of a coin is measured in

_____.

The symbol for cents is

_____.

A _____

is 50 cents or 50¢.

A _____

is 25 cents or 25¢.

My Word Cards Study the words on the front of the card. Complete the activity on the back.

A-Z
Glossary

greatest value

The quarter has the greatest value.

least value

The dime has the least value.

dollar

$1 or 100¢

dollar sign

$37

↑
dollar sign

dollar bills

tally mark

Ways to Show 30¢			
Quarter	Dime	Nickel	Total
I		I	30¢
	III		30¢
	II	II	30¢
	I	IIII	30¢
		IIIII I	30¢

My Word Cards

Use what you know to complete the sentences.
Extend learning by writing your own sentence using each word.

One _____

equals 100¢.

The coin that has the

_____

_____

is the coin that is worth the least.

The coin that has the

_____

_____

is the coin that is worth the most.

Use a _____

_____

to keep track of each piece of information in an organized list.

_____

can have different dollar values, such as $1, $5, $10, or $20.

A _____

_____

is a symbol used to show dollar money values.

Study the words on the front of the card.
Complete the activity on the back.

quarter past

It is quarter past 4.

half past

It is half past 9.

quarter to

It is quarter to 4.

a.m.

breakfast time

p.m.

dinner time

My Word Cards

Use what you know to complete the sentences.
Extend learning by writing your own sentence using each word.

A ____________________

____

is 15 minutes before the hour.

30 minutes past the hour is

____

________________________.

A ____________________

____

is 15 minutes after the hour.

Clock time from noon to midnight can be shown as

________________________.

Clock time from midnight to noon can be shown as

________________________.

Name _____

Solve & Share

Kelsey had 10 cents in her piggybank.
She finds 5 cents more and puts it in her bank.
Then Kelsey's mother gives her 20 cents to put in her bank.

How many cents does Kelsey have in her bank now?

I can ...
solve problems with coins.

© **Content Standards** 2.MD.C.8,
2.NBT.A.2
Mathematical Practices MP.1,
MP.2, MP.3, MP.5

_____ cents

 **dime** 10¢

  **nickel** 5¢

  **penny** 1¢

 **quarter** 25¢

 half-dollar 50¢

Micah has the coins shown below. How many cents does Micah have? Count on to find the total value.

Micah has 91 cents. The cent sign is ¢.

50¢   75¢   85¢   90¢   91¢

Do You Understand?

Show Me! How many quarters have the same value as a half-dollar?

How many dimes have the same value as a half-dollar?

How many cents would Micah have if he didn't have the half-dollar?

☆ **Guided Practice**   Count on to find each total value.

1. Li has these coins. How many cents does Li have?

      ➡

25¢   50¢   ____   ____   ____   **Total**

---

2. Manny has these coins. How many cents does Manny have?

    ➡

Total

____   ____   ____   ____

Name _____

Tools Assessment

Independent Practice ⭐ Count on to find each total value.

3. Jan has these coins. How many cents does Jan have?

_____   _____   _____   _____

Total _____

---

4. Tim has these coins. How many cents does Tim have?

_____   _____   _____   _____   _____

Total _____

---

5. Manny has these coins. How many cents does Manny have?

_____   _____   _____   _____   _____

Total _____

---

6. Algebra Stacey had 92¢ this morning. She lost a coin.
Write the name of the coin Stacey lost.

_____

Total 92¢

7. © **MP.3 Explain** Tori has 2 quarters, 1 dime, and 1 nickel. How many cents does Tori have? Show how you found your answer.

8. **Higher Order Thinking** Write a story about what coins you could use to buy an orange for 60¢.

9. © **Assessment** Lucas has these coins.

He is buying a gift for his brother. If he had one more nickel, which item would he have exactly enough money to buy?

Ⓐ 41¢   Ⓑ 51¢   Ⓒ 76¢   Ⓓ 84¢

10. © **Assessment** Jamie has 90¢. Which coins could she have? Choose all that apply.

Topic 8 | Lesson 1

Name _____

Another Look! You can count on to find the total value of a group of coins.

Luanne has one quarter and two nickels. How many cents does Luanne have?

Start with 25¢. Count on by fives.

Think: 25¢   5¢ more   5¢ more

25¢   30¢   35¢

Tim has one half-dollar and two dimes. How many cents does Tim have?

Start with 50¢. Count on by tens.

Think: 50¢   10¢ more   10¢ more

50¢   60¢   70¢

 Count on to find each total value.

1. Sarah has these coins. How many cents does Sarah have?

25¢   ___   ___   ___   ___   Total

2. Marc has these coins. How many cents does Marc have?

___   ___   ___   ___   ___   Total

3. **Higher Order Thinking** Find the coins needed to buy each toy. Use the fewest coins possible. Write how many of each coin to use.

Count on as you use each coin.

4. **© Assessment** Will has 37¢. Which coins could he have? Choose all that apply.

5. **© Assessment** Jamal has these coins.

He needs 85¢ to buy a toy car.
How many more cents does Jamal need?
Draw the coin or coins he needs.

© Pearson Education, Inc. 2

Solve & Share

Choose 5 coins. Which coin has the least value? Which coin has the greatest value? What is the total value of money you have?

I can ...
solve problems with coins.

Ⓒ **Content Standards** 2.MD.C.8, 2.NBT.A.2
Mathematical Practices MP.3, MP.4, MP.5, MP.6

_____ greatest _____ ¢

_____ least _____ ¢

Total: _____ ¢

Seline has these coins.

How many cents does Seline have?

Start with the coin of **greatest value**.

Count on to the coin of **least value**.

So, Seline has 90¢.

50¢   75¢   85¢   90¢

Do You Understand?

Show Me! Why is it a good idea to put 1 nickel, 1 penny, and 1 quarter in a different order to find the total?

Guided Practice Draw the coins from the greatest to the least value. Count on to find each total. You can use coins.

1.

25¢   50¢   55¢   60¢

60¢ **Total**

2.

_____

Total

Topic 8 | Lesson 2

Name _____

Independent Practice   Count on to find each total value.

3. Eboo has these coins. How many cents does Eboo have?

It helps to put the coins in order from greatest value to least value.

_____ _____ _____ _____   The total is _____.

4. Hanna has these coins. How many cents does Hanna have?

_____ _____ _____ _____   The total is _____.

5. Mary has 3 dimes and 2 nickels.
How many cents does she have?

_____

6. Danny has 4 nickels, 1 quarter, 2 dimes, and 3 pennies. How many cents does he have?

_____

7. **Number Sense** What 4 coins have a total value of 20¢? Draw the coins. Label the value of each coin.

8. Math and Science Greg's science class wants to sort these coins by their color. What is the total value of the silver coins?

_____ ¢

9. © MP.4 Model Draw the fewest number of coins to show 80¢.

10. Higher Order Thinking Write a story about finding 75¢. Draw the coins.

_____

_____

_____

11. © Assessment Lydia has 3 coins. The total value is 40¢. She has 1 quarter and 1 nickel. Which shows her third coin?

40¢

Ⓐ

Ⓒ

Ⓑ

Ⓓ

© Pearson Education, Inc. 2

Help Tools Games

Homework & Practice 8-2

Continue to Solve Problems with Coins

Another Look! To count coins, start with the coin that has the greatest value. Count on from the greatest to the least value.

Find the total value of the coins Seth has.
Draw an X on the coin with the greatest value.

  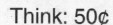

Think: 50¢   60¢   70¢   75¢

Start with 50¢.   50¢   60¢   70¢   75¢

Find each total value. Draw an X on the coin with the greatest value.

1.

Start with _____.

___ ___ ___ ___

2.

Start with _____.

___ ___ ___ ___

3. Megan had 50¢. She lost 1 nickel.
Circle the 5 coins that show how much she has left.

4. Yoshi had 55¢. He gave his sister a dime.
Circle the 3 coins that show how much he has left.

5. Kayla had 60¢. She gave her brother 4 pennies.
Circle the 3 coins that show how much she has left.

6. **A-Z** **Vocabulary** Circle the **nickel**. Put a square around the **half-dollar**. What is the total value of all the money?

_____ ¢

7. © **Assessment** Karen has 85¢. She has a half-dollar and a dime. Which other coin does Karen have?

Ⓐ   Ⓒ

Ⓑ   Ⓓ

Solve & Share

What is one way you can show 100¢ with coins? Use coins to model. Draw and label the coins you use.

Lesson 8-3

Solve Problems with Dollar Bills

I can ...

solve problems with dollar bills and coins that model 100 cents.

© **Content Standards** 2.MD.C.8, 2.NBT.A.2
Mathematical Practices MP.2, MP.4, MP.6, MP.7

100¢

This is 1 **dollar**.
The **dollar sign** is $.

$1 bill
$1 = 100¢

Here are some other **dollar bills**.

$5 bill

$10 bill

$20 bill

Maria had these dollar bills. What is the total value?

$20 $30 $40 $45 $50 $51

20 + 10 + 10 + 5 + 5 + 1

Count on from the greatest bill to the least bill. Maria has $51.

Do You Understand?

Show Me! How is counting dollar bills like counting coins? How is it different?

☆ Guided Practice   Solve each problem.

1. Mr. Park has these dollar bills. Count on to find the total value.

_____

2. Ms. Lenz has these dollar bills. Count on to find the total value.

_____

Remember to count from the greatest bill to the least bill.

© Pearson Education, Inc. 2

Topic 8 | Lesson 3

Tools Assessment

Independent Practice ☆ Solve each problem.

3. Mr. Higgins has these dollar bills.
Count on to find the total value.

_____

4. Ms. Nguen has these dollar bills.
Count on to find the total value.

5. Mr. Abreu has these dollar bills.
Count on to find the total value.

_____

6. Ms. Wills has these dollar bills.
Count on to find the total value.

_____

7. Number Sense Mr. Anson has $26 in his wallet.
What is the least number of bills he can have?
Draw the bills.

_____ bills

8. © **MP.4 Model** Diana buys shoes on sale for $28. Draw dollar bills that she could use to pay for the shoes.

9. Mrs. Baker has two $10 bills and three $5 bills in her purse. Does she have enough money to buy a dress that costs $33? Explain.

10. **Higher Order Thinking** Roger buys a baseball bat that costs $27. He pays the clerk with two $20 bills. What bills can the clerk give him back as change?

11. © **Assessment** The dollar bills below show the total cost of tickets for a soccer game.

How much do the tickets cost?

$5 $31 $40 $41

Ⓐ   Ⓑ   Ⓒ   Ⓓ

© Pearson Education, Inc. 2

Name _____

Another Look! What is the total value of the dollar bills shown below?

Count on from greatest bill to least bill to find the total value of dollar bills.

HOME ACTIVITY Have your child make different groups of dollar bills that total $37.

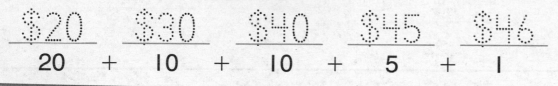

$20 $30 $40 $45 $46

20 + 10 + 10 + 5 + 1

Solve each problem.

1. Ms. Lopez has these dollar bills. Count on to find the total value.

_____

2. Ms. Lenz has these dollar bills. Count on to find the total value.

3. Jack buys a bicycle on sale for $59. Draw dollar bills that he could use to pay for the bike.

4. ⓒ **MP.7 Look for Patterns** Marvin counts six $5 bills. Write each value that he counts. What pattern do you see in the ones digits of the values he counts?

_____

_____

_____

_____

5. Higher Order Thinking Maria has two $20 bills, three $5 bills, and four $1 bills. What other bill or bills does she need to buy a present that costs $69?

6. ⓒ **Assessment** The dollar bills below show the money that Sam has saved.

How much money has Sam saved?

$52	$43	$42	$5
Ⓐ	Ⓑ	Ⓒ	Ⓓ

© Pearson Education, Inc. 2

Solve & Share

Timmy takes money out of his piggy bank.
He takes out two $10 bills, three $5 bills, and 6 $1 bills.
How much money does Timmy take out?

Draw a picture to show your work.

I can ...
solve problems with dollar bills.

© **Content Standards** 2.MD.C.8,
2.OA.A.1
Mathematical Practices MP.1,
MP.2, MP.4, MP.6

$ _____

Chloe has a $20 bill and a $1 bill. Her sister Violet has $6 less than Chloe. Do they have enough money to buy a $35 scarf for their mother?

$35

You can show how much money Chloe has with a $20 bill and a $1 bill.

$20 + $1 = $21

$20

$1

You can find how much money Violet has by subtracting $21 − $6.

$21 − $6 = $15

$10

$5

Add to find if Chloe and Violet have enough money to buy the scarf.

$21 + $15 = $36

Violet could have a $10 bill and a $5 bill.

$36 is enough to buy a $35 scarf.

Do You Understand?

Show Me! How can you keep track of the amounts of money in the word problem?

☆ Guided Practice ☆

Solve each problem any way you choose. Show your work.

1. Sam had some money in his wallet. He went to the carnival and spent $12. Now Sam has $5. How much was in his wallet before the carnival?

$ _?_ − $_12_ = $_5_

$_12_ + $_5_ = $_17_

$_17_

2. Morgan has $7. Her grandmother gives her a $10 bill and a $5 bill. How much money does Morgan have now?

$____

Independent Practice ☆ Solve each problem any way you choose. Show your work.

3. Mia has two dollars. Ethan gives her two $5 bills. Noah gives her one $10 bill. How much money does Mia have in all?

$_____

4. A sweater costs $38. Charlie has one $20 bill, one $10 bill, and two $1 bills. How much more money does he need to buy the sweater?

$_____

5. Eli has $64 dollars. One of the bills is a $20 bill. What are the other bills Eli could have?

Draw a picture to show one solution.

6. **Higher Order Thinking** Jen bought three $5 raffle tickets and eight $1 raffle tickets. How much did Jen spend on raffle tickets?

Jen spent $_____ on raffle tickets.

Explain how you solved the problem.

7. © MP.I Make Sense Lily has two $10 bills, three $5 bills, and one $1 bill. She gives Grace $11. How much money does Lily have left?

$_____

8. © MP.I Make Sense Isaac wants to buy a backpack for $20. He has two $5 bills and nine $1 bills. How much more money does he need to buy the backpack?

$_____

How much is two $10 bills?

9. Higher Order Thinking Henry has two $10 bills, two $5 bills, and three $1 bills. Mr. Harper has one $100 bill. Henry says he has more money because he has seven bills and Mr. Harper only has one bill. Is Henry correct? Explain.

10. © Assessment Olivia has one $20 bill, three $5 bills, and nine $1 bills. How much more money does Olivia need to buy a coat that costs $49? Explain.

What bills can you use to show how much money Olivia needs?

Name _____

Another Look! Kim has $4 in her bank.
She needs $20 to buy the gift she picked out for her mom.
How much more money does Kim need?

Add to check your work.
$4 + $16 = $20
So, the answer makes sense.

$20 − $4 = $ __16__

Kim needs $16 more.

$10 + $5 + $1 = $16

HOME ACTIVITY Have your child use coins and bills to show various amounts in different ways.

Solve each problem any way you choose. Show your work.

1. Mrs. Brown had $16 dollars in her wallet. After shopping at the store, she now has $8. How much money did Mrs. Brown spend at the store?

$ _____

2. Evelyn has $7. Liz gives her one $5 bill and two $1 bills. How much money does Evelyn have now?

$ _____

Solve each problem. Show your work.

3. @ **MP.6 Be Precise** Aiden has three $20 bills and two $10 bills. He wants to save a total of $95. How much more money does he need? What bills could they be?

_____

_____

4. Carter has one $20 bill, one $10 bill, four $5 bills and two $1 bills. Aubrey has two $10 bills, five $5 bills, and seven $1 bills. Who has more money? Explain.

_____

_____

_____

5. Higher Order Thinking Mark has $24. His brother has $8 more than Mark has. How much do they have in all?

Step 1

$_____ ◯ $_____ = $_____

Step 2

$_____ ◯ $_____ = $_____

Mark and his brother have $_____ in all.

6. @ **Assessment** Emma has two $10 bills, three $5 bills, and two $1 bills. How much more money does she need to buy a game that costs $45? Explain.

_____

_____

_____

What bills can you use to show how much more money Emma needs?

_____

© Pearson Education, Inc. 2

Name _____

Solve & Share

Suppose you want to buy a pencil that costs 35¢. How many different ways can you use nickels, dimes, or quarters to make 35¢? Show each way. Tell how you know.

Lesson 8-5
Reasoning

I can ...
reason about values of coins and dollar bills, and find different ways to make the same total value.

© **Mathematical Practices** MP.2 Also MP.1, MP.3, MP.4, MP.8 **Content Standards** 2.MD.C.8, 2.OA.A.1

Quarter	Dime	Nickel	Total Amount
			35¢
			35¢
			35¢
			35¢
			35¢
			35¢

Thinking Habits

What do the numbers and symbols in the problem mean?

How do the values of the coins relate to the total?

I have some quarters, dimes, and nickels. I want to buy a banana.

30¢

How many ways can I make 30¢?

How can I reason about the different ways to make a total?

A table can show the coins. I can use **tally marks** to record the number of coins.

Ways to Show 30¢			
Quarter	Dime	Nickel	Total
I		I	30¢
	III		30¢

$25¢ + 5¢ = 30¢$
$10¢ + 10¢ + 10¢ = 30¢$

Tally marks make it easy to show the different ways.

Ways to Show 30¢			
Quarter	Dime	Nickel	Total
I		I	30¢
	III		30¢
II	II		30¢
I		IIII	30¢
		ⅢⅠ I	30¢

I can write an equation to show and check each way.

I can make 30¢ in 5 different ways.

Do You Understand?

Show Me! Use the chart above. Write equations to show the ways to make 30¢ using dimes and nickels.

Guided Practice   Use reasoning. Complete the table.

1. Tony wants to buy a pencil.

55¢

He has half-dollars, quarters, and nickels. Find all the ways he can make 55¢.

How do the tally marks relate to money values?

Half-Dollar	Quarter	Nickel	Total
I		I	55¢

© Pearson Education, Inc. 2

Name _____

Independent Practice ✧ Use reasoning. Complete each table.

2. Sue needs $12 to buy a book. She has $1 bills, $5 bills, and $10 bills. Find 3 more ways Sue can make $12.

$10 Bill	$5 Bill	$1 Bill	Total
I		II	$12

3. Raul wants to buy a bookmark for 14¢. He has dimes, nickels, and pennies. Find all of the ways he can make 14¢.

You can write equations to check your work.

Dime	Nickel	Penny	Total
	II	IIII	14¢

Number Sense What is the least number of bills or coins that you could use to make each amount? You can use the tables above to help.

4. $12

Number of bills: _____
Bills I would use:

_____

5. 14¢

Number of coins: _____
Coins I would use:

_____

6. Write an equation to show the total value of 2 nickels and 4 pennies.

_____

Math Practices and Problem Solving

© **Performance Assessment**

Carnival Game Money

Don wants to use these coins to play as many carnival games as he can. Each game costs 40¢.

How can Don spend the coins that are shown at the right?

7. **MP.4 Use Models** Choose from the coins shown. Show one way Don can spend 40¢ on one game. Write an equation.

_____

_____

8. **MP.1 Make Sense** You used some of the coins for one of the ways. How will you know which coins are left to spend?

_____

_____

9. **MP.2 Reasoning** Show how Don can spend the coins to play games. Use tally marks in the table.

Which coin is left over?

_____

Quarter	Dime	Nickel	Penny	Total

© Pearson Education, Inc. 2

Name _____

Another Look! Show three ways to make 25¢.
Two ways are shown in the table.

Use coins to help you find a third way. Show I dime.
Make I tally mark.
How many nickels do you need to add 15¢?

_3_

Make 3 tally marks.

Ways to Show 25¢

Quarter	Dime	Nickel	Total
I			25¢
	II	I	25¢
	I	III	25¢

Use reasoning to solve each problem.

1. Show three ways to make $20.
Use tally marks to record the bills.

Ways to Show $20

$20 Bill	$10 Bill	$5 Bill	Total

2. What is the least number of coins you could use to make 45¢?
Make a table, if needed.

Number of coins: _____

Coins I would use: _____

_____

Least Number of Bills

The Williams family wants to buy these toys. They have $20 bills, $10 bills, $5 bills, and $1 bills. They want to use the least number of bills to pay for each item.

Which bills will they use to pay for each item?

3. **MP.3 Explain** Marci thinks the family should use three $5 bills and three $1 bills to buy the doll. Does Marci's way use the least number of bills? Explain.

_____

_____

_____

4. **MP.8 Generalize** How can you find the least number of bills to use to pay for any of the 3 items?

_____

_____

_____

5. **MP.2 Reasoning** Complete the Williams's shopping card. Record the least number of bills they could use to pay for each item. Use tally marks.

Item	$20 Bill	$10 Bill	$5 Bill	$1 Bill
Doll				
Basketball				
Bicycle				

Lesson 8-6
Tell Time to Five Minutes

Solve & Share

An airplane is due to arrive at 3:15.
How can you show this time on the clock below? Explain.

I can …
tell time to the nearest 5 minutes.

© **Content Standards** 2.MD.C.7, 2.NBT.A.2
Mathematical Practices MP.2, MP.5, MP.6, MP.8

Both clocks show 8:05.

minute hand

8:05

The minute hand moves from number to number in 5 minutes.

To tell time to five minutes, count by 5s. Both clocks show 8:35.

8:35

I can start at 8:00 and count by 5s to tell the time.

There are 60 minutes in 1 hour.

hour hand

9:00

The minutes start over again each hour.

Do You Understand?

Show Me! The time is 9:35. What time will it be in 5 minutes?

In 15 minutes?

In 25 minutes?

☆ Guided ☆ Practice

Complete the clocks so both clocks show the same time.

1.

6:45

2.
3:25

3.

:

4.
5:40

Name _____

Independent Practice

Complete the clocks so both clocks show the same time.

5.

6.

7.

8.

9.

10.

---

11. Number Sense Complete the pattern.

 7:00    7:05    7:10   :

Topic 8 | Lesson 6

four hundred seventy-five **475**

12. © **MP.2 Reasoning** One of the clocks is running a little slow. The other clock is running a little fast. Estimate the correct time.

_____

13. Number Sense Look at the time on the first clock.
What time will it be in 5 minutes?
Write that time on the second clock.

14. Higher Order Thinking Draw a clock that shows your favorite time of the day. Explain why it is your favorite time.

_____

_____

15. © **Assessment** The minute hand is pointing to the 7. Which number will it be pointing to 10 minutes later?

Ⓐ 5

Ⓑ between 7 and 8

Ⓒ 8

Ⓓ 9

Name _____

Another Look! You can use two kinds of clocks to tell time.

The minute hand moves from mark to mark in 1 minute. There are 5 moves between each number. So, the minute hand moves from number to number in 5 minutes.

There are 30 minutes in a half hour and 60 minutes in an hour. The hour hand moves from number to number every 60 minutes.

HOME ACTIVITY Draw three clock faces showing 3:20, 10:50, and 7:05. Have your child tell you the time each clock shows.

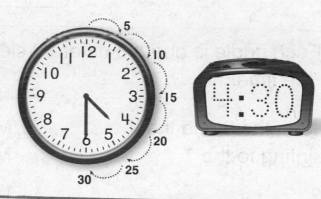

Count by 5s. Write the time.

1.

2.

3. © **MP.8 Generalize** The time is shown on the clock below.

6:05

Draw the time on the clock in the box at the right. Then complete each sentence.

The minute hand is pointing to the _____.

The hour hand is between _____ and _____.

Higher Order Thinking Each riddle is about a different clock. Solve the riddle and write the time.

4. My hour hand is between the 3 and the 4. My minute hand is pointing to the 7.

What time do I show? _____

5. My hour hand is between the 5 and the 6. My minute hand is pointing to the 4.

What time do I show? _____

6. My hour hand is between the 11 and the 12. My minute hand is pointing to the 3.

What time do I show? _____

7. My hour hand is between the 1 and the 2. My minute hand is pointing to the 9.

What time do I show? _____

8. © **Assessment** The clock shows the time that Sharon starts to walk to the library. The walk takes 10 minutes. At what time does Sharon get to the library?

5:00 Ⓐ   5:10 Ⓑ   5:20 Ⓒ   5:30 Ⓓ

© Pearson Education, Inc. 2

Solve & Share

Name _____

 Solve

Both of these clocks show the same time.
How many different ways can you say this time?
Write each way.

I can ...
say the time in different ways.

© **Content Standards** 2.MD.C.7, 2.NBT.A.2
Mathematical Practices MP.3, MP.4, MP.6, MP.8

6:45

_____

_____

_____

Look at the times. Count by 5s to tell the time.
What are other ways to name the same times?

1:15

15 minutes
after 1,
quarter past 1

1:30

30 minutes
after 1,
half past 1

1:50

50 minutes
after 1

Times after the half hour are often read as times
before the next hour.

3:30

30 minutes
before 4

3:45

15 minutes
before 4,
quarter to 4

3:50

10 minutes
before 4

Do You Understand?

Show Me! Write two ways
to say 5:30.

☆ **Guided Practice** ☆ Complete so both clocks show the same time.
Then circle another way to say the time.

1.

(half past 2)

30 minutes before 2

2.

quarter to 7

quarter past 6

© Pearson Education, Inc. 2

Name _____

Tools   Assessment

Independent Practice Complete so both clocks show the same time.
Then write the time before or after the hour.

3.

4:45

_____ minutes before 5

4.

12:15

quarter past _____

5.

:

25 minutes after _____

Higher Order Thinking Look at the clock to solve each problem.

6. What time will it be in 30 minutes?
Write this time in two different ways.

_____

_____

7. What time will it be in 50 minutes?
Write this time in two different ways.

_____

_____

8. **(A-Z) Vocabulary** Miguel is meeting a friend at **half past** 4.
Complete both clocks to show this time.

9. **© MP.8 Generalize** A train left the station at 6:55.
What are two other ways to say this time?

_____

_____

10. **Higher Order Thinking** Draw a clock with hands that show 11:45.
Then write two ways to say the time.

_____

11. **© Assessment** James gets home at 6:00. He starts his homework at quarter past 6. At what time does James start his homework?

Ⓐ

Ⓒ

Ⓑ

Ⓓ

Name _____

Another Look! Here are different ways to say time before and after the hour.

6:15
15 minutes after 6 or quarter past 6

6:30
30 minutes after 6 or half past 6

6:45
45 minutes after 6 or quarter to 7

2:40
20 minutes before 3 or 40 minutes after 2

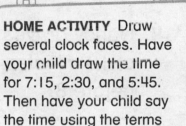

HOME ACTIVITY Draw several clock faces. Have your child draw the time for 7:15, 2:30, and 5:45. Then have your child say the time using the terms *quarter past, half past,* and *quarter to.*

Count by 5s to tell the time. Write the time on the line below the clock. Then write the missing numbers.

1.

_30_ minutes after _____

or half past _____

_____

2.

_____ minutes after _____ or

_____ minutes before _____

_____

3. **© MP.3 Explain** The time is 6:10.
Is the hour hand closer to 6 or 7?
Explain your reasoning.

Higher Order Thinking Write the time. Then answer each question.

4. Nancy arrives
at 10 minutes
before 8.

School starts at

Is Nancy early
or late for school?

_____

_____

5. Sean arrives at
quarter to 7.

Dinner starts at

Is Sean early
or late for dinner?

_____

_____

6. **© Assessment** Joyce wakes up at 10 minutes after 7. It takes her 40 minutes
to get ready and walk to school. What time does Joyce get to school?

Ⓐ

Ⓑ

Ⓒ

Ⓓ

© Pearson Education, Inc. 2

Solve & Share

Look at the clock and tell what time Ethan wakes up for school. Write the time on the digital clock and circle morning or evening.

Solve

Lesson 8-8
A.M. and P.M.

I can ...
tell time and use reasoning to state if the event is happening in the a.m. or p.m.

© **Content Standards** 2.MD.C.7, 2.NBT.A.2
Mathematical Practices MP.2, MP.6, MP.8

Ethan wakes up at:

Circle

morning

evening

Learn Glossary

You can use the terms **a.m.** and **p.m.** to tell about time.

Use a.m. for morning times. I wake up at 8 a.m.

Use p.m. for afternoon or evening times. I go to bed at 8 p.m.

I eat breakfast at:

8:20

(a.m.) p.m.

I eat lunch at school at:

11:45

(a.m.) p.m.

I eat dinner with my family at:

6:30

a.m. (p.m.)

Do You Understand?

Show Me! What might you be doing at 6:15 a.m.? At 6:15 p.m.?

Guided Practice

Complete the clocks so both clocks show the same time. Then circle a.m. or p.m. to tell when you would do each activity.

1. Ride the bus to school

8:45

(a.m.) p.m.

2. Do your homework

4:30

a.m. p.m.

© Pearson Education, Inc. 2

Topic 8 | Lesson 8

Independent Practice

Complete the clocks so both clocks show the same time.
Circle a.m. or p.m. to tell when you would do each activity.

3. Take the bus home from school

a.m.   p.m.

4. Walk the dog before breakfast

a.m.   p.m.

5. Read a book before bedtime

a.m.   p.m.

6. Take swimming lessons on Saturday morning

10:15

a.m.   p.m.

7. Watch a movie on Friday night

7:20

a.m.   p.m.

8. Go to a party on Saturday afternoon

2:00

a.m.   p.m.

9. Higher Order Thinking Jen and Maria have dance lessons at the time shown on the clock.
Write the time two different ways. Is it a.m. or p.m.? Explain.

10. © MP.6 Be Precise Draw hands on the clock to show what time your school begins each day. Then write the time. Include a.m. or p.m.

11. Math and Science Stargazing is looking at the stars. The best time to stargaze is on a clear moonless night.

Gina went outside to stargaze at 9:00. Is this 9:00 a.m. or 9:00 p.m.? Explain.

_____

_____

12. Higher Order Thinking Grace starts her homework at 4:15.
She finishes her homework 45 minutes later. Draw the hands on the clocks to show both times. Write both times on the digital clocks.

Circle a.m. or p.m. below to tell when Grace does her homework.

a.m.   p.m.

13. © Assessment Circle a.m. or p.m. to tell when you would do each activity.

Brush your teeth before bedtime   a.m.   p.m.   Walk the dog before dinner   a.m.   p.m.

Go to soccer practice after school   a.m.   p.m.   Watch the sunrise   a.m.   p.m.

Name _____

Help · Tools · Games

Another Look! Circle a.m. or p.m. to tell when each activity takes place.

Mom goes swimming in the morning.	I go to soccer practice after school.	Dad goes for a walk after dinner in the evening.

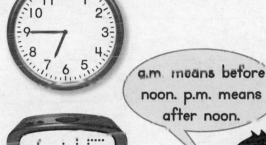

a.m. means before noon. p.m. means after noon.

HOME ACTIVITY Write three things that you do at different times of the day. Have your child tell you whether you do these things in the a.m. or the p.m.

(a.m.) p.m.   a.m. (p.m.)   a.m. (p.m.)

Complete the clocks so both clocks show the same time. Circle a.m. or p.m. to tell when each activity takes place.

1. Eat a snack in the morning

  10:15

(a.m.) p.m.

2. Brush your teeth after lunch

:

a.m. p.m.

Solve each problem.

3.  **Vocabulary** Write an example of an event that could happen in the **a.m.** Write an example of an event that could happen in the **p.m.**

_____

_____

_____

4. **Higher Order Thinking** Guess what time it is. Right now, it is p.m.

In 10 minutes it will be a.m. What time is it now? Explain.

_____

_____

Write the time in the clock.

5. © **Assessment** Alexis wakes up in the morning at the time shown on the clock. What time does Alexis wake up?

Ⓐ 7:15 a.m.

Ⓑ 8:15 a.m.

Ⓒ 7:15 p.m.

Ⓓ 8:15 p.m.

6. © **Assessment** Circle a.m. or p.m. to tell when you would do each activity.

Watch the sunset   a.m.   p.m.

Eat breakfast   a.m.   p.m.

Walk home from school   a.m.   p.m.

Take the bus to school   a.m.   p.m.

© Pearson Education, Inc. 2

Topic 8 | Lesson 8

Name _____

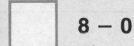 Find a Match

Find a partner. Point to a clue. Read the clue.

Look below the clues to find a match. Write the clue letter in the box next to the match.

Find a match for every clue.

Clues

A Is equal to $12 - 5$

B Is equal to $9 + 2$

C Is equal to $12 - 10$

D Is equal to $8 + 9$

E Is equal to $3 + 3$

F Is equal to $15 - 7$

G Is equal to $8 + 6$

H Is equal to $12 - 8$

I Is equal to $17 - 8$

J Is equal to $6 + 9$

K Is equal to $8 - 5$

L Is equal to $9 + 9$

☐ $8 - 0$	☐ $10 + 8$	☐ $10 + 5$	☐ $9 + 8$
☐ $10 - 6$	☐ $4 + 7$	☐ $7 - 4$	☐ $3 + 4$
☐ $8 - 6$	☐ $9 + 5$	☐ $14 - 8$	☐ $12 - 3$

A-Z
Glossary

Word List
- a.m.
- cents (¢)
- dime
- dollar
- dollar bills
- dollar sign
- greatest value
- half-dollar
- half past
- least value
- nickel
- penny
- p.m.
- quarter
- quarter past
- quarter to
- tally mark

Understand Vocabulary

1. Circle the name of the coin with the *greatest value*.

   quarter   nickel   dime

2. Circle the name of the coin with the *least value*.

   half-dollar   penny   quarter

3. Cross out the time that is **NOT** quarter past 5 or quarter to 5.

   4:45   5:15   5:25

4. Cross out the time that is **NOT** half past 8 or quarter past 8.

   8:30   8:45   8:15

When does each event happen? Write a possible time.
Use a.m. or p.m.

5. school ends

_____

6. eat breakfast

_____

7. sunrise

_____

Use Vocabulary in Writing

8. Explain how you can show ways to make 1 dollar (100¢) using coins. Use terms from the Word List. Give examples.

Set A

When you count coins, start with the coin of greatest value.

Randi has the coins shown below. Count on to find the total value.

quarter (25¢)   dime (10¢)   nickel (5¢)

25¢   35¢   40¢

Randi has 40¢ .

Another Example

Duane has the coins below. How much money does Duane have?

25¢ 50¢ 60¢ 70¢

Duane has 70¢ .

Reteaching

Solve each problem.
Count on to find the total value.

I. These coins are in a jar. How many cents are in the jar?

Draw the coins in order.

Count on. _____ _____

There is _____ in the jar.

2. The coins shown below are in a box. How much money is in the box?

There is _____ in the box.

Dollar bills are paper money and can have different dollar values.

$1 bill
$1 = 100¢

$5 bill

$10 bill

$20 bill

Matt has $56. Two of his bills are $20 bills. What other bills could Matt have? You can count on to get to $56.

$20, $40, $50 , $55 , $56
        +$10   +$5   +$1

The other bills Matt could have are a $10 bill, a $5 bill, and a $1 bill.

Solve each problem.

3. Mr. Park has these dollar bills. Count on to find the total value.

Remember to count from the greatest bill to the least bill.

_____

4. A cookbook costs $36. Mrs. Beeson has a $10 bill and a $5 bill. How much more money does Mrs. Beeson need to buy the cookbook?

$_____

© Pearson Education, Inc. 2

Set C

Thinking Habits

Reasoning

What do the numbers and symbols in the problem mean?

How do the values of the coins relate to the total?

Use reasoning. Finish the table.

5. Mitch has dimes, nickels, and pennies. Find ways he can make 11¢. Show a tally mark for each coin you use.

Dime	Nickel	Penny	Total
l		l	11¢

Did you find all the different ways?

Set D

It takes 5 minutes for the minute hand to move from one number to the next. Count on by 5s.

8:20

Read the time.
Write the same time on the digital clock.

6.

You can say the number of minutes before the hour or after the hour.

Circle the time each clock shows.

10 minutes before 5

(10 minutes after 5)

(10 minutes before 5)

10 minutes after 5

7.

5 minutes before 3

5 minutes after 3

8.

15 minutes before 10

15 minutes after 10

Use a.m. from midnight to noon.
Use p.m. from noon to midnight.

Circle a.m. or p.m. to tell when you would do each activity.

Walking the
dog before bed

Eating a morning
snack

9. Afternoon recess   10. Feeding fish after breakfast

a.m. (p.m.)

(a.m.) p.m.

a.m.   p.m.

a.m.   p.m.

1. Chen has these coins.
How much money does Chen have?

Count on to find the total.

_____ cents

2. Ellen has 4 coins.
The total value is 46¢.
She has 1 quarter, 1 dime,
and 1 penny.
Which shows her fourth coin?

Ⓐ   Ⓑ   Ⓒ   Ⓓ

3. Nancy has 31¢.
Which coins could she have?
Choose all that apply.

☐

☐

☐

☐

4. George has quarters, dimes, and nickels.
Show all the ways he can make 25¢. Use
tally marks.

Circle the way that uses the least number
of coins.

Ways to Show 25¢			
Quarter	Dime	Nickel	Total

5. Mr. Zink has the dollar bills shown below.

How many dollars does Mr. Zink have?

$36 $31 $26 $5

Ⓐ   Ⓑ   Ⓒ   Ⓓ

6. Claire has two $20 bills, two $5 bills, and three $1 bills. How much more money does Claire need to buy a bike that costs $89? Explain.

What bills can you use to show how much money Claire needs?

7. Kay has saved $30.
Show three different ways to make $30.
Use tally marks in the table at the right.

Circle the way that uses the least number of bills.

Ways to Show $30			
$20 Bill	$10 Bill	$5 Bill	Total

© Pearson Education, Inc. 2

Name _____

8. Sandy wakes up in the morning at the time shown on the clock.

What time does Sandy wake up?

Ⓐ 5:10 a.m

Ⓒ 5:10 p.m.

Ⓑ 6:10 a.m.

Ⓓ 6:10 p.m.

9. Sara's baseball game starts at the time shown on the clock.

Is this the time her game starts?
Choose Yes or No.

45 minutes after 4	○ Yes	○ No
15 minutes before 5	○ Yes	○ No
quarter to 4	○ Yes	○ No
quarter to 5	○ Yes	○ No

10. The clock shows the time that Holly leaves for school.
It takes 15 minutes to walk to school.
At what time will Holly arrive at school?
Choose all that apply.

☐ half past 7

☐ quarter past 8

☐ 30 minutes after 8

☐ half past 8

11. The first clock shows the time the sun rises.
Write the same time on the second clock.
Then circle a.m. or p.m.

a.m.   p.m.

12. Look at the time on the first clock. What time will it be in 10 minutes? Write that time on the second clock.

13. Circle a.m. or p.m. to tell when you would do each activity.

Watch the sunset at 7:40.   a.m.   p.m.

Take a music lesson after school.   a.m.   p.m.

Brush your teeth before school.   a.m.   p.m.

Eat breakfast at 6:45.   a.m.   p.m.

14. Draw lines to match the time on each clock in the first row to the same time shown in the second row.

Name _____

The Toy Store

Terry's family owns a toy store.
These are some of the things
that they sell.

$14 $21 $1   38¢

1. Lorna paid for a box of crayons
with 6 coins.
Ken paid for a box of crayons
with 7 coins.
Draw the coins that each of them used.

Lorna's 6 coins	Ken's 7 coins

2. Kim goes to the toy store
with these coins.

Part A

What is the total value of the coins Kim
has? Explain how you know.

_____

_____

_____

Part B

How much more money does Kim need to
buy the book? Explain.

3. Kay's father buys a toy train at the toy store for $50.

Part A

Show five different ways that he could have paid $50. Use tally marks to complete the table.

Ways to Show $50			
$20 Bill	$10 Bill	$5 Bill	Total
			$50
			$50
			$50
			$50
			$50

Part B

Which way uses the least number of bills to make $50? Explain.

4. Ted walks to the toy store in the afternoon.

Part A

He starts walking at the time shown on the digital clock. Draw hands on the second clock to show the same time.

Is the time on the clocks above 3:35 a.m. or 3:35 p.m.? Explain how you know.

_____

_____

Part B

Ted gets to the store 10 minutes later. Write this time in two different ways.

Glossary

A

add

When you add, you join groups together.

$$3 + 4 = 7$$

addend

numbers that are added

 $2 + 5 = 7$

addends

after

424 comes after 423.

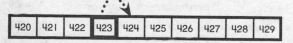

a.m.

clock time from midnight until noon

angle

the corner shape formed by two sides that meet

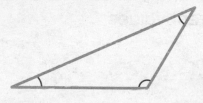

array

a group of objects set in equal rows and columns that forms a rectangle

B

bar diagram

a model for addition and subtraction that shows the parts and the whole

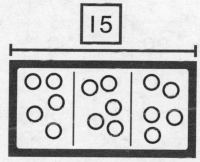

bar graph

A bar graph uses bars to show data.

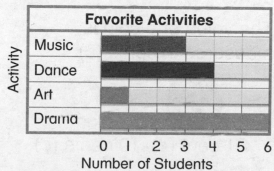

before

| 420 | 421 | 422 | 423 | 424 | 425 | 426 | 427 | 428 | 429 |

421 comes before 422.

break apart

You can break apart a number into its place value parts.

$$27 + 35 = ?$$

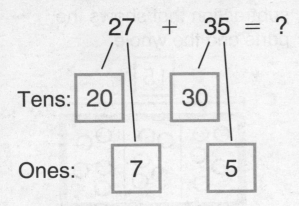

Tens: 20   30

Ones: 7   5

C

cents

The value of a coin is measured in cents (¢).

1 cent (¢)   10 cents (¢)

centimeter (cm)

a metric unit of length that is part of 1 meter

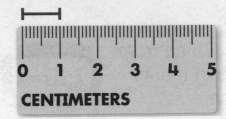

CENTIMETERS

coins

money that is made out of metal and that can have different values

1¢   5¢   10¢   25¢   50¢

column

objects in an array or data in a table that are shown up and down

column

1	2	3	4	5
11	12	13	14	15
21	22	23	24	25
31	32	33	34	35

compare

When you compare numbers, you find out if a number is greater than, less than, or equal to another number.

$$147 > 143$$

147 is greater than 143.

compatible numbers

numbers that are easy to add or subtract using mental math

$$8 + 2$$
$$20 + 7$$
$$53 + 10$$

compensation

a mental math strategy you can use to add or subtract

$$38 + 24 = ?$$
$$+2 \quad -2$$

You add 2 to 38 to make 40. Then subtract 2 from 24 to get 22. 40 + 22 = 62. So, 38 + 24 = 62.

cone

a solid figure with a circle shaped base and a curved surface that meets at a point

cube

a solid figure with six faces that are matching squares

cylinder

a solid figure with two matching circle shaped bases

 D

data

information you collect and can be shown in a table or graph

Favorite Fruit	
Apple	7
Peach	4
Orange	5

decrease

to become lesser in value

$$600 \longrightarrow 550$$

600 decreased by 50 is 550.

denominator

the number below the fraction bar in a fraction, which shows the total number of equal parts

$$\frac{3}{4} \longleftarrow \text{denominator}$$

difference

the answer in a subtraction equation or problem

$$14 - 6 = 8$$

$\uparrow$

difference

digits

 43

Numbers are made up of 1 or more digits. 43 has 2 digits.

dime

10 cents or 10¢

division

an operation that tells how many equal groups there are or how many are in each group

$$12 \div 3 = 4$$

divided by

what you say to read a division symbol

$$18 \div 3 = 6$$

↰ divided by

---

dollar

One dollar equals 100¢.

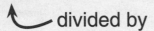

---

dollar bills

paper money that can have different dollar values, such as $1, $5, $10, or $20

dollar sign

a symbol used to show that a number represents money

$37

↑
dollar sign

---

doubles

addition facts that have two addends that are the same

$$4 + 4 = 8$$

↑ ↑
addend addend

E

edge

a line formed where two faces of a solid figure meet

← edge

eighths

When a whole is separated into 8 equal shares, the parts are called eighths.

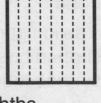

---

equal groups

groups that have the same number of items or objects

2   2   2

---

equal shares

parts of a whole that are the same size

All 4 shares are equal.

---

equals (=)

has the same value

$$36 = 36$$

36 is equal to 36.

equation

a math sentence that uses an equal sign (=) to show that the value on the left is equal to the value on the right

$$3 + ? = 7$$

$$14 - 6 = 8$$

estimate

When you estimate, you make a good guess.

This table is about 3 feet long.

even

a number that can be shown as a pair of cubes.

8 is even.

expanded form

a way of writing a number that shows the place value of each digit

$$400 + 60 + 3 = 463$$

face

a flat surface of a solid figure that does not roll

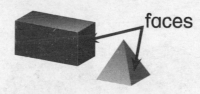

faces

fact family

a group of related addition and subtraction facts

$$2 + 4 = 6$$

$$4 + 2 = 6$$

$$6 - 2 = 4$$

$$6 - 4 = 2$$

factors

numbers that are multiplied together to give a product

$$7 \times 3 = 21$$

factors

flat surface

flat surfaces that are **NOT** faces

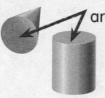

foot (ft)

a standard unit of length equal to 12 inches

fourths

When a whole is divided into 4 equal shares, the shares are called fourths.

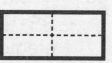

fraction

a number, such as $\frac{1}{2}$ or $\frac{3}{4}$, that names part of a whole or part of a set

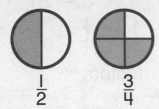

$\frac{1}{2}$ $\frac{3}{4}$

G

greater than (>)

has greater value

$$5 > 1$$

5 is greater than 1.

greatest

the number in a group with the largest value

 35 47 58 61

greatest

greatest value

The coin that has the greatest value is the coin that is worth the most.

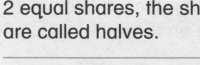

The quarter has the greatest value.

H

half-dollar

50 cents or 50¢

half past

30 minutes past the hour

It is half past 9.

halves (half)

When a whole is divided into
2 equal shares, the shares are called halves.

height

how tall an object is from bottom to top

heptagon

a polygon that has 7 sides

hexagon

a polygon that has 6 sides

hour

An hour is 60 minutes.

hundred

10 tens make 1 hundred.

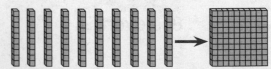

inch (in.)

a standard unit of length that is part of 1 foot

increase

to become greater in value

550 ⟶ 600

550 increased by 50 is 600.

least

the number in a group with the smallest value

35 47 58 61
↳ least

least value

The coin that has the least value is the coin that is worth the least.

The dime has the least value.

length

the distance from one end to the other end of an object

less than (<)

has less value

2 < 6

2 is less than 6.

line plot

A line plot uses dots above a number line to show data.

Lengths of Shells

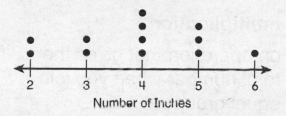

Number of Inches

mental math

Start at 23. Count on 2 tens. 33, 43

math you do in your head

23 + 20 = 43

meter (m)

a metric unit of length equal to 100 centimeters

A long step is about a meter.

minute

a standard length of time
There are 60 minutes in 1 hour.

multiplication

an operation that gives the total number when you join equal groups

$$3 \times 2 = 6$$

To multiply 3×2 means to add 2 three times.

$$2 + 2 + 2 = 6$$

near doubles

addition facts that have two addends that are close

$$4 + 5 = 9$$

addend   addend

nearest centimeter

The whole number centimeter mark closest to the measure is the nearest centimeter.

about 2 cm long

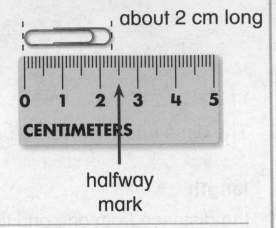

CENTIMETERS

halfway mark

nearest inch

The whole number inch mark closest to the measure is the nearest inch.

about 2 inches long

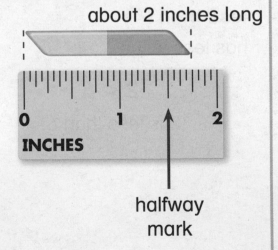

INCHES

halfway mark

next ten

the first ten greater than a number

30 is the next ten after 27.

nickel

5 cents or 5¢

nonagon

a polygon that has 9 sides

number line

a line that shows numbers in order from left to right

1 2 3 4 5 6 7 8 9 10

numerator

the number above the fraction bar in a fraction, which shows how many equal parts are described

$\dfrac{3}{4}$ ← numerator

octagon

a polygon that has 8 sides

odd

a number that can **NOT** be shown as pairs of cubes

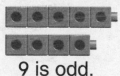

9 is odd.

ones

digits that shows how many ones are in a number

$54 + 14 = 68$

↑   ↑   ↑

open number line

An open number line is a tool that can help you add or subtract. It can begin at any number.

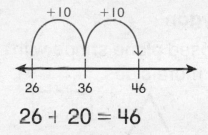

$26 + 20 = 46$

order

to place numbers from least to greatest or from greatest to least

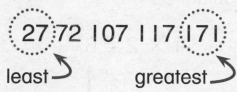

least   greatest

parallelogram

a quadrilateral that has 4 sides and opposite sides parallel

part

a piece of a whole or of a number

2 and 3 are parts of 5.

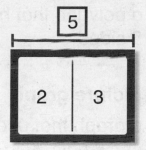

partial sum

When you add numbers, the sum of one of the place values is called a partial sum.

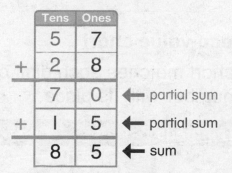

Tens	Ones	
5	7	
+ 2	8	
7	0	← partial sum
+ 1	5	← partial sum
8	5	← sum

penny

1 cent or 1¢

pentagon

a polygon that has 5 sides

picture graph

a graph that uses pictures to show data

Favorite Ball Games	
Baseball	👤👤
Soccer	👤👤👤👤👤👤👤
Tennis	👤👤👤👤

Each 👤 = 1 student

place-value chart

a chart matches each digit of a number with its place

Hundreds	Tens	Ones
3	4	8

plane shape

a flat shape

circle   rectangle   square   triangle

p.m.

clock time from noon until midnight

7:10 PM

polygon

a closed plane shape with 3 or more sides

product

the answer to a multiplication problem

$$4 \times 2 = 8$$

↑
product

pyramid

a solid figure with a base that is a polygon and faces that are triangles that meet in a point

Q

quadrilateral

a polygon that has 4 sides

quarter

25 cents or 25¢

quarter past

15 minutes after the hour

4:15

It is quarter past 4.

quarter to

15 minutes before the hour

3:45

It is quarter to 4.

rectangular prism

a solid figure with bases and faces that are rectangles

regroup

to name a number or part in a different way

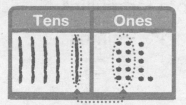

Tens	Ones

10 ones can be regrouped as 1 ten. 1 ten can be regrouped as 10 ones.

related

Addition facts and subtraction facts are related if they have the same numbers.

$$2 + 3 = 5$$
$$5 - 2 = 3$$

---

repeated addition

adding the same number repeatedly

$$3 + 3 + 3 + 3 = 12$$

right angle

an angle that forms a square corner

row

objects in an array or data in a table that are shown across

1	2	3	4	5
11	12	13	14	15
21	22	23	24	25
31	32	33	34	35

← row

S

separate

to subtract or to take apart into two or more parts

$$5 - 2 = 3$$

---

side

a line segment that makes one part of a plane shape

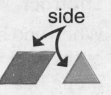
side

solid figure

a shape that has length, width, and height

These are all solid figures.

sphere

a solid figure that looks like a ball

standard form

a way to write a number using only digits

436

Glossary

G11

subtract

When you subtract, you find out how many are left or which group has more.

$$5 - 3 = 2$$

sum

the answer to an addition equation or problem

$$3 + 4 = 7$$

$$\begin{array}{r} 4 \\ + 3 \\ \hline 7 \end{array}$$

sum ⟶ 7

symbol

a picture or character that stands for something

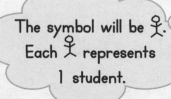

The symbol will be ⚇.
Each ⚇ represents
1 student.

tally mark

a symbol used to keep track of each piece of information in an organized list

Ways to Show 30¢			
Quarter	Dime	Nickel	Total
I		I	30¢
	III		30¢
	II	II	30¢
	I	IIII	30¢
		ℍ I	30¢

tens

the digit that shows how many groups of ten are in a number

2**3**8
↑

thirds

When a whole is divided into 3 equal shares, the shares are called thirds.

thousand

10 hundreds make 1 thousand.

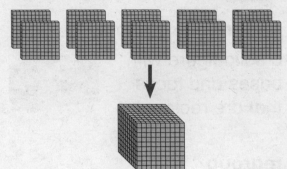

times

another word for multiply

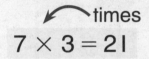

times

$$7 \times 3 = 21$$

trapezoid

a polygon with 4 sides and one pair of sides are parallel

triangular prism

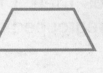

a solid figure that has two triangle shaped bases and three faces that have rectangle shapes.

U

unequal

Unequal parts are parts that are not equal.

5 unequal parts

unit

You can use different units to measure.

about 12 inches
about 1 foot

unit fraction

a fraction that reperesents one equal part of a whole or a set

$\frac{1}{2}$ $\frac{1}{4}$ $\frac{1}{8}$

unknown

a symbol that stands for a number in an equation

$$34 + ? = 67$$

↑
unknown

V

vertices (vertex)

corner points where 2 sides of a polygon meet or where edges of a solid figure meet

vertex

W

whole

a single unit that can be divided into parts

The two halves make one whole circle.

width

the distance across an object

word form

a way to write a number using only words

The word form for 23 is twenty-three.

Y

yard (yd)

a standard unit of length equal to 3 feet

A baseball bat is about a yard long.

Photographs

Every effort has been made to secure permission and provide appropriate credit for photographic material. The publisher deeply regrets any omission and pledges to correct errors called to its attention in subsequent editions.

Unless otherwise acknowledged, all photographs are the property of Pearson Education, Inc.

Photo locators denoted as follows: Top (T), Center (C), Bottom (B), Left (L), Right (R), Background (Bkgd)

F13C Pearson Education;**F13CL** Pearson Education;**F13CR** Pearson Education;**F13L** Pearson Education;**F13R** Pearson Education;**001BL** Lori Martin/Shutterstock;**001BR** An Nguyen/Shutterstock;**001C** Africa Studio/Fotolia;**001L** Africa Studio/Fotolia;**001R** karandaev/Fotolia;**077BL** michaklootwijk/Fotolia;**077BR** Jitka Volfova/Shutterstock;**077L** Charles Brutlag/Shutterstock;**077R** Erni/Fotolia;**119L** FiCo74/Fotolia;**119R** Antonio Scarpi/Fotolia;**189** Beboy/Shutterstock;**253** Deborah Benbrook/Fotolia;**321** GlebStock/Shutterstock;**389** Paylessimages/Fotolia;**435** Ambient Ideas/Shutterstock;**456** Pearson Education;**494C** Pearson Education;**494** Pearson Education;**494B** Pearson Education;**494T** Pearson Education;**503** Es0lex/Fotolia;**504B** Pearson Education;**504BL** Pearson Education;**504BR** Pearson Education;**504C** Pearson Education;**504CL** Pearson Education;**504CR** Pearson Education;**504T** Pearson Education;**504TC** Pearson Education;**504TL** Pearson Education;**583** kalafoto/Fotolia;**635** Klagyivik Viktor/Shutterstock;**675** Nagel Photography/Shutterstock;**678** Optionm/Shutterstock;**687** Ant Clausen/Fotolia;**759** Bonita R. Cheshier/Shutterstock;**788** Lledó/Fotolia;**790** Ivan Kruk/Fotolia;**799L** Karichs/Fotolia;**799R** Ivonne Wierink/Fotolia;**845B** Pearson Education;**845BC** Pearson Education;**845CT** Pearson Education;**845T** Pearson Education;**851** Yurakr/Shutterstock;**868** StudioSmart/Shutterstock;**932** Pearson Education;**934** Pearson Education;**G2L** Pearson Education;**G2R** Pearson Education;**G3L** Pearson Education;**G3R** Pearson Education;**G4B** Pearson Education;**G4C** Pearson Education;**G4CB** Pearson Education;**G4CT** Pearson Education;**G4T** Pearson Education;**G6BL** Pearson Education;**G6BR** Pearson Education;**G6TC** Pearson Education;**G6TL** Pearson Education;**G6TR** Pearson Education;**G7C** Pearson Education;**G7L** Pearson Education;**G7R** Pearson Education;**G8L** Pearson Education;**G8R** Pearson Education;**G9L** Pearson Education;**G9R** Pearson Education;**G10L** Pearson Education;**G10R** United State Mint.